WordPress Plugin Development Cookbook

Second Edition

Create powerful plugins to extend the world's most popular CMS

Yannick Lefebvre

BIRMINGHAM - MUMBAI

WordPress Plugin Development Cookbook

Second Edition

First published: July 2012

Second edition: July 2017

Production reference: 1140717

Published by Packt Publishing Ltd.
Livery Place
35 Livery Street
Birmingham
B3 2PB, UK.

ISBN 978-1-78829-118-7

www.packtpub.com

Credits

Author
Yannick Lefebvre

Reviewers
Cyril Pierron
Ardian Yuli Setyanto

Commissioning Editor
Smeet Thakkar

Acquisition Editor
Shweta Pant

Content Development Editor
Arun Nadar

Technical Editor
Ralph Rosario

Copy Editor
Akshada Lobo

Project Coordinator
Ritika Manoj

Proofreader
Safis Editing

Indexer
Mariammal Chettiyar

Graphics
Jason Monteiro

Production Coordinator
Shantanu Zagade

About the Author

Yannick Lefebvre is a plugin developer who has published eight projects to the official WordPress repository. His first creation, *Link Library*, has been used on thousands of sites around the world. With a background in Computer Science and working for CM Labs Simulations — a company providing software tools and simulators for vehicle and heavy equipment simulation — he started writing plugins for his own WordPress site in 2004 and quickly started sharing his creations with the community. He is actively involved in the Montreal WordPress community, has presented multiple times at WordCamp Montreal, and offers WordPress plugin development services. You can find out more about him and his plugins on his website, Yannick's Corner.

I would like to thank the WordCamp Montreal organizers for giving me a chance to speak at multiple editions of the event, for creating great videos of the presentations, and giving me the opportunity to get involved in the community. This project would not have existed without them.

I would also like to thank Richard Archambault for his great feedback and encouragement while I wrote the first edition of this book, as well as the entire Packt Publishing team for proposing this great project to me, supporting me through the entire process, and coming back to me to put together this second edition.

Finally, I would like to thank my parents for always believing in me and encouraging me in all my projects.

About the Reviewers

Cyril Pierron is a tech-savvy, life-curious engineer. He started programming at the age of 8. He worked in the telecommunications industry for 13 years, leading network value added service application development. Since 2011 he has been working as an ecommerce solution architect, supporting customers and partners, building transactional sites on Salesforce Commerce Cloud platform. He is married and the father of a lovely 7-year old girl.

As an ecommerce expert, Cyril has witnessed over the past few years the convergence of content sites and online stores into one unified experience for the consumer. He has integrated with various content management platforms in the context of his projects.

> *I would like to thank Packt Publishing for giving me the opportunity to work on this book as a reviewer. I would also like to thank Yannick Lefebvre, who did a wonderful job writing it, and my wife, who showed quite a lot of patience and support as I kept working on this book after hours.*
>
> *Content management systems (CMS) are key for brands to share information and reach out to their communities and fans. WordPress is a reference in the CMS world, one of the best known systems in the market. This book will definitely help plugin developers quickly start building on it.*

Ardian Yuli Setyanto, S.Kom, has played with programming since in high school. He joined national selection for Tim Olimpiade Komputer Indonesia (TOKI, Indonesia Computer Olympiad Team) in 2002 and 2003, which convinced him to study computer science at Gadjah Mada University (UGM), and he graduated in 2009 firstly among his other friends with a score 3.5/4.

He also used WordPress as his essay topic for bachelor degree, he developed his own plugin and combined it with a GSM phone to read and send SMS, instead of the usual email, to manage WordPress comments in his essay. After graduating from university, he start working as freelancer using WordPress and Prestashop. These CMS are widely used in his home country, Indonesia.

Now he is working as a backend developer using Symfony2, Rails, and Sinatra. You can reach him on Twitter: @ardianys.

> *I would like to thank Packt for giving me this wonderful opportunity as a reviewer on their book once again. I would like to thank Arun Nadar, who assisted me while I was reviewing Yannick's wonderful content. I would also like to thank my family, Niela, Nain, Nusa, and Mazaya. All praise to God.*

www.PacktPub.com

For support files and downloads related to your book, please visit www.PacktPub.com.

Did you know that Packt offers eBook versions of every book published, with PDF and ePub files available? You can upgrade to the eBook version at www.PacktPub.com and as a print book customer, you are entitled to a discount on the eBook copy. Get in touch with us at service@packtpub.com for more details.

At www.PacktPub.com, you can also read a collection of free technical articles, sign up for a range of free newsletters and receive exclusive discounts and offers on Packt books and eBooks.

https://www.packtpub.com/mapt

Get the most in-demand software skills with Mapt. Mapt gives you full access to all Packt books and video courses, as well as industry-leading tools to help you plan your personal development and advance your career.

Why subscribe?

- Fully searchable across every book published by Packt
- Copy and paste, print, and bookmark content
- On demand and accessible via a web browser

Customer Feedback

Thanks for purchasing this Packt book. At Packt, quality is at the heart of our editorial process. To help us improve, please leave us an honest review on this book's Amazon page at `https://www.amazon.com/dp/1788291182`.

If you'd like to join our team of regular reviewers, you can email us at `customerreviews@packtpub.com`. We award our regular reviewers with free eBooks and videos in exchange for their valuable feedback. Help us be relentless in improving our products!

To my wife, Andrée, for her everlasting love, her patience throughout the writing process, and for being a great first proofreader.
To my daughters, Évelyne and Gabrielle, for always making me smile, giving the best hugs in the world, and growing up to become wonderful young ladies.

Table of Contents

Preface   1

Chapter 1: Preparing a Local Development Environment   7

   Introduction   7
   Installing a web server on your computer   8
      How to do it...   8
      How it works...   12
      There's more...   13
         Creating a remote web development environment   13
      See also   14
   Downloading and configuring a local WordPress installation   14
      Getting ready   14
      How to do it...   15
      How it works...   18
   Creating a local Subversion repository   19
      How to do it...   19
      How it works...   21
      There's more...   21
         Manual repository creation   22
         Other version control systems   22
      See also   22
   Importing initial files to a local Subversion repository   22
      Getting ready   22
      How to do it...   23
      How it works...   24
      See also   24
   Checking out files from a Subversion repository   24
      Getting ready   24
      How to do it...   25
      How it works...   26
      There's more...   26
         Subversion file statuses   26
      See also   27
   Committing changes to a Subversion repository   27
      Getting ready   28
      How to do it...   28

How it works...   30
There's more...   30
   Viewing the differences in modified files   30
   Updating files to latest repository version   31
   Reverting uncommitted file changes   31
   Viewing file history   31
Installing a dedicated code editor/text editor   31
Getting ready   32
How to do it...   33
How it works...   34

Chapter 2: Plugin Framework Basics   35

Introduction   35
Creating a plugin file and header   36
Getting ready   36
How to do it...   37
How it works...   38
See also   39
Adding output content to page headers using plugin actions   40
How to do it...   40
How it works...   41
There's more...   43
   Action hooks online listings   43
   Searching for hooks in the WordPress source code   43
See also   44
Using WordPress path utility functions to load external files and images   44
How to do it...   44
How it works...   46
There's more...   46
See also   47
Modifying the site generator meta tag using plugin filters   47
How to do it...   47
How it works...   48
There's more...   49
   preg_replace function   49
   Filter hooks online listings and the apply_filters function 49
See also   50
Adding text after each item's content using plugin filters   50
How to do it...   50
How it works...   52

There's more...	53
get_the_title and get_permalink functions	53
See also	53
Inserting link statistics tracking code in page body using plugin filters	53
Getting ready	54
How to do it...	54
How it works...	55
See also	56
Troubleshooting coding errors and printing variable content	56
How to do it...	56
How it works...	59
There's more...	60
Built-in WordPress debugging features	60
See also	61
Creating a new simple shortcode	61
How to do it...	62
How it works...	63
See also	63
Creating a new shortcode with parameters	63
How to do it...	64
How it works...	65
See also	66
Creating a new enclosing shortcode	66
How to do it...	66
How it works...	67
See also	67
Loading a style sheet to format plugin output	68
Getting ready	68
How to do it...	68
How it works...	69
See also	69
Writing plugins using object-oriented PHP	70
Getting ready	70
How to do it...	70
How it works...	71
See also	72
Chapter 3: User Settings and Administration Pages	73
Introduction	74
Creating default user settings on plugin initialization	74

How to do it... 75
How it works... 76
There's more... 77
    Deactivation function 77
See also 78
Storing user settings using arrays 78
Getting ready 78
How to do it... 78
How it works... 80
See also 81
Removing plugin data on deletion 81
Getting ready 82
How to do it... 82
How it works... 83
See also 84
Creating an administration page menu item in the settings menu 84
Getting ready 84
How to do it... 85
How it works... 87
There's more... 87
    Settings hook priority to determine menu order 88
See also 88
Creating a multi-level administration menu 88
How to do it... 88
How it works... 90
See also 91
Adding menu items leading to external pages 91
Getting ready 91
How to do it... 92
How it works... 92
See also 93
Hiding items which users should not access from the default menu 93
How to do it... 93
How it works... 94
Rendering the admin page contents using HTML 95
Getting ready 95
How to do it... 95
How it works... 97
There's more... 97
    wp_nonce_field 98

See also   98
Processing and storing plugin configuration data   98
   Getting ready   99
   How to do it...   99
   How it works...   101
   See also   102
Displaying a confirmation message when options are saved   102
   Getting ready   102
   How to do it...   102
   How it works...   104
   See also   104
Adding custom help pages   104
   Getting ready   105
   How to do it...   105
   How it works...   107
   See also   108
Rendering the admin page contents using the Settings API   108
   How to do it...   108
   How it works...   112
   There's more...   114
     Rendering a drop-down list settings field   114
     Rendering a text area settings field   115
   See also   115
Accessing user settings from action and filter hooks   116
   Getting ready   116
   How to do it...   116
   How it works...   117
   See also   118
Formatting admin pages using meta boxes   118
   Getting ready   118
   How to do it...   118
   How it works...   122
   See also   124
Splitting admin code from the main plugin file to optimize site performance   124
   Getting ready   125
   How to do it...   125
   How it works...   126
   See also   126
Storing style sheet data in user settings   127

Getting ready	127
How to do it...	127
How it works...	131
See also	132
Managing multiple sets of user settings from a single admin page	132
Getting ready	133
How to do it...	133
How it works...	138
See also	139
Creating network-level admin pages	139
Getting ready	139
How to do it...	139
How it works...	142
See also	142
Chapter 4: The Power of Custom Post Types	143
Introduction	143
Creating a custom post type	144
Getting ready	145
How to do it...	145
How it works...	148
There's more...	149
Changing the custom post type permalinks slug	149
Adding a new section to the custom post type editor	150
Getting ready	150
How to do it...	150
How it works...	153
See also	154
Displaying single custom post type items using a custom layout	154
Getting ready	155
How to do it...	155
How it works...	157
See also	158
Displaying custom post type data in shortcodes	158
Getting ready	159
How to do it...	159
How it works...	162
There's more...	162
do_shortcode function	163
Adding custom categories for custom post types	163

Getting ready	163
How to do it...	164
How it works...	166
See also	166
Adding custom fields to categories	**166**
Getting ready	167
How to do it...	167
How it works...	169
See also	169
Hiding the category editor from the custom post type editor	**170**
Getting ready	170
How to do it...	170
How it works...	172
See also	172
Displaying additional columns in the custom post list page	**173**
Getting ready	173
How to do it...	173
How it works...	176
See also	177
Adding filters for custom categories to the custom post list page	**177**
Getting ready	177
How to do it...	178
How it works...	179
See also	180
Adding Quick Edit fields for custom categories	**180**
Getting ready	181
How to do it...	181
How it works...	186
Updating page title to include custom post data using plugin filters	**187**
Getting ready	188
How to do it...	188
How it works...	189
Chapter 5: Customizing Post and Page Editors	**191**
Introduction	191
Capturing and displaying information using custom meta boxes	**192**
Getting ready	192
How to do it...	192
How it works...	195
There's more...	196

Adding a new meta box to all post types (including custom ones)   196
Displaying custom post data using filter functions   196
   Getting ready   197
   How to do it...   197
   How it works...   198
   See also   198
Hiding the Custom Field section in the post editor   199
   Getting ready   199
   How to do it...   199
   How it works...   201
Extending the post editor to allow users to upload files directly   201
   Getting ready   201
   How to do it...   202
   How it works...   206
   See also   207

Chapter 6: Accepting User Content Submissions   209

Introduction   209
Creating a client-side content submission form   210
   Getting ready   210
   How to do it...   210
   How it works...   213
   See also   213
Saving user-submitted content in custom post types   213
   Getting ready   214
   How to do it...   214
   How it works...   216
   There's more...   217
     Moderating user-submitted content   217
   See also   218
Sending email notifications upon new submissions   218
   Getting ready   218
   How to do it...   219
   How it works...   220
   See also   221
Implementing a CAPTCHA on user forms using an online service   221
   Getting ready   221
   How to do it...   222
   How it works...   224
   See also   225

Using a local library to implement a CAPTCHA on user forms	225
Getting ready	226
How to do it...	226
How it works...	228
See also	228
Chapter 7: Customizing User Data	229
Introduction	229
Adding custom fields to the user editor	229
Getting ready	230
How to do it...	230
How it works...	232
See also	232
Processing and storing user custom data	233
Getting ready	233
How to do it...	233
How it works...	234
See also	234
Displaying new user data in user list page	235
Getting ready	235
How to do it...	235
How it works...	239
See also	239
Using custom user data in containing shortcode	240
Getting ready	240
How to do it...	240
How it works...	241
See also	242
Chapter 8: Creating Custom MySQL Database Tables	243
Introduction	244
Creating new database tables	244
Getting ready	244
How to do it...	245
How it works...	246
There's more...	247
Using phpMyAdmin to simplify code creation	248
Create tables in network installation	249
Deleting custom tables on plugin removal	251
Getting ready	251
How to do it...	251

How it works...	253
See also	253
Updating custom table structure on plugin upgrade	253
Getting ready	253
How to do it...	254
How it works...	255
See also	255
Displaying custom table data on an admin page	256
Getting ready	256
How to do it...	256
How it works...	258
See also	259
Inserting and updating records in custom tables	259
Getting ready	259
How to do it...	260
How it works...	264
See also	265
Deleting records from custom tables	265
Getting ready	265
How to do it...	265
How it works...	267
See also	268
Displaying custom database table data in shortcodes	269
Getting ready	269
How to do it...	269
How it works...	271
See also	271
Implementing a search function to retrieve custom table data	272
Getting ready	272
How to do it...	272
How it works...	274
See also	274
Importing data from a user file into custom tables	275
Getting ready	275
How to do it...	275
How it works...	278
See also	278
Chapter 9: Leveraging JavaScript, jQuery, and AJAX Scripts	279
Introduction	279

Safely loading jQuery onto WordPress web pages	280
Getting ready	280
How to do it...	280
How it works...	282
There's more...	282
jQuery noconflict mode	282
Displaying a pop-up dialog using the built-in ThickBox plugin	283
Getting ready	283
How to do it...	283
How it works...	285
There's more...	286
Removing the dialog close button	286
Displaying pop-up dialogs on select pages	286
Controlling pop-up dialog display using shortcodes	287
Getting ready	287
How to do it...	287
How it works...	290
See also	290
Displaying a calendar day selector using the Datepicker plugin	290
Getting ready	290
How to do it...	291
How it works...	293
Adding tooltips to admin page form fields using the TipTip plugin	293
Getting ready	294
How to do it...	294
How it works...	296
See also	296
Using AJAX to dynamically update partial page contents	296
Getting ready	297
How to do it...	297
How it works...	301
See also	302
Chapter 10: Adding New Widgets to the WordPress Library	303
Introduction	303
Creating a new widget in WordPress	304
Getting ready	304
How to do it…	304
How it works…	305
There's more…	306

Plugins extending other plugins   306
See also   306
Displaying configuration options   307
Getting ready   307
How to do it...   307
How it works...   309
See also   310
Validating configuration options   310
Getting ready   310
How to do it...   311
How it works...   311
See also   312
Implementing the widget display function   312
Getting ready   312
How to do it...   313
How it works...   314
See also   315
Adding a custom dashboard widget   315
Getting ready   315
How to do it...   315
How it works...   317
See also   318
Adding a custom widget to the network dashboard   318
Getting ready   318
How to do it...   319
How it works...   320
See also   321
Chapter 11: Enabling Plugin Internationalization   323
Introduction   323
Changing the WordPress language configuration   324
Getting ready   324
How to do it...   324
How it works...   325
Adapting default user settings for translation   325
Getting ready   325
How to do it...   326
How it works...   327
See also   327
Making admin page code ready for translation   327

Getting ready	328
How to do it…	328
How it works…	330
See also	330
Modifying shortcode output for translation	330
Getting ready	331
How to do it…	331
How it works…	332
See also	332
Translating text strings using Poedit	332
Getting ready	333
How to do it…	333
How it works…	335
There's more…	335
Translation template file	335
See also	336
Loading a language file in the plugin initialization	336
Getting ready	336
How to do it…	336
How it works…	337
There's more…	338
Updating a translation file	338
Advanced translation functions	338
Localizing JavaScript files	339
See also	339
Chapter 12: Distributing Your Plugin on wordpress.org	341
Introduction	341
Creating a README file for your plugin	342
Getting ready	343
How to do it…	343
How it works…	344
There's more…	345
Releasing specific plugin versions using tags	345
Applying for your plugin to be hosted on WordPress.org	346
How to do it…	346
How it works…	346
See also	347
Uploading your plugin using Subversion	347
Getting ready	347
How to do it…	348

How it works…   350
There's more…   350
  Checking out plugins to your development installation   350
See also   351
Providing plugin banner and thumbnail images   351
Getting ready   351
How to do it…   351
How it works…   353
See also   354
Index   355

Preface

Developing plugins for WordPress is the next big thing for you if you are an administrator looking to enhance a personal site with custom functionality for which no plugin exists, a developer looking to enhance the WordPress platform with new ideas for the community, or a website designer building a specific project for a client. Learning how to create WordPress plugins will allow you to unleash the full potential of the most popular web content management system.

As an early WordPress adopter, before version 1.0 was out, I started building plugins to add functionality to my personal site. Once I got these new elements in place, I quickly realized that other users could benefit from these extensions, and started distributing them online. To this day, I always love hearing back from users of my creations and finding out how they have put them to use and what new functionality they think would make them even better.

While developing plugins might initially sound a little bit like black magic, this book shows you how easy creating plugins actually is through a series of step-by-step recipes. If you have previously added code to a theme's functions file, you may even be familiar with some of the mechanics explained in this book. With all of the information contained in this book, you will quickly be able to create your own plugins or dissect existing ones to add that extra bit of missing functionality that you require. Before you know, you'll be publishing your own creations to the official WordPress plugin repository!

Let's start learning how to cook up great WordPress plugins!

What this book covers

Chapter 1, *Preparing a Local Development Environment*, shows plugin developers how to install and configure an efficient development environment.

Chapter 2, *Plugin Framework Basics*, explains the basic mechanics of registering user functions with WordPress to be executed at key points when web pages are displayed, forming the basis of plugin creation.

Chapter 3, *User Settings and Administration Pages*, covers the creation of administration pages that will allow users to configure the plugins you create.

Chapter 4, *The Power of Custom Post Types*, empowers developers to add whole new content management sections to the WordPress environment.

Chapter 5, *Customizing Post and Page Editors*, demonstrates how to alter the default administration post and page editing environment to add new capabilities.

Chapter 6, *Accepting User Content Submissions*, allows users to submit their own content to new content sections that will be managed by your plugins.

Chapter 7, *Customizing User Data*, explains how to store additional information for users and how to modify site output based on this data.

Chapter 8, *Creating Custom MySQL Database Tables*, leverages the power of MySQL to create custom database tables in a site database to store and retrieve custom data.

Chapter 9, *Leveraging JavaScript, jQuery, and AJAX Scripts*, makes plugin output very dynamic by using a number of popular script libraries.

Chapter 10, *Adding New Widgets to the WordPress Library*, indicates how to add new widgets that users will be able to easily drag and drop to add content to their web pages.

Chapter 11, *Enabling Plugin Internationalization*, prepares your plugin to be translated into any language to make it easier to be used by non-English speakers.

Chapter 12, *Distributing Your Plugin on wordpress.org*, shows you how to prepare your plugin for sharing with the global WordPress community.

What you need for this book

Chapter 1, *Preparing a Local Development Environment*, walks you through all of the tools that are useful to have when developing plugins for WordPress, including a local web server, a Subversion client, and a dedicated code editor. While this book will always describe all of the steps necessary to perform its recipes, having a good understanding of WordPress will allow you to fully appreciate the information contained in these pages.

Who this book is for

This book is for WordPress users, developers, or site integrators with basic knowledge of WordPress and PHP and an interest in creating new plugins to address their personal needs, client needs, or share new ideas with the WordPress community.

Conventions

In this book, you will find a number of text styles that distinguish between different kinds of information. Here are some examples of these styles and an explanation of their meaning.

Code words in text, database table names, folder names, filenames, file extensions, pathnames, dummy URLs, user input, and Twitter handles are shown as follows: "create a text file called `uninstall.php` in the `ch8-bug-tracker` directory and open it in a code editor."

A block of code is set as follows:

```
add_filter( 'the_generator', 'ch2gf_generator_filter', 10, 2 );
```

When we wish to draw your attention to a particular part of a code block, the relevant lines or items are set in bold:

```
echo '<tr style="background: #FFF">';
echo '<td><input type="checkbox" name="bugs[]" value="';
echo intval( $bug_item['bug_id'] ) . '" /></td>';
echo '<td>' . $bug_item['bug_id'] . '</td>';
```

New terms and **important words** are shown in bold. Words that you see on the screen, for example, in menus or dialog boxes, appear in the text like this: "Here, we added an inner grid with two full-size columns; one for the **Price** of an item and the other will wrap up the **Quantity** component."

> Warnings or important notes appear in a box like this.

> Tips and tricks appear like this.

Reader feedback

Feedback from our readers is always welcome. Let us know what you think about this book-what you liked or disliked. Reader feedback is important for us as it helps us develop titles that you will really get the most out of.

To send us general feedback, simply email `feedback@packtpub.com`, and mention the book's title in the subject of your message.

If there is a topic that you have expertise in and you are interested in either writing or contributing to a book, see our author guide at `www.packtpub.com/authors`.

Customer support

Now that you are the proud owner of a Packt book, we have a number of things to help you to get the most from your purchase.

Downloading the example code

You can download the example code files for this book from your account at `http://www.packtpub.com`. If you purchased this book elsewhere, you can visit `http://www.packtpub.com/support`and register to have the files emailed directly to you.

You can download the code files by following these steps:

1. Log in or register to our website using your email address and password.
2. Hover the mouse pointer on the **SUPPORT** tab at the top.
3. Click on **Code Downloads & Errata**.
4. Enter the name of the book in the **Search** box.
5. Select the book for which you're looking to download the code files.
6. Choose from the drop-down menu where you purchased this book from.
7. Click on **Code Download**.

Once the file is downloaded, please make sure that you unzip or extract the folder using the latest version of:

- WinRAR / 7-Zip for Windows
- Zipeg / iZip / UnRarX for Mac
- 7-Zip / PeaZip for Linux

The code bundle for the book is also hosted on GitHub at `https://github.com/PacktPublishing/WordPress-Plugin-Development-Cookbook-Second-Edition`. We also have other code bundles from our rich catalog of books and videos available at `https://github.com/PacktPublishing/`. Check them out!

Errata

Although we have taken every care to ensure the accuracy of our content, mistakes do happen. If you find a mistake in one of our books-maybe a mistake in the text or the code-we would be grateful if you could report this to us. By doing so, you can save other readers from frustration and help us improve subsequent versions of this book. If you find any errata, please report them by visiting http://www.packtpub.com/submit-errata, selecting your book, clicking on the **Errata Submission Form** link, and entering the details of your errata. Once your errata are verified, your submission will be accepted and the errata will be uploaded to our website or added to any list of existing errata under the Errata section of that title.

To view the previously submitted errata, go to https://www.packtpub.com/books/content/support and enter the name of the book in the search field. The required information will appear under the **Errata** section.

Piracy

Piracy of copyrighted material on the Internet is an ongoing problem across all media. At Packt, we take the protection of our copyright and licenses very seriously. If you come across any illegal copies of our works in any form on the Internet, please provide us with the location address or website name immediately so that we can pursue a remedy.

Please contact us at copyright@packtpub.com with a link to the suspected pirated material.

We appreciate your help in protecting our authors and our ability to bring you valuable content.

Questions

If you have a problem with any aspect of this book, you can contact us at questions@packtpub.com, and we will do our best to address the problem.

1
Preparing a Local Development Environment

We will cover the following topics in this chapter:

- Installing a web server on your computer
- Downloading and configuring a local WordPress installation
- Creating a local Subversion repository
- Importing initial files to a local Subversion repository
- Checking out files from a Subversion repository
- Committing changes to a Subversion repository
- Installing a dedicated code/text editor

Introduction

Before we start writing our first WordPress plugin, it is important to have a good set of tools in place that will allow you to work locally on your computer and be more efficient in your work. While it is possible to perform some development tasks with the built-in tools that are provided with the operating system, creating a solid local development environment will help you develop plugins quickly and have full control over your server settings to be able to test different configurations.

This chapter proposes a set of free tools that can easily be installed on your computer, regardless of your preferred operating system, to facilitate the development of your future WordPress plugins. These tools include a local web server to speed up page access and avoid sending files constantly to a remote server, a version control system to keep incremental backups of your work, and a code editor to enhance your editing capabilities. In addition to installing and learning how to use these tools, this chapter also shows how to download and configure a local WordPress installation on a local web server.

Installing a web server on your computer

The first step to configure a local development environment is to install a local web server on your computer. This will transform your computer into a system capable of displaying web pages and performing all tasks related to rendering a WordPress website locally.

Having a local web server has many benefits, as follows:

- It provides a quick response to the frequent page refreshes that are made as plugin code is written, tested, and refined, since all information is processed locally
- It removes the need to constantly upload new plugin file versions to a remote web server to validate code changes
- It allows development to take place when no internet connection is available (for example, when traveling on an airplane)
- It offers a worry-free programming environment, where you cannot bring down a live website with a programming error or an infinite loop

There are many free packages available online that contain all of the web server components necessary to run a WordPress installation. This recipe shows you how to easily install one of these packages.

How to do it...

1. Visit the XAMPP website (`https://www.apachefriends.org/`) and download the appropriate XAMPP package for your computer.

XAMPP is available for Windows, macOS, and Linux platforms. The screenshots in this recipe were taken from XAMPP version 5.6.30 on Windows 10. The installation steps and exact dialog content might vary based on your choice of platform.

2. Optional on Windows: Disable the Windows **User Access Control (UAC)** feature to give full permissions to XAMPP to install itself on your system (look up the steps to perform this procedure on your favorite search engine).
3. Launch the XAMPP installer (`xampp-win32-5.6.30-0-VC11-installer.exe` on the Windows platform).
4. Acknowledge the warning message about **User Access Control (UAC)** and click on **Next** to start the installation process.
5. On the following screen, which lists all of the components that can be installed, uncheck the boxes for **FileZilla FTP Server**, **Mercury Mail Server**, **Tomcat**, **Perl**, and **Webalizer**, then click on **Next**:

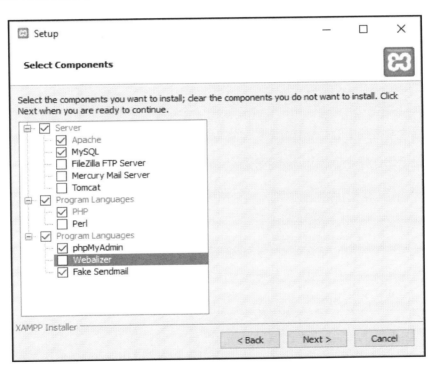

6. On the **Installation folder** screen, leave the default value for the installation directory if possible (c:\xampp), since some references to this folder will be made in this book, then click on **Next**.

7. Click on the **Next** button to proceed with the web server installation.

8. Make sure that the option to start the **Control Panel** is checked and click on **Finish** once the installation is complete.

9. Select your preferred language for the **XAMPP Control Panel** and click on **Save** to launch the application.

10. Click the **Start** buttons for **Apache** and **MySQL** to launch these modules. Their names will be highlighted in green once they have been successfully started, as shown in the following screenshot:

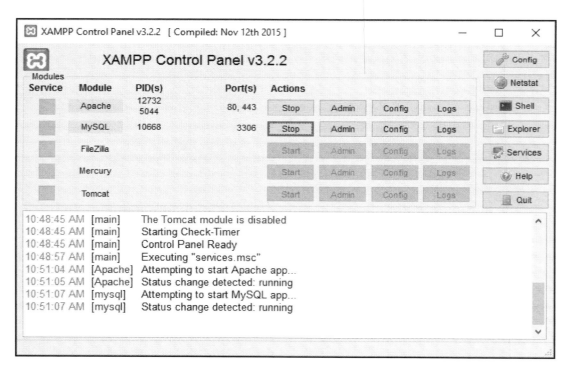

11. Open a web browser and navigate to the address `http://localhost` to display your local web server's welcome page:

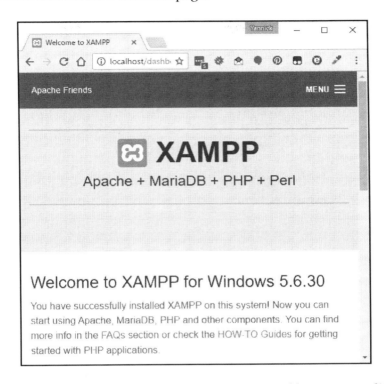

12. Open the `c:\xampp\apache\conf\httpd.conf` file in a text editor (for example, Notepad).
13. Search for the `DocumentRoot` configuration option and change its value to a different location on the disk to avoid keeping your project files under the original installation directory. For example, you could set it to a new directory designed to hold your local development installation of WordPress, such as `DocumentRoot "C:/WPDev"`.

 Notice that forward slashes are used in this path. You should be careful if you copy and paste a path from a file explorer window.

14. Search for the `Directory` option and change it to the same path that was used for `DocumentRoot`, that is, `<Directory "C:/WPDev">`.

15. Save and close the `httpd.conf` file.

16. Create the directory specified as `DocumentRoot`, if it does not already exist on your computer.

17. Open **XAMPP Control Panel**.

18. Stop and re-start the **Apache** service for the new configuration to take effect.

 Trying to access the local web server's welcome page will no longer work after having performed steps 14 through 20, since the new directory specified is currently empty. This will be corrected in the next recipe.

How it works...

The XAMPP package contains all of the components necessary to run a web server capable of hosting a WordPress website on your computer. These components include:

- Apache web server
- PHP interpreter
- MySQL database server
- phpMyAdmin database management interface

The XAMPP package also includes other components, which are not required to run a local WordPress development site.

Once XAMPP is installed and started, the keyword `localhost` that we type in the web browser is recognized by the operating system as a request to communicate with the web server on the local computer and the Apache web server displays the welcome page from its documentation.

The XAMPP documentation is a set of flat HTML files located in the `c:\xampp\htdocs` directory on the Windows platform. This is the web server's default working directory.

The last few steps of the recipe instruct the Apache web server to look for the local website's content in a new directory. This is a safety precaution to be sure that site files are not deleted inadvertently if XAMPP is uninstalled. It can also help in managing multiple sites on a single computer.

There's more...

While XAMPP is a full-featured local web server package and is available on the three major operating systems, there are many others available online. Most of these packages will run the required web services on the computer directly, while more advanced packages, such as **Varying Vagrant Vagrants (VVV)**, will virtualize a Linux-based web server on your computer to create a more accurate replica of a final deployment environment optimized for WordPress. Here is a list of some of the most popular local web server packages:

For Windows:

- WampServer (http://www.wampserver.com/en/)
- EasyPHP (http://www.easyphp.org/)

For macOS X:

- MAMP (https://www.mamp.info/en)

For Windows, Mac, or Linux:

- Varying Vagrant Vagrants (https://varyingvagrantvagrants.org)

 For a more complete list of web server packages, visit https://en.wikipedia.org/wiki/List_of_AMP_packages.

Creating a remote web development environment

If it's not possible for you to set up a local web server to develop WordPress plugins, or if you are planning to share the development tasks with one or more people, then an alternative to setting up a local web server is to create a remote development environment.

The easiest way to create such an environment, assuming that you already have a web hosting account set up, is to create a sub-domain off your main domain. This will allow you to create a standalone test installation for WordPress that will still provide safety from affecting a live site, but will not carry the other benefits of a local installation.

See also

- The *Downloading and configuring a local WordPress installation* recipe

Downloading and configuring a local WordPress installation

The next component of our local development environment is to install WordPress on your local web server to run a fully working website and have all of its files hosted locally.

WordPress has always prided itself with its easy five minutes installation process. Installing it on a local web server is even easier and quicker than it would be on a live remote server. This recipe covers the creation of a MySQL database to store all data related to our new WordPress installation and the actual setup process.

Getting ready

This recipe assumes that you have a local web server installed on your computer. This web server can be a fresh install performed using the previous recipe or can be from a previous installation. The steps in the following section are written with a focus on new local web servers. If you have created a new account to access the MySQL database or changed the root user's password, some of the steps will change slightly. The location of the phpMyAdmin tool might also be different if you are using a different web server than XAMPP. You should refer to your web server's documentation to find out what that address is.

How to do it...

1. In the web browser, navigate to the address `http://localhost/phpmyadmin/` to access your web server's database administration tool.
2. Click on **Databases** tab in **phpMyAdmin**.
3. Type the name of the new database to be created in the empty field following to the words **Create database**. In this case, we will use the name `wordpressdev`:

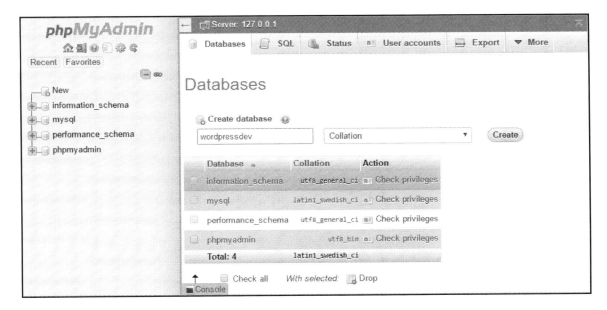

4. Click on the **Create** button to complete the database creation process.
5. Download the latest WordPress installation package from the official WordPress website (`https://wordpress.org`). The download link can be found on the very first page of the website and the download package will work on any web server, local, or remote.

 The following instructions have been tested against WordPress version 4.8. While the installation process does not usually change much between versions, there may be slight differences in these steps on newer versions.

6. Extract the WordPress archive file contents using your favorite file archiver utility or your operating system's built-in capabilities.

7. Copy the contents of the resulting `wordpress` folder to your local web server's web content directory (`c:\WPDev`, if you followed the previous recipe). You should not copy the `wordpress` folder itself unless you want the address of your WordPress website to be `http://localhost/wordpress`.

8. Direct your web browser to `http://localhost` to start the WordPress installation process.

9. Select your preferred language and click on **Continue**.

10. On the next page, click on the **Let's Go** button to start your development site's configuration.

11. Update the **Database Name** field to reflect the name of our newly-created database (`wordpressdev`).

12. Set the MySQL **User Name** to `root`.

13. Delete all the characters from MySQL **Password** to leave it empty, since local MySQL server root accounts are typically configured without any password.

14. Leave the **Database Host** field with its default value (`localhost`).

15. Change the **Table Prefix** field from its default value to `wpdev_`:

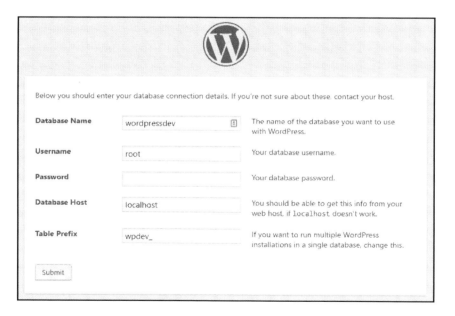

16. Click on the **Submit** button to validate the information entered. If any parameters are not entered correctly, or if the WordPress installation process cannot correctly access your database server, it will display an error page and give you an opportunity to make corrections.

17. Click on the **Run the install** button for WordPress to create the required table structure in the designated MySQL database.

18. Specify a **Site Title** (for example, `Development Site`).

19. Set **Username** for the admin user. For increased security, it's always best to choose a username that people would not be able to easily guess. Obvious names such as admin or administrator should be avoided.

20. Optionally, change the randomly generated password with a password of your own choice. If WordPress determines that your new password is weak, you will need to check the additional checkbox that appears to confirm that you want to use a weak password.

21. Enter your email address in the appropriate field (although no email will actually be sent on most local development installations).

22. If you are configuring a live external development server, check the **Discourage search engines from indexing this site** option, since we do not want this development site to appear anywhere.

23. Click on **Install WordPress** to complete the installation and you will be automatically logged in to the site's WordPress **Dashboard**.

24. Click on the **Development Site** link in the Dashboard admin bar to see your new site:

How it works...

In the first few steps, the phpMyAdmin interface is used to create a database on the local MySQL server. This web-based database management tool comes bundled with XAMPP and most other web servers. The `http://localhost/phpmyadmin` address will always take you to the database administration tool, even if you relocate your web server's document root directory as documented in the previous recipe.

Once a database is created and the WordPress files have been copied to the correct location, pointing your browser to the local web server gets it to search through the document root directory to find HTML files to send back to the browser or PHP files to execute. In the case of WordPress, the web server finds the `index.php` file and executes it using its PHP interpreter. As the WordPress code is executed, it checks if a configuration file is present and launches the installation process when it does not find one. The WordPress code does not see any difference between the local web server that we are running it on and a remote live web server that would be accessible anywhere online.

While we specified an email address for the administrator during the installation, many local web servers are not configured to send out email messages so we will never receive any email communication in these cases. It is preferable to use a remote server when developing and testing email functionality in a plugin.

Once this recipe has been completed, you will have a functional WordPress installation in place.

Creating a local Subversion repository

Version control is an important part of any code development project, to keep track of a project's history, to have full and organized backups, and to be able to easily roll back changes to get back to a known working state. Version control is also the best and most efficient way to share code and other files when developing a project in a team environment. In addition to being a great version control system that is easy to use and configure, Subversion (often referred to as SVN) is also the technology that manages all submissions on the official WordPress plugin directory. Therefore, by setting up and using a local Subversion repository during your initial plugin development, you will immediately be ready to share your creations with the community.

How to do it...

1. Visit the **TortoiseSVN** website (`https://tortoisesvn.net/downloads.html`) and download the free Subversion client for your version of Windows (32-bit or 64-bit).

While this recipe focuses on the creation of a local repository on the Windows platform, equivalent tools for other platforms are discussed after the recipe steps, in the *There's more...* section.

2. Launch the TortoiseSVN installation program and install it using all the default installation options.
3. Create a new folder on your hard drive that will host the local Subversion repository (for example, `c:\WPSVN`).
4. Right-click on the new folder and select the **TortoiseSVN | Create repository here** menu item, then click on **Start Repobrowser**. TortoiseSVN will create the required file structure in the target directory and display the contents of the repository, which is currently empty:

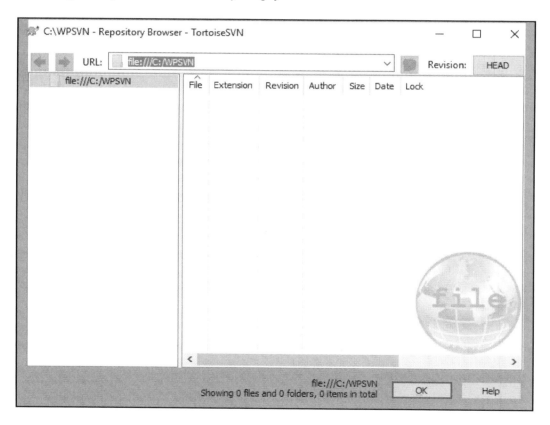

How it works...

Subversion is a free, open source version control system that is designed to keep file revisions organized and backed up over the course of a project's development, as well as provide access to older versions of all files at any time. If you have ever found yourself copying a directory on your computer and giving each copy sequentially numbered names or adding dates to their names, then you will recognize that version control is really just a more organized and efficient method of achieving the same goal of keeping backups of known working versions of code files and being able to access any older version of a file.

While the default Subversion interface is a set of command-line utilities, TortoiseSVN and many other client applications provide graphical tools to create, access, and manage local and remote repositories.

In addition to familiarizing yourself with this system for later use on wordpress.org, using a local Subversion repository will ensure that you will always have older versions of your plugins easily accessible in case a code change that you perform breaks your work and you cannot figure out how to get back to a working state.

There's more...

While there are many Subversion clients available online to interact with a repository, not all of them include the necessary administration tools to easily create a repository, as shown in this recipe. You should look for these administration capabilities when searching for a Subversion client for non-Windows platforms.

On macOS X, versions (http://versionsapp.com/) and Cornerstone (https://www.zennaware.com/cornerstone) offer similar capabilities but are paid applications.

On Linux, PagaVCS is a free TortoiseSVN clone (https://code.google.com/p/pagavcs/) while SmartSVN (http://smartsvn.com) is a paid SVN client.

Manual repository creation

If your Subversion client does not offer the ability to create a local repository, you can download the Subversion command-line tools from the official Subversion website (https://subversion.apache.org/packages.html) and create a repository manually following instructions found in the online Subversion reference manual (http://svnbook.red-bean.com/).

Other version control systems

While Subversion is easy to learn and is the system that is used by WordPress on its official plugin repository, other version control systems, such as Git (https://git-scm.com/) and Mercurial (https://mercurial-scm.org/), are gaining traction in the open source development community and could also be considered to manage your plugin code.

See also

- The *Importing initial files to a local Subversion repository* recipe

Importing initial files to a local Subversion repository

Once you have a local repository in place, this recipe describes the steps required to add files and start tracking their revisions over time. To have the flexibility to create multiple plugins, as discussed throughout this cookbook, without having to worry about adding each of them to the repository individually, we will add the entire WordPress plugin directory to your local repository.

Getting ready

You should have already installed a Subversion client on your computer and created a local repository, as described in the *Creating a local Subversion repository* recipe. These steps will be slightly different based on the Subversion client that you have selected and your operating system.

How to do it...

1. Navigate to the `wp-content/plugins` directory of your local WordPress installation (for example, `c:\WPDev\wp-content\plugins`, if you followed the previous recipe) with the file explorer.
2. Right-click on the folder and select the **TortoiseSVN | Import** menu item.
3. Enter the file location of your local Subversion repository in the **URL of repository** field (for example, `file:///c:/WPSVN`), if it is not already specified.
4. Write a message in the **Import message** field that gives an overview of the files that are being imported into the repository:

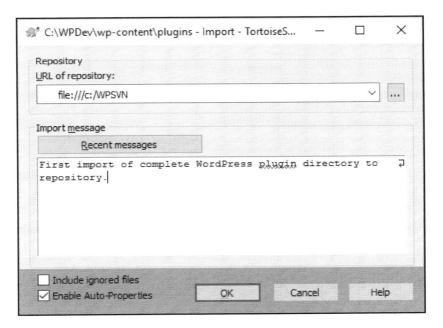

5. Click on the **OK** button to complete the import process.

Once the import operation has started, TortoiseSVN sends all the selected files to the repository, displaying each of their names in the process. At the end of the import operation, it also displays the revision number that it assigned to this first set of files.

How it works...

Using the **Import** Subversion feature copies all the selected files to the repository. In addition to storing the files themselves, Subversion identifies each file with a revision number and an import message. The revision number is generated by Subversion and incremented every time a group of files is added. It is especially useful when searching through a file's history.

The import message is specified by the user and is actually optional. That being said, it is important to set meaningful import messages when adding files to a repository, as it will make it easier for you to identify what these files are, the state that they are in, and the reason they were added to the repository when performing future searches.

While these steps have led to a successful import, you may be wondering why nothing changed in the plugin directory. The reason is that the import process only makes copies of the selected files to the Subversion repository. An additional step, called the checkout process, needs to take place to start keeping track of changes and file history.

See also

- The *Checking out files from a Subversion repository* recipe

Checking out files from a Subversion repository

After performing an initial import of the files to a Subversion repository, the files need to be checked out to really start working in a version control environment. This recipe explains how to check out files from your local repository and what the resulting file structure changes will be.

Getting ready

You should have already installed a Subversion client, created a local repository, and imported files before following this recipe. These steps will be slightly different based on the Subversion client that you have selected and the operating system you are using.

How to do it...

1. Navigate to the WordPress plugin directory of your local installation in the file explorer if you are not already there.
2. Right-click in the white space of the directory window and select the **SVN Checkout...** menu item.
3. Enter the file location of your local Subversion repository in the **URL of repository** field (for example, `file:///c:/WPSVN`), if it is not already specified.
4. Set **Checkout directory** to the plugin folder of your local WordPress installation (for example, `C:\WPDev\wp-content\plugins`).

 By default, the TortoiseSVN client adds the word `WPSVN` at the end of the path used when performing checkouts. Be sure to remove that last part of the path so that all files that are checked out go to the correct location.

5. Click **Yes** on the dialog asking if files should be checked in a folder that is not empty. At this time, TortoiseSVN will retrieve all the files that were added to the repository and copy them locally.
6. Once the operation is complete, look back at the file listing in the `plugins` directory to see that it has changed from its previous state:

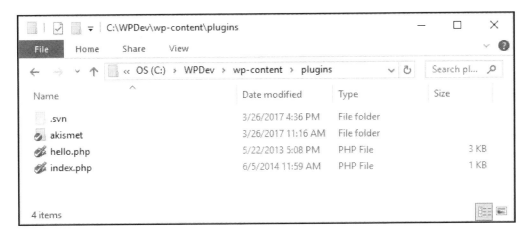

How it works...

Performing a checkout operation takes copies of all files from the repository and places them in the target directory. It also creates a `.svn` directory at the top level of the file hierarchy to store files that will support the version control functionality.

By default, most operating systems do not show folders that have a period at the beginning of their name, since this usually identifies hidden files and directories. To display hidden folders on the Windows 10 platform, carry out the following steps:

1. Open **Windows Explorer**.
2. Click on the **View** tab and check the option labeled **Hidden Items**.

The `.svn` directory contains information on the address of the repository that is associated with the files in the current folder. It also contains an original version of each file that was checked out. These original files are used for Subversion to determine when changes have been made to each file relative to their state when they were checked out or updated. While it might seem a bit redundant to have an original copy of all the files in the `.svn` folders when our repository is locally hosted, this functionality allows Subversion to identify file changes when working on a remote repository, such as the official WordPress plugin server, even when your computer is not connected to the internet.

There's more...

As you work with Subversion and TortoiseSVN, files that you create, modify, and delete will go through a number of different states. The following section explains what each of them represents.

Subversion file statuses

The green check mark indicator shown over each file icon, after performing this recipe, shows us that our files and directories have not been modified since they were last checked out or updated. These indicators will change over time as we start modifying existing files and creating new ones. The following is a list of the most common statuses that files will have as you work on a project, along with their associated TortoiseSVN icons:

- **Normal** (green check mark): The file or directory is in a normal state and has not changed since it was last checked out or updated.

- **Modified** (red exclamation mark): The file or directory has been modified since it was last checked out or updated.
- **Non-versioned** (blue question mark): The file or directory is not under version control.
- **Added** (blue plus sign): The file or directory is new and has been marked to be committed to the repository in the next commit operation.
- **Deleted** (red x icon): The directory has been deleted and will be removed from the repository in the next commit operation.
- **Ignored** (grey do not pass symbol): This file or directory will never be sent to the repository and Subversion should stop checking for changes. This state is useful for keeping private files, such as personal documentation or to-do lists, in the same directory as the plugin but without uploading them to the repository and tracking their history over time.
- **Conflicted** (yellow exclamation mark): This icon appears in situations of conflict, typically when more than one person works on the same repository and multiple users have made changes to the same file. While the Subversion client will normally try to merge these changes to create a single file, a conflicted state indicates that the system was not able to merge these changes automatically. Conflicted files need to be manually merged or the user needs to indicate if the file has priority over the version that is currently stored in the repository.

See also

- The *Committing changes to a Subversion repository* recipe

Committing changes to a Subversion repository

During the course of a project, plugin files will typically be created, modified, or deleted. These changes should be transmitted regularly to the Subversion repository to have proper backups of all the files in a project. A good practice is to commit changes at least once a day, with more frequent commit operations taking place when specific milestones are reached in the implementation of a plugin's features.

This recipe indicates how to manage file creation, modification, and deletion operations to keep everything organized and mirrored in the Subversion repository.

Getting ready

You should have already installed a Subversion client, created a local repository, and imported and checked out files before performing the steps in this recipe. These steps will be slightly different based on the Subversion client that you have selected and the operating system you are using.

How to do it...

1. Navigate to the WordPress plugin directory of your local installation in the file explorer if you are not already there.
2. Open the `hello.php` file in a text editor.
3. Edit the plugin name on line 7 to change it from `Plugin Name: Hello Dolly` to `Plugin Name: Goodbye Dolly`.
4. Save and close the file. You should now notice that the modified file is identified by a red exclamation mark icon in the file explorer, indicating that it has been modified.
5. Create a new folder in the `plugins` directory named `chapter1`.
6. Right-click on the new folder and select the **TortoiseSVN | Add...** menu item to bring up the **Add** dialog.
7. Click on the **OK** button to queue the file to be added to the repository when changes are next committed. You will see a blue plus sign appear over the folder name to indicate that it will be added to the repository on the next code commit.
8. Navigate to the `chapter1` directory and create a new text document named `example.txt`.
9. Navigate back to the `plugins` directory.
10. Right-click on the `index.php` file and select the **TortoiseSVN | Delete** menu item. The selected file is immediately deleted and disappears from the file explorer.

11. Right-click in an empty part of the `plugins` directory and select the **SVN Commit...** menu item. This last step will display the **Commit** dialog, with a top section to write a message detailing the changes that are being committed, and a bottom section containing a file listing. Notice that all files but one have check marks next to them, since they have either been recognized as being changed by the Subversion client or have been added or deleted through the TortoiseSVN interface. The file that does not have a check mark next to it is the text file that was created but not tagged to be included in the next commit operation using the TortoiseSVN contextual menu:

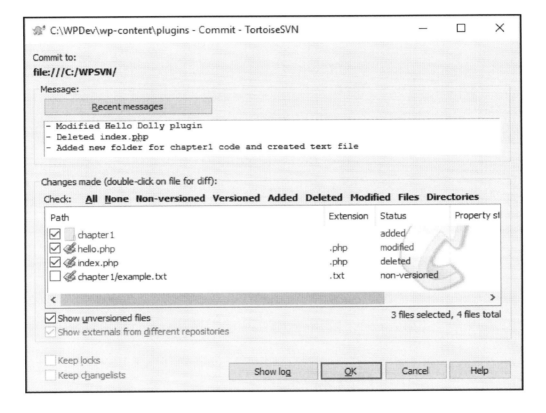

12. Type a message in the appropriate field indicating the reason for the operation.
13. Right-click on the `chapter1/example.txt` file and select the **Add** menu item to add it to the operation.
14. Click on the **OK** button to send all the changes to the Subversion repository.

How it works...

Using the local data stored in the `.svn` folder, the Subversion client is able to analyze the directory contents and identify all the files that are new, have been modified, or are missing since the last checkout or update operation was performed, and then generate a list of these changes.

When the commit operation is performed, new files are added to the repository, modified files are uploaded and stored next to their previous versions, while deleted files are tagged as no longer being part of the current project version. While some of these behaviors might seem strange, it's by preserving previous versions of files and even keeping files that are no longer part of a project that Subversion is able to let us navigate through a project's entire history.

While it is preferable to use the TortoiseSVN menu to mark files and directories for addition and to delete items that are no longer needed, it is also possible to perform these operations when the commit is about to take place, as we saw in the recipe steps.

There's more...

Before files are committed to the repository, many programmers and developers want to see what changes were made to the modified files, especially in an environment that promotes peer reviews before committing code changes.

Viewing the differences in modified files

By right-clicking on any modified file in the Commit dialog and selecting the **Diff** menu item, the TortoiseSVN client will display its built-in file difference viewer tool, highlighting the parts that are different between the last version of the file in the repository and the current version of this file. This allows users to see what changed at a glance and be sure that no code was modified inadvertently.

Updating files to latest repository version

If you are the only person committing files to a repository and you are working on a single computer, then you will never need to use the **SVN Update** menu item. This function is designed to compare your local files with the repository and check if new files or new revisions are available in the repository that are not present locally. It will then apply all the necessary changes to the local versions of these files. Remember to use the **SVN Update** option in TortoiseSVN regularly if you are working in a team environment or are developing a project across multiple computers.

Reverting uncommitted file changes

Until a file is committed to a repository, it's possible to reverse all the changes made to it since the last checkout, update, or committal by using the **Revert** item in the **TortoiseSVN** menu. This can be useful if you made changes to the code that broke its functionality and want to get back to a known good state.

Viewing file history

As multiple versions of files are committed to a repository over time, Subversion keeps track of all the versions of these files along with the messages that were associated with each commit operation. The **Show Log** tool, accessible from the TortoiseSVN menu, allows you to see a full history of changes made to one more files, use the difference viewer to see changes between previous and current versions of each file, and easily restore a specific revision of these files.

Installing a dedicated code editor/text editor

Most operating systems provide a built-in text editor. While it is possible to create WordPress plugins using such a simple tool, it is highly recommended to install a dedicated code editor on your computer to simplify your plugin development work.

Getting ready

Of course, not all code editors are equal. Here are some of the features that you should look for when selecting a code editing application:

- PHP syntax highlighting
- Completion of PHP function names
- Ability to search in multiple files simultaneously
- Ability to highlight all instances of search keyword(s) or selected text
- Line numbering
- Ability to resize the editor text or specify a replacement font
- Possibility of opening multiple files simultaneously

The following editors contain most or all of these key features. Most are free tools, but some are paid applications:

On the Windows platform:

- Programmer's Notepad (http://www.pnotepad.org)
- Notepad++ (https://notepad-plus-plus.org/)
- Visual Studio Code (https://code.visualstudio.com)

On the Mac platform:

- TextMate (https://macromates.com)
- TextWrangler (https://www.barebones.com/products/TextWrangler)

On the Linux platform:

- Screem (http://www.screem.org/)

Cross-platform:

- Sublime Text (https://www.sublimetext.com)

This recipe explains how to install a dedicated code editor and shows basic editor operations. It provides detailed steps using Programmer's Notepad for Windows.

How to do it...

1. Download the installation package for one of the text editors listed previously.
2. Run the installation program for the editor and select the default settings.
3. Launch the text editor.
4. Open the `hello.php` file from the `plugin` directory of your local WordPress installation. You will see that different parts of the code are displayed in different colors based on the type of code.
5. Double-click on a word to select it. You will see any other instance of that same word highlighted across the file contents:

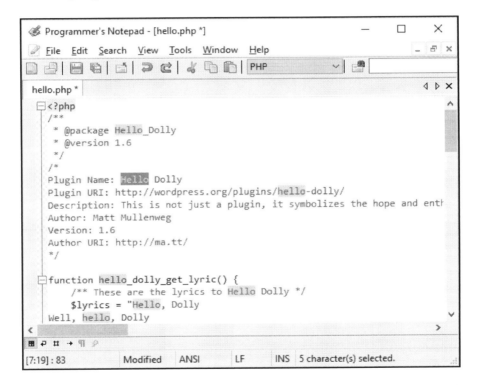

6. Select the **View | Line Numbers** menu item (or similarly named item based on your selected text editor) to display line numbers in the editor.

How it works...

Code editors have built-in parsers that enable them to identify the parts of the code that are comments, PHP language functions, text strings, and a variety of other elements. Having these elements colored on the screen makes it much easier to read through code and to see that a function's name is not spelled correctly, or to quickly identify comments.

Another functionality that is crucial when developing plugins for WordPress is the ability to see line numbers in the editor. This function comes in handy, especially when PHP code errors come up, since the filename and line of code that was being processed at the time of the error are normally displayed. In most code editors, the developer can either scroll to the specific line or enter the line number in a quick **Go To** dialog box to jump to that line right away.

2
Plugin Framework Basics

In this chapter, we will cover the following topics:

- Creating a plugin file and header
- Adding output content to page headers using plugin actions
- Using WordPress path utility functions to load external files and images
- Modifying the site generator meta tag using plugin filters
- Adding text after each item's content using plugin filters
- Inserting link statistics tracking code in page body using plugin filters
- Troubleshooting coding errors and printing variable content
- Creating a new simple shortcode
- Creating a new shortcode with parameters
- Creating a new enclosing shortcode
- Loading a style sheet to format plugin output
- Writing plugins using object-oriented PHP

Introduction

From its very first versions, WordPress has always been designed as a very open platform. This openness has been exemplified not only through its open source licensing and distribution model, but also its open plugin architecture, providing developers with the ability to deliver an even richer experience to its users.

While a basic WordPress installation provides a great amount of functionality that continues to expand from one release to the next, users often have the need to add one more feature to make it the perfect website management system. This is where the plugins come into play. They can fill this gap by augmenting or manipulating virtually any aspect of a WordPress website's display and administrative tasks.

Just like WordPress, plugins are written in the PHP programming language, which is structurally similar to more traditional languages such as C and C++. This code is stored in plain ASCII text files that are read and executed on the web server when pages are requested to be displayed. The secret ingredient that enables plugins to have such great power in WordPress is the inclusion of callback mechanisms, called **hooks**, throughout the platform's source code. These hooks come in two flavors, called action and filter hooks, which allow plugins to add content to a site and modify data before it is displayed, respectively. Whether it's rendering a site's front page, a single article, or its administration pages, WordPress has hundreds of entry points where custom functions can be executed.

Beyond their ability to augment WordPress functionality, a side benefit of plugins is that most functionalities they add to a site are independent of the active theme. Therefore, users who like to change their theme frequently don't have to worry about manually adding back custom elements to their new themes when they make a switch.

This chapter explains the difference between action and filter hooks and shows how to use them to write a first set of plugins that will range in functionality from adding information to the page header to defining new custom shortcodes.

Creating a plugin file and header

The first step of creating a WordPress plugin is to create a PHP file inside of the plugins directory and add the necessary information to have it recognized by the system. This first recipe shows you how to create a basic plugin file for WordPress and how to see and activate this new extension from the administration interface.

Getting ready

You should have access to a WordPress development environment, either on your local computer or a remote server, where you will be able to load your new plugin files.

How to do it...

1. Navigate to the WordPress plugin directory (`wp-content/plugins`) of your development installation.
2. Create a new subdirectory called `ch2-plugin-header` within the plugin directory.
3. Navigate to this directory and create a new text file called `ch2-plugin-header.php`.
4. Open the new file in a text editor and add the following text:

```php
<?php
/*
Plugin Name: Chapter 2 - Plugin Header
Plugin URI:
Description: Declares a plugin that will be visible in the
WordPress admin interface
Version: 1.0
Author: Yannick Lefebvre
Author URI: http://ylefebvre.ca
License: GPLv2
*/
```

While the Description text is shown on two separate lines in the code example, it should all be entered on a single line in your code to be completely displayed in the WordPress Installed Plugins list.

Downloading the example code

You can download the example code files for all Packt books you have purchased from your account at `https://www.packtpub.com`. If you purchased this book elsewhere, you can visit `https://www.packtpub.com/support` and register to have the files emailed directly to you.

5. Save and close the new file.
6. Log in to the administration page of your development WordPress installation.

7. Click on **Plugins** in the left-hand navigation menu to show a list of all the installed plugins. You should see your new plugin listed next to the two default ones that come pre-packaged with WordPress:

8. Enable the plugin by clicking on the **Activate** link under its name. You will see that the background color of your new plugin changes to indicate that it has been activated, along with a message specifying that the activation was successful.

How it works...

Plugin files can either be located directly in the `wp-content/plugins` directory or in a subdirectory under this location. When you access the installed plugins list in the administration interface, WordPress scans all potential plugin locations, looking for PHP files that contain comments following the format specified in this recipe. There can actually be one or more PHP files containing plugin header data in any of these directories, and each of them will show up as an entry in the plugin list.

Taking a closer look at the code that we entered in the file, the first line of the plugin file is a tag that identifies the beginning of the PHP code that will be analyzed and executed by the PHP interpreter. Optionally, we could include a closing PHP tag (?>) at the end of the file. However, most PHP developers omit the closing tag, since having any spaces after that tag will cause warnings to be displayed by the interpreter.

 To ensure compatibility with most WordPress installations, it is important to use the complete <?php open tag syntax in your plugin code instead of the <? short-hand version, since not all PHP installations are configured to support the short version and many users don't have access to change this type of configuration on their server.

The second and last lines indicate that the enclosed text should be considered as text comments. Finally, each line within the comment contains a specific label, indicating the type of information that follows it. When this information is found, WordPress retrieves data about the plugin and adds it to the list.

When a plugin is activated, WordPress validates the file's content to be sure that it is valid PHP code. It will then execute this content every time any page is rendered on the site, whether that page is front-facing or a backend administration section. For this reason, it is preferable to activate plugins only when they are in use, to avoid site slowdowns.

Of course, at this point, our new plugin does not add or modify any functionality in our WordPress installation, since it does not contain real code, but this is still an important first step.

See also

- The *Installing a web server on your computer* recipe in Chapter 1, *Preparing a Local Development Environment*
- The *Downloading and configuring a local WordPress installation* recipe in Chapter 1, *Preparing a Local Development Environment*

Adding output content to page headers using plugin actions

A common action performed by plugins is to add extra content to the header of visitor-facing pages generated by WordPress. This recipe shows you how to register an action hook function to be able to add such additional content. To make this example more concrete, we will use the Google Analytics page header JavaScript code that so many people use to get good page view statistics for their site.

How to do it...

1. Navigate to the WordPress plugin directory of your development installation.
2. Create a new directory called `ch2-page-header-output`.
3. Navigate to this directory and create a new text file called `ch2-page-header-output.php`.
4. Open the new file in a code editor and add an appropriate header at the top of the plugin file, naming the plugin `Chapter 2 - Page Header Output`.
5. Add the following line of code to register a function that will be called when WordPress renders the page header:

```
add_action( 'wp_head', 'ch2pho_page_header_output' );
```

6. Add the following code section to provide an implementation for the `ch2pho_page_header_output` function:

```
function ch2pho_page_header_output() { ?>
    <script>
        (function(i,s,o,g,r,a,m){i['GoogleAnalyticsObject']=r;
        i[r]=i[r]||function(){
        (i[r].q=i[r].q||[]).push(arguments)},i[r].l=1*new Date();
        a=s.createElement(o),
        m=s.getElementsByTagName(o)[0];a.async=1;a.src=g;
        m.parentNode.insertBefore(a,m)})(window,document,'script',
        'https://www.google-analytics.com/analytics.js','ga');

        ga('create', 'UA-0000000-0', 'auto');
        ga('send', 'pageview');
    </script>
<?php }
```

7. Save and close the plugin file.
8. Log in to the administration page of your development WordPress installation.
9. Click on **Plugins** in the left-hand navigation menu.
10. **Activate** your new plugin.
11. Navigate to your website's front page and use your browser's **View Page Source** function to see the HTML source code for the site. The exact name of this function will be slightly different based on which browser you are using. Reading through the page source code, all of the code contained between the two curled brackets of our new function will be visible on your website's header:

```
50    <script>
51        (function(i,s,o,g,r,a,m){i['GoogleAnalyticsObject']=r;
52        i[r]=i[r]||function(){
53        (i[r].q=i[r].q||[]).push(arguments)},i[r].l=1*new Date();
54        a=s.createElement(o),
55        m=s.getElementsByTagName(o)[0];a.async=1;a.src=g;
56        m.parentNode.insertBefore(a,m)})(window,document,'script',
57        'https://www.google-analytics.com/analytics.js','ga');
58
59        ga('create', 'UA-0000000-0', 'auto');
60        ga('send', 'pageview');
61    </script>
```

If you are copying and pasting code from a digital version of this book, you will lose the original code indentation and should correct it in your code editor.

How it works...

The `add_action` function is used to associate custom plugin code to one of the two types of WordPress hooks, the action hook. As mentioned briefly in this chapter's introduction, hooks are the enabling functionality that make plugins possible in WordPress. Action hooks enable the execution of additional code at specific points when either public-facing or administration pages are prepared to be displayed. This code usually adds content to a site or changes the way a given action is performed.

In this recipe, the first line of code that we wrote registered a function named `ch2pho_page_header_output` with an action hook called `wp_head`. This action is one among more than 2,400 action hooks that are available in current versions of WordPress and it allows any registered function to output additional content to the page header. Since all echoed content will be displayed, we can write our callback function very simply by placing `?>` and `<?php` tags around the Google Analytics code. This will tell PHP to display all the content that is within that function's body, as opposed to interpreting it.

As you may have noticed, the current code is not very flexible, since you would need to hardcode your Google Analytics account number in the output for it to function properly. The creation of a configuration panel in `Chapter 3`, *User Settings and Administration Pages*, will provide a way to configure such information to make our plugins more flexible.

Now, to fully understand its syntax, let's take a closer look at the complete `add_action` function:

```
add_action ( 'hook_name', 'your_function_name', [priority],
             [accepted_args] );
```

The first parameter, the hook name, indicates the name of the WordPress hook that we want our custom function to be associated with. This name must be accurately spelled; otherwise, our function will not be called and no error message will be displayed.

The second parameter is the name of the plugin function that will be called to perform an action. This function can have any name, with the only condition being that this name must be unique enough to avoid conflicts with function names from other plugins or from the core WordPress code. In this recipe, the function name starts with an acronym representing the name of the plugin, making it much more unique.

The priority parameter is optional, as indicated by the square brackets, and has a default value of 10. It indicates the execution priority of this plugin relative to other plugin functions that hook into the same action, with a lower number indicating a higher priority.

Any plugin can register one or more functions with an action hook using the `add_action` function. As it is rendering web pages, WordPress keeps a queue of all entries and calls them at the appropriate moment. It is interesting to note that the hook mechanism is also used by WordPress itself, as it regularly calls the `add_action` function in its own code to register functions to be called at the right time. If you realize that you need your function to be called before or after other plugins that are registering with the same hook, change the value of the priority parameter.

The last parameter of the `add_action` function, `accepted_args`, has a default value of 1 and should be assigned a number. It should also only be set to a different value for some particular hooks where more than one parameter should be passed to the registered function. Some of these hooks will be covered in later recipes.

There's more...

Finding the right hooks to register plugin functions is a large part of WordPress plugin development. Fortunately, there are a number of ways to get information on existing hooks and learn when they get called during the WordPress page generation process.

Action hooks online listings

The WordPress Codex (`https://codex.wordpress.org/`) and WordPress Code Reference (`https://developer.wordpress.org/reference/`) are documentation sites that contain a multitude of information that is useful to users and developers alike. When it comes to action hooks, the Codex contains information on the most commonly used hooks, with basic descriptions indicating how they can be used, and can be found here: `https://codex.wordpress.org/Plugin_API/Action_Reference`. That being said, this is not a complete listing.

There are many third-party sites that parse the WordPress source code and provide their own hook listings (for example, `http://hookr.io`). While hooks are not as eloquently documented in these types of raw listings, they do provide basic information on their names and where they are called as WordPress generates pages for visitors and administrators. These details can be enough to find a hook based on the functionality that you are trying to implement.

Searching for hooks in the WordPress source code

Since WordPress is open source, another way to find information about hooks is to search directly within its code. For every action hook that accepts user functions, you will see a call to the `do_action` function to execute all the registered items. As can be seen, the function takes two or more arguments, with the second one(s) being optional:

```
do_action ( 'tag', [$arg] );
```

For the example shown in this recipe, a search for `do_action( 'wp_head' )` reveals that it is the only function that is called when a theme makes a call to the `wp_head()` function in its header file:

```
do_action( 'wp_head' );
```

See also

- The *Creating a plugin file and header* recipe

Using WordPress path utility functions to load external files and images

On occasion, plugins need to refer to external files (for example, images, JavaScript, or jQuery script files) that are stored in the plugin directory. Since users are free to rename a plugin's folder or even install plugin files straight into the WordPress plugin directory, paths to any external files must be built dynamically based on the actual plugin location. Thankfully, a number of utility functions are present to simplify this task. In this recipe, we will write a simple plugin that will add a favicon meta tag to a website's header, pointing to an image file located in the plugin directory.

How to do it...

1. Navigate to the WordPress plugin directory of your development installation.
2. Create a new directory called `ch2-favicon`.
3. Use a web service, such as `http://getfavicon.org`, to retrieve a website's favicon (for example, `http://www.packtpub.com`) and store it in the plugin directory with its default name (`favicon.ico`).
4. Navigate to the plugin directory and create a new text file called `ch2-favicon.php`.
5. Open the new file in a code editor and add an appropriate header at the top of the plugin file, naming the plugin `Chapter 2 - Favicon`.

6. Add the following line of code to register a function that will be called when WordPress renders the page header:

```
add_action( 'wp_head', 'ch2fi_page_header_output' );
```

7. Add the following code section to provide an implementation for the ch2fi_page_header_output function:

```
function ch2fi_page_header_output() {
    $site_icon_url = get_site_icon_url();
    if ( !empty( $site_icon_url ) ) {
        wp_site_icon();
    } else {
        $icon_url = plugins_url( 'favicon.ico', __FILE__ );
    ?>

    <link rel="shortcut icon" href="<?php echo $icon_url; ?>" />
    <?php }
}
```

8. Save and close the plugin file.
9. Log in to the administration page of your development WordPress installation.
10. Click on **Plugins** in the left-hand navigation menu.
11. **Activate** your new plugin.
12. Navigate to your website's front page and refresh it to see that the icon file that you assigned through your plugin code now appears in your browser's address bar, title bar, or navigation tab, depending on your preferred browser. The following screenshot shows how the favicon file is rendered in Internet Explorer, Mozilla Firefox, and Google Chrome, from top to bottom:

13. Navigate to your development site's dashboard and select the **Customize** submenu under the **Appearance** menu.

14. Under **Site Identity**, assign a square image that is at least 512 x 512 pixels in dimension as **Site Icon**; then, press the **Save & Publish** button at the top of the customizer.

15. Refresh your website to see that the newly assigned site icon is now displayed instead of the `favicon.ico` file.

How it works...

The `plugins_url` utility function, used in conjunction with the `__FILE__` PHP constant and the name of our favicon file, enables us to quickly get the URL of the directory where our plugin files are located and print out the appropriate HTML command to notify browsers of the location of this file:

```
plugins_url( $path, $plugin );
```

The `plugins_url` function can be called with or without parameters. In the first case, it builds a URL by appending the path found in the first parameter to the location of the file specified in the second argument. In the second situation, it simply returns the location of the plugin directory.

Before we display our plugin's favicon file, we also check to see whether the user has already assigned a site icon using the WordPress customizer. If that is the case, we give priority to that icon and display it using the built-in `wp_site_icon` function.

There's more...

The `plugins_url` function is one of the many functions that can be used in plugins to help find the location of files in a WordPress installation. Other useful functions include:

- `get_theme_root()`: Returns the address of the theme installation directory
- `get_template_directory_uri()`: Retrieves the URI to the current theme's files
- `admin_url()`: Provides the address of the WordPress administrative pages
- `content_url()`: Indicates where the `wp-content` directory can be found

- `site_url()` and `home_url()`: Returns the site address
- `includes_url()`: Provides the location of WordPress `include` files
- `wp_upload_dir()`: Indicates the directory where user-uploaded files are stored

See also

- The *Creating a plugin file and header* recipe
- The *Adding output content to page headers using plugin actions* recipe

Modifying the site generator meta tag using plugin filters

Beyond adding functionality or content to a site, the other major task commonly performed by plugins is to augment, modify, or reduce information before it is displayed on the screen. This is done by using WordPress filter hooks, which allow plugins to register a custom function through the WordPress API to be called, since content is prepared before it is sent to the browser. In this recipe, you will learn how to implement your first filter callback function to modify the contents of the generator meta tag that is output as part of the site header.

How to do it...

1. Navigate to the WordPress plugin directory of your development installation.
2. Create a new directory called `ch2-generator-filter`.
3. Navigate to this directory and create a new text file called `ch2-generator-filter.php`.
4. Open the new file in a code editor and add an appropriate header at the top of the plugin file, naming the plugin `Chapter 2 - Generator Filter`.
5. Add the following line of code to register a function that will be called when WordPress is preparing data to output the generator meta tag as part of the page header:

```
add_filter( 'the_generator', 'ch2gf_generator_filter', 10, 2 );
```

6. Add the following code section to provide an implementation for the `ch2gf_generator_filter` function:

```
function ch2gf_generator_filter ( $html, $type ) {
    if ( $type == 'xhtml' ) {
        $html = preg_replace( '("WordPress.*?")',
                              '"Yannick Lefebvre"', $html );
    }
    return $html;
}
```

7. Save and close the plugin file.
8. Log in to the administration page of your development WordPress installation.
9. Click on **Plugins** in the left-hand navigation menu.
10. **Activate** your new plugin.
11. Use a web browser to visit your website and display the page source. Searching for the keyword `generator` will reveal that the content generator meta tag has been modified and now reads:

```
<meta name="generator" content="Yannick Lefebvre" />
```

How it works...

The `add_filter` function is used to associate a custom plugin function to the second type of WordPress hooks, the filter hook. Filter hooks give plugins the chance to augment, modify, delete, or completely replace information while WordPress is executed. To enable this, filter functions are sent data that can be modified as a function parameter. They must return the resulting set of data back to WordPress once they have finished making the changes.

Unlike action hooks, filter functions must not output any text or HTML code, since they are executed while output is being prepared and that would likely result in the output showing up in unexpected places in the site layout. Instead, they should return the filtered data.

Taking a closer look at the parameters of the `add_filter` function, we can see that it is very similar to the `add_action` function that we saw in the previous recipes:

```
add_filter( 'hook_name', 'your_function_name', [priority],
            [accepted_args] );
```

The first parameter, the hook name, indicates the name of the WordPress hook that we want our custom function to be associated with. This name must be accurately spelled; otherwise, our function will not be called and no error message will be displayed.

The second parameter is the name of the plugin function that will be called to filter data. This function can have any name, with the only condition being that this name must be unique enough to avoid conflicting with functions from other plugins or from the WordPress code.

The `priority` parameter is optional, as indicated by the square brackets, and has a default value of 10. It indicates the execution priority of this plugin relative to other plugins that are loaded by WordPress, with a lower number indicating a higher priority.

The last parameter of the function, `accepted_args`, has a default value of 1 and indicates how many parameters will be sent to your custom filter function. It should only be set to higher values when you are using filters that will send multiple parameters, as shown in this recipe with the `$html` and `$type` arguments.

There's more...

Beyond demonstrating how to change the site generator name, this plugin also shows how to use an advanced PHP function to perform the actual text replacement. We also take a look at resources to learn more about filter hooks.

preg_replace function

The `preg_replace` function is a PHP function that can be used to perform a search and replace operation within a string based on a search pattern. We use this function rather than the simpler `str_replace`, since we want to find and replace both the WordPress keyword and its associated version number, which changes with every version.

Filter hooks online listings and the apply_filters function

Similar to action hooks, information about commonly used filter hooks can be found on the WordPress Codex (https://codex.wordpress.org/Plugin_API/Action_Reference) or on sites that provide raw function lists (for example, http://hookr.io).

It is also possible to learn about filter hooks by searching for occurrences of the `apply_filters` function in the WordPress code. As can be seen in the following code, this function has a variable number of arguments, with the first one being the name of the filter hook, the second representing the value that the registered function will be able to modify, and the remaining optional parameters containing additional data that may be useful in the implementation of the filter function:

```
apply_filters( $tag, $value, $var ... );
```

For the example shown in this recipe, a search for `apply_filters( 'the_generator'` in the WordPress code reveals that it is called within the `the_generator` template function:

```
echo apply_filters( 'the_generator',
                    get_the_generator( $type ), $type );
```

See also

- The *Creating a plugin file and header* recipe

Adding text after each item's content using plugin filters

After making a number of changes to the page header, the generator meta tag, and the site favicon, this recipe takes a more active role by adding a link to each post or page, allowing visitors to email a link to the item that they are currently viewing. This functionality is implemented using a filter hook attached to the page and post content, allowing our custom function to append custom output code to all entries that get displayed on the screen.

How to do it...

1. Navigate to the WordPress plugin directory of your development installation.
2. Create a new directory called `ch2-email-page-link`.
3. Navigate to this directory and create a new text file called `ch2-email-page-link.php`.
4. Open the new file in a code editor and add an appropriate header at the top of the plugin file, naming the plugin `Chapter 2 - Email Page Link`.

5. Visit an icon download website, such as `http://iconarchive.com`, and download an email icon in a small size (32 x 32 pixels) in PNG format to the new plugin's directory, giving it the name `mailicon.png`.

6. Add the following line of code to register a function that will be called when WordPress is preparing data to display the content of a post or page:

```
add_filter( 'the_content', 'ch2epl_email_page_filter' );
```

7. Add the following code section to provide an implementation for the `ch2epl_email_page_filter` function:

```
function ch2epl_email_page_filter ( $the_content ) {
    // build url to mail message icon downloaded from
    // iconarchive.com
    $mail_icon_url = plugins_url( 'mailicon.png', __FILE__ );

    // Set initial value of $new_content variable to previous
    // content
    $new_content = $the_content;

    // Append image with mailto link after content, including
    // the item title and permanent URL
    $new_content .= '<div class="email_link">';
    $new_content .= '<a href="mailto:someone@somewhere.com?';
    $new_content .= 'subject=Check out this interesting article ';
    $new_content .= 'entitled ' . get_the_title();
    $new_content .= '&body=Hi!%0A%0AI thought you would enjoy ';
    $new_content .= 'this article entitled ';
    $new_content .= get_the_title() . '.%0A%0A' . get_permalink();
    $new_content .= '%0A%0AEnjoy!">';

    if ( !empty( $mail_icon_url ) ) {
        $new_content .= '<img alt="Email icon" ';
        $new_content .= ' src="';
        $new_content .= $mail_icon_url. '" /></a>';
    } else {
        $new_content .= 'Email link to this article';
    }
    $new_content .= '</div>';

    // Return filtered content for display on the site
    return $new_content;
}
```

8. Save and close the plugin file.

9. Log in to the administration page of your development WordPress installation.

10. Click on **Plugins** in the left-hand navigation menu.
11. **Activate** your new plugin.
12. Visit your website to see the new mail icon at the end of each post and page.
13. Click on one of the mail links. Your default mail client will come up with information about the item you were reading. The only information that needs to be updated is the recipient address, and visitors can quickly send an email:

How it works...

Similar to the previous recipe, this plugin uses the add_filter function to register a custom function to be called by WordPress as it prepares an item's content to be displayed on the screen. When the filter function is called, the first action that it performs is to create a URL to the email icon that was downloaded in the recipe. It then goes on to modify the original content by appending the HTML code to display a mailto link. The same technique could be used to create links to popular social media and link sharing sites, with simple changes to the syntax of the link. Once the new content is ready, it is returned back to WordPress to be sent to any other registered filters and subsequently be displayed on the site.

There's more...

This recipe also introduces a pair of useful WordPress utility functions to get access to the current item's content.

get_the_title and get_permalink functions

While these two functions are mainly seen within theme template files, they can also be used by plugins to get easy access to the content of items that are currently being processed.

More specifically, the two utility functions that are used in this recipe are as follows:

- `get_the_title()`: This function gives us quick access to the item's title
- `get_permalink()`: A function that returns the item's permalink (a URL that is always associated with this post or page, even after it is no longer featured on a website's front page)

See also

- The *Creating a plugin file and header* recipe
- The *Using WordPress path utility functions to load external files and images* recipe
- The *Modifying the site generator meta tag using plugin filters* recipe

Inserting link statistics tracking code in page body using plugin filters

After creating two filter functions that append text to the existing content, this recipe shows you how to modify the page content before it is displayed on the screen. More specifically, the following plugin will expand on the Google Analytics header plugin created earlier and add a JavaScript function to all the links that are included in posts and pages to track when they are clicked by visitors.

Getting ready

You should have already followed the *Adding output content to page headers using plugin actions* recipe to have a starting point for this recipe and the resulting plugin should be active in your development site. Alternatively, you can download the resulting code (Chapter 2/ch2-page-header-output/ch2-page-header-output.php) for that recipe from the Packt Publishing website (https://www.packtpub.com/support).

How to do it...

1. Navigate to the ch2-page-header-output folder in the WordPress plugin directory of your development installation.

2. Open the ch2-page-header-output.php file in a text editor.

3. Add the following line of code after the existing functions to register a function that will be called when WordPress is preparing data to display a page or post's content:

```
add_filter( 'the_content', 'ch2lfa_link_filter_analytics' );
```

4. Add the following code section to provide an implementation for the ch2lfa_link_filter_analytics function:

```
function ch2lfa_link_filter_analytics ( $the_content ) {
    $new_content = str_replace( 'href',
        'onClick="recordOutboundLink( this );return false;" href'
        , $the_content );
    return $new_content;
}
```

5. Add the following line of code to register a function that will be called when WordPress renders the page footer:

```
add_action( 'wp_footer', 'ch2lfa_footer_analytics_code' );
```

6. Add the following code section to provide an implementation for the ch2lfa_footer_analytics_code function:

```
function ch2lfa_footer_analytics_code() { ?>
<script type="text/javascript">
    function recordOutboundLink( link ) {
        ga( 'send', 'event', 'Outbound Links', 'Click',
            link.href, {
```

```
                    'transport': 'beacon',
                    'hitCallback': function() {
                        document.location = link.href;
                    }
                } );
            }
        </script>

        <?php }
```

7. Save and close the plugin file.

8. Go to the **Pages** section of the Dashboard and edit the home page (or any other page). Add a link to the content, pointing to a location of your choice.

9. In your web browser, refresh your website and navigate to the page modified in the previous step.

10. Open the source view for the page and find the link you added. You will see that the link tag has additional onClick JavaScript code that will be called when visitors follow it:

```
132            <span class="edit-link"><a class="post-edit-link" href="http://localhost/wp-
   admin/post.php?post=7&#038;action=edit">Edit<span class="screen-reader-text"> "Home"</span></a>
   </span>
133            </header><!-- .entry-header -->
134
135            <div class="entry-content">
136                <p>Welcome to your site! This is your homepage, which is what most visitors will
   see when they come to your site for the first time.</p>
137    <p><a onClick="recordOutboundLink(this);return false;" href="http://www.packtpub.com">Packt
   Publishing</a></p>
138            </div><!-- .entry-content -->
139
140        </div><!-- .wrap -->
141    </div><!-- .panel-content -->
```

11. Scroll to the bottom of the page to see the implementation of the recordOutboundLink JavaScript function that was added to the page footer.

How it works...

The content filter function that is put in place by calling add_filter receives the entire content of all the posts and pages before they are rendered to the browser and is allowed to make any number of changes to this information. In this case, we are using the PHP str_replace function to search for any occurrence of the string href, which indicates a link. When the string is found, it is replaced with a call to a JavaScript function as well as the original href tag.

To make this plugin complete, it also needs to provide an implementation for the JavaScript `recordOutboundLink` function. This is done by registering a custom function with the `wp_footer` hook that will output extra content with the function code in the website's footer.

The resulting plugin automates many of the tasks related to tracking usage data on a website using Google Analytics.

See also

- The *Adding output content to page headers using plugin actions* recipe
- The *Adding text after each item's content using plugin filters* recipe

Troubleshooting coding errors and printing variable content

As you transcribe code segments from the pages of this book or start writing your own plugins, there is a strong chance that you will have to troubleshoot problems with your code or have trouble working with data that your plugin is meant to manipulate. This recipe shows the basic techniques to identify and quickly resolve these errors while creating a plugin that will hide an item from the navigation menu for users who are not logged in to your site.

How to do it...

1. Navigate to the WordPress plugin directory of your development installation.
2. Create a new directory called `ch2-nav-menu-filter`.
3. Navigate to this directory and create a new text file called `ch2-nav-menu-filter.php`.
4. Open the new file in a code editor and add an appropriate header at the top of the plugin file, naming the plugin `Chapter 2 - Nav Menu Filter`.

5. Add the following line of code to register a function that will be called when WordPress is preparing data to display the site's navigation menu:

```
add_filter( 'wp_nav_menu_objects', 'ch2nmf_new_nav_menu_items',
        10, 2 );
```

6. Add the following code section to provide an implementation for the `ch2nmf_new_nav_menu_items` function. Notice that the word `functio` is mistyped on purpose at the beginning of the first line:

```
functio ch2nmf_new_nav_menu_items( $sorted_menu_items, $args ) {
    print_r( $sorted_menu_items );
    return $sorted_menu_items;
}
```

If you are using a dedicated code editor, you should be able to tell that the text font is not a recognized keyword since it will not be colored as a PHP keyword.

7. Save the plugin file and leave your code editor open.
8. Log in to the administration page of your development WordPress installation.
9. Click on **Plugins** in the left-hand navigation menu.
10. **Activate** your new plugin.
11. WordPress will display a fatal error message indicating that the plugin could not be activated, since a syntax error was found. It also indicates the exact filename and line where the error occurred, helping to narrow down where the problem occurred:

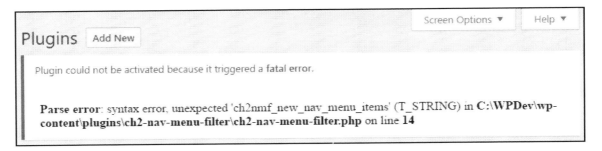

12. Go back to your code editor, correct the spelling of the word `function`, and save the file.
13. **Activate** the plugin a second time. It should now activate correctly.

14. Back in the code editor, remove the last letter of the word kbd>function to reintroduce a syntax error.

15. Visit your website. You will now see that the entire site has disappeared and your browser only displays a blank page with an error message similar to the one we just saw. You may also only get a blank page, depending on your web server configuration.

16. Correct the spelling error once again and your website will go back to normal. You will also see a lot of information printed before the navigation menu. This output is generated by the print_r function and is meant to help us understand how the data received by our filter function is organized. Once we have a good understanding of that data, we will be able to properly make changes to this information in a further step.

17. In the WordPress dashboard, navigate to the **Appearance** | **Menus** item and create an additional item in your menu as **Custom Link,** setting the **URL** to /privatearea and the **Link Text** to Private Area:

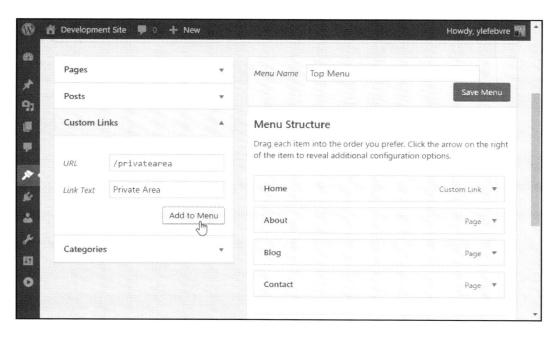

18. Click on the **Save Menu** button to store all of your updates.

19. Back in the code editor, replace the `print_r` function call inside of the filter function with the following code:

```
// Check if used is logged in, continue if not logged
if ( is_user_logged_in() == FALSE ) {
    // Loop through all menu items received
    // Place each item's key in $key variable
    foreach ( $sorted_menu_items as $key => $sorted_menu_item ) {
        // Check if menu item title matches search string
        if ( 'Private Area' == $sorted_menu_item->title ) {
            // Remove item from menu array if found using
            // item key
            unset( $sorted_menu_items[ $key ] );
        }
    }
}
```

20. Refresh your website and you will see that the large array printout has disappeared. If you are logged in as the administrator, you will also notice the **Private Area** link in your menu. Log out or use another browser where you are not logged in to your development site to hide the menu item.

How it works...

As WordPress assembles a list of all available plugins to display them in the administration interface, it does not check to see if each plugin's PHP code is valid. This check is actually done when a plugin is activated. At that time, any syntax error will be caught immediately and the newly-activated plugin will remain inactive, preventing a failure of the entire website.

That being said, once a plugin is activated, its code is evaluated every time WordPress renders a web page, and any subsequent code error that gets saved to the plugin file will cause the site to stop working correctly. For this reason, it is highly recommended to set up a local development environment, as shown in Chapter 1, *Preparing a Local Development Environment*, to avoid affecting a live site when an inevitable error creeps up in your plugin code. On a live website, to avoid potential outages, a safer method is to deactivate plugins before making changes to them, then reactivating them once changes have been made so that they are revalidated before their functionality is enabled. It should be noted that, with this method, the plugin's functionality won't be available on your site while you make changes, so it is not an optimal way to modify deployed code.

Once the code is working correctly, the second part of this recipe shows us how to visualize the information that is received by a custom filter function. While the WordPress Codex website provides great documentation about the purpose of most filters available, it does not go into details about the structure of the information that is sent to each filter function. Thankfully, the PHP `print_r` function comes in very handy, since it can display the content of any variable on the screen, no matter what information is stored in the variable it receives as an argument.

Last, but not least, the implementation of the custom filter function uses the WordPress API function `is_user_logged_in()` to see whether the person viewing the site has provided login credentials, and then goes on to parse all the menu items and remove the **Private Area** menu item if the visitor is not logged in.

There's more...

In addition to the debugging techniques used in this recipe, WordPress offers a number of built-in tools to facilitate plugin troubleshooting.

Built-in WordPress debugging features

While the `wp-config.php` file, located at the top of the WordPress file structure, is primarily used to store basic site configuration data, it can also be used to trigger a number of debugging features. The first of these is the debug mode, which will display all PHP errors, warnings, and notices at the top of site pages. For example, having this option active will show all the undefined variables that you try to access in your code along with any deprecated WordPress function. To activate this tool, change the second parameter of the line defining the `WP_DEBUG` constant from `false` to `true` in `wp_config.php`:

```
define( 'WP_DEBUG', true );
```

To prevent debug messages from affecting the site's layout, you can download a useful plugin called Debug Bar (`https://wordpress.org/plugins/debug-bar/`) to collect messages and display them in the admin bar:

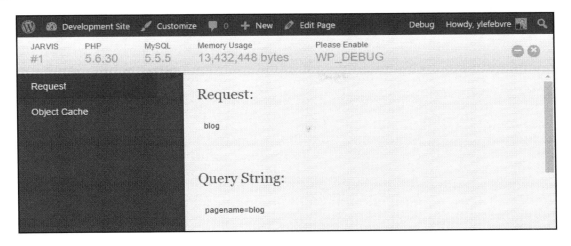

Other debugging features that can be activated from the `wp-config.php` file are as follows:

- `WP_DEBUG_LOG`: Stores all debug messages in a file named `debug.log` in the site's `wp-content` directory for later analysis
- `WP_DEBUG_DISPLAY`: Indicates whether or not error messages should be displayed on the screen
- `SAVEQUERIES`: Stores database queries in a variable that can be displayed in the page footer (see `https://codex.wordpress.org/Editing_wp-config.php#Save_queries_for_analysis` for more information)

See also

- The *Modifying the site generator meta tag using plugin filters* recipe

Creating a new simple shortcode

Shortcodes are a very popular tool in WordPress that allow users to easily add content generated by plugins or themes to any page or post without needing to be familiar with PHP code and editing theme template files. As they are very simple to create, shortcodes can also be used to easily automate the output of content that repeatedly needs to be included in your site's content.

This recipe explains how to create a new custom shortcode that will be used to quickly add a link to a Twitter page in any post or page, automating a repetitive task.

How to do it...

1. Navigate to the WordPress plugin directory of your development installation.
2. Create a new directory called `ch2-twitter-shortcode`.
3. Navigate to this directory and create a new text file called `ch2-twitter-shortcode.php`.
4. Open the new file in a code editor and add an appropriate header at the top of the plugin file, naming the plugin `Chapter 2 - Twitter Shortcode`.
5. Add the following line of code to declare a new shortcode, simply using the two characters `tl`, and specify the name of the function that should be called when the code is encountered in posts or pages:

    ```
    add_shortcode( 'tl', 'ch2ts_twitter_link_shortcode' );
    ```

6. Add the following code section to provide an implementation for the `ch2ts_twitter_link_shortcode` function:

    ```
    function ch2ts_twitter_link_shortcode( $atts ) {
        $output = '<a href="https://twitter.com/ylefebvre">';
        $output .= 'Twitter Feed</a>';
        return $output;
    }
    ```

7. Save and close the plugin file.
8. Log in to the administration page of your development WordPress installation.
9. Click on **Plugins** in the left-hand navigation menu.
10. **Activate** your new plugin.
11. Edit an existing post on your site and use the shortcode **[tl]** in the code editor:

12. Save and view the post to see that the shortcode was replaced by a link to a Twitter page attached to the words **Twitter Feed**.

How it works...

Shortcodes have similarities with both action hooks and filter hooks, since their associated custom function is called when it is time to perform a task, just like an action hook, but they must return their output through a return value, just like a filter hook. In terms of external data, the function associated with a shortcode will receive data in the case of some types of codes, while it will only produce output in other cases.

When used in the text of a post or page, any shortcode surrounded by a pair of square brackets is identified by the WordPress engine, which then searches for functions registered for that specific code. If found, the associated function is called and the expected result is used to replace the original shortcode text in the item's content. Just like filter functions, shortcode functions must not output any text directly, since it would likely appear in an unexpected place in the page layout, as WordPress calls all shortcode-processing functions before displaying the body of an item.

For simple shortcodes, such as those in this recipe, the plugin functions associated with them must return information, but they do not receive any additional data through function parameters. That being said, they can rely on utility functions, such as get_the_ID, get_the_title, and other WordPress utility functions, to be able to produce the appropriate output. Other types of shortcodes seen in later recipes will have more context and configuration options. It is also possible for shortcodes to access stored options data, which will be covered in Chapter 3, *User Settings and Administration Pages*.

See also

- The *Creating a plugin file and header* recipe

Creating a new shortcode with parameters

While simple shortcodes already provide a lot of potential to output complex content to a page by entering a few characters in the post editor, shortcodes become even more useful when they are coupled with parameters that will be passed to their associated processing function. Using this technique, it becomes very easy to create a shortcode that accelerates the insertion of external content in WordPress posts or pages by only needing to specify the shortcode and the unique identifier of the source element to be displayed.

We will illustrate this concept in this recipe by creating a shortcode that will be used to quickly add Twitter feeds to posts or pages.

How to do it...

1. Navigate to the WordPress plugin directory of your development installation.
2. Create a new directory called `ch2-twitter-embed`.
3. Navigate to this directory and create a new text file called `ch2-twitter-embed.php`.
4. Open the new file in a code editor and add an appropriate header at the top of the plugin file, naming the plugin `Chapter 2 - Twitter Embed`.
5. Add the following line of code to declare a new shortcode and specify the name of the function that should be called when the shortcode is found in posts or pages:

```
add_shortcode( 'twitterfeed', 'ch2te_twitter_embed_shortcode' );
```

6. Add the following code section to provide an implementation for the `ch2te_twitter_embed_shortcode` function:

```
function ch2te_twitter_embed_shortcode( $atts ) {
    extract( shortcode_atts( array(
        'user_name' => 'ylefebvre'
    ), $atts ) );

    if ( !empty( $user_name ) ) {
        $output = '<a class="twitter-timeline" href="';
        $output .= esc_url( 'https://twitter.com/' . $user_name );
        $output .= '">Tweets by ' . esc_html( $user_name );
        $output .= '</a><script async ';
        $output .= 'src="//platform.twitter.com/widgets.js"';
        $output .= ' charset="utf-8"></script>';
    } else {
        $output = '';
    }
    return $output;
}
```

7. Save and close the plugin file.
8. Log in to the administration page of your development WordPress installation.
9. Click on **Plugins** in the left-hand navigation menu.
10. **Activate** your new plugin.

11. Create a new page and use the shortcode [twitterfeed user_name='WordPress'] in the page editor, where WordPress is the Twitter username of the feed to display:

12. **Publish** and **view** the page to see that the shortcode has been replaced by an embedded Twitter feed on your site.
13. **Edit** the page and remove the user_name parameter and its associated value, only leaving the core [twitterfeed] shortcode in the post, then **Update** to save changes.
14. Refresh the page and see that the feed is still being displayed, but now shows tweets from another account.

How it works...

When shortcodes are used with parameters, these extra pieces of data are sent to the associated processing function in the $atts parameter variable. By using a combination of the standard PHP extract and WordPress-specific shortcode_atts functions, our plugin is able to parse the data sent to the shortcode and create an array of identifiers and values that are subsequently transformed into PHP variables that we can use in the rest of our shortcode implementation function. In this specific example, we expect a single variable to be used, called user_name, which will be stored in a PHP variable called $user_name. If the user enters the shortcode without any parameter, a default value of ylefebvre will be assigned to the username variable to ensure that the plugin still works. Since we are going to accept user input in this code, we also verify that the user did not provide an empty string and we use the esc_html and esc_url functions to remove any potentially harmful HTML characters from the input string and make sure that the link destination URL is valid.

Once we have access to the Twitter username, we can put together the required HTML code that will embed a Twitter feed in our page and display the selected user's tweets.

While this example only has one argument, it is possible to define multiple parameters for a shortcode.

See also

- The *Creating a new simple shortcode* recipe

Creating a new enclosing shortcode

A different type of shortcode is available in WordPress that encloses content in posts and pages. Using a syntax similar to HTML tags, enclosing shortcodes can be used to identify parts of an item's content that need to be treated in a special way. For example, it is possible to use this type of shortcode to style a part of the post.

As an example of how to create enclosing shortcodes, this recipe shows you how to create a set of tags that will identify part of a post or page that should only be shown to visitors that are logged in to a site. In this way, the shortcode acts similarly to a filter hook, with the added bonus that you do not need to parse for instances of these tags, as would normally be done in a filter.

How to do it...

1. Navigate to the WordPress plugin directory of your development installation.
2. Create a new directory called `ch2-private-item-text`.
3. Navigate to this directory and create a new text file called `ch2-private-item-text.php`.
4. Open the new file in a code editor and add an appropriate header at the top of the plugin file, naming the plugin `Chapter 2 - Private Item Text`.
5. Add the following line of code to declare a new shortcode and specify the name of the function that should be called when the shortcode is found in posts or pages:

```
add_shortcode( 'private', 'ch2pit_private_shortcode' );
```

6. Add the following code section to provide an implementation for the `ch2pit_private_shortcode` function:

```
function ch2pit_private_shortcode( $atts, $content = null ) {
    if ( is_user_logged_in() ) {
        return '<div class="private">' . $content . '</div>';
    } else {
```

```
        $output = '<div class="register">';
        $output .= 'You need to become a member to access ';
        $output .= 'this content.</div>';
        return $output;
    }
}
```

7. Save and close the plugin file.
8. Log in to the administration page of your development WordPress installation.
9. Click on **Plugins** in the left-hand navigation menu.
10. **Activate** your new plugin.
11. Create a new post and wrap some of the content with the **[private]** and **[/private]** tags:

12. Save and view the post to see that the text is visible while you are logged in to your site.
13. Log out and refresh the page to see that the enclosed text has been replaced by a general message.

How it works...

Similar to a filter function, enclosing shortcodes receive a copy of the text that has been wrapped with the new tags. It is then possible to return this text with additional HTML code, or completely replace it with new content. In this specific case, we used the `is_user_logged_in` WordPress function to determine whether the current visitor is logged in to the site. Based on the result of that query, the code determines whether the original content should be displayed with some additional styling code, or if the visitor should see a message encouraging them to join the website.

See also

- The *Creating a new simple shortcode* recipe

Loading a style sheet to format plugin output

When a plugin adds custom content or inserts styling tags to a post or page's existing content, as was done in the previous recipe showing how to create an enclosing shortcode, it usually needs to load a custom style sheet to style these new elements. This recipe shows how to add a style sheet in the WordPress style queue to format the private output created in the previous recipe. This queue is processed when the page header is rendered, listing all the style sheets that need to be loaded to display the site correctly.

Getting ready

You should have already followed the *Creating a new enclosing shortcode* recipe to have a starting point for this recipe and the resulting plugin should still be active in your development site. Alternatively, you can download the resulting code (Chapter 2/ch2-private-item-text/ch2-private-item-text.php) of that recipe from the Packt website (https://www.packtpub.com/support).

How to do it...

1. Navigate to the ch2-private-item-text folder of the WordPress plugin directory of your development installation.
2. Open the ch2-private-item-text.php file in a text editor.
3. Add the following line of code after the existing functions to register a function that will be called at the beginning of the WordPress page display process:

```
add_action( 'wp_enqueue_scripts', 'ch2pit_queue_stylesheet' );
```

4. Add the following code section to provide an implementation for the ch2pit_queue_stylesheet function:

```
function ch2pit_queue_stylesheet() {
```

```
wp_enqueue_style( 'privateshortcodestyle',
                  plugins_url( 'stylesheet.css', __FILE__ ) );
}
```

5. Save and close the plugin file.
6. Create a new text file in the plugin's directory called `stylesheet.css` and open it in a code editor.
7. Add the following content to the file:

```
.private {
    color: #6E6A6B;
}

.register {
    background-color: #ff4d4d;
    color: #fff;
    padding-left: 10px;
}
```

8. Save and close the text file.
9. Navigate to your website, making sure you are logged in, and refresh the page containing the private text content. You should notice that the text is now displayed in gray.
10. Log out of the site and refresh the page to see that the registration message styling has also changed.

How it works...

While it would have been possible to write straight HTML code to load the CSS file by registering a function with the `wp_head` action hook, as we have done previously, WordPress has utility functions designed to help avoid loading duplicate style sheets or scripts on a site. In this specific example, `wp_enqueue_script` is used to place the plugin's style sheet file in a queue that will be processed when the plugin header is rendered, with the associated name `privateshortcodestyle`. Once WordPress has processed all the plugins and boiled down all the style sheet requests to single instances, it will output the necessary HTML code to load all of them.

The content of the `stylesheet.css` file is normal CSS code that specifies that any text that is assigned the `private` class should be displayed in gray, while the text displayed to non-registered users should be displayed in white on a red background.

See also

- The *Creating a new enclosing shortcode* recipe

Writing plugins using object-oriented PHP

So far, all plugin examples that have been covered in this chapter have been written using the procedural PHP programming style, with all the functions declared directly in the main body of the plugin and the hook registration functions having direct access to these functions.

WordPress can also be written using an object-oriented PHP approach. This recipe explains how to convert the code from the previous recipe into a class-based version of the same functionality.

Getting ready

You should have already followed the *Loading a style sheet to format plugin output* recipe to have a starting point for this recipe. Alternatively, you can download the resulting code (`Chapter 2/ch2-private-item-text/ch2-private-item-text-v2.php`) for that recipe from the Packt Publishing website (`https://www.packtpub.com/support`).

How to do it...

1. Log in to the administration page of your WordPress installation.
2. Click on **Plugins** in the left-hand navigation menu.
3. Check whether the `Chapter 2 - Private Item Text` plugin is currently active and deactivate it if it is.
4. Copy the entire contents of the `ch2-private-item-text` directory and rename the copy `ch2-oo-private-item-text`.
5. Navigate to the newly renamed folder and rename the main PHP code file `ch2-oo-private-item-text.php`.
6. Open the newly renamed plugin file in a code editor.

7. Update the plugin header to change the name of the plugin to `Chapter 2 - Object-Oriented - Private Item Text`.

8. Right after the plugin header, add the following text to declare a new class for our plugin and specify a constructor method for this class:

```
class CH2_OO_Private_Item_Text {
    function __construct() {
    }
}
$my_ch2_oo_private_item_text = new CH2_OO_Private_Item_Text();
```

9. Move the calls to the `add_shortcode` and `add_action` functions to be placed inside of the class constructor.

10. Modify the second argument of the `add_shortcode` and `add_action` functions as follows:

```
add_shortcode( 'private', array( $this,
                'ch2pit_private_shortcode' ) );

add_action( 'wp_enqueue_scripts', array( $this,
            'ch2pit_queue_stylesheet' ) );
```

11. Move the complete `ch2pit_private_shortcode` and `ch2pit_queue_stylesheet` functions inside of the class body (after the constructor method and before the class closing bracket).

12. Save and close the modified file.

13. Log in to the administration page of your development WordPress installation.

14. Click on **Plugins** in the left-hand navigation menu.

15. **Activate** the new plugin.

16. Visit your site to see that the private item content functionality is still in place and works as it did before.

How it works...

The code changes that we applied to the plugin first declare a class for all of our plugin's functionality and also contain a constructor method for that class. The constructor method is called once, as soon as the class is instantiated by the last line in the plugin's code, and can be used to associate custom functions with all action hooks, filter hooks, and shortcodes.

The main benefit of using an object-oriented approach is that you don't have to be as careful when naming your hook callbacks and all other functions, since these names are local to the class and can be the same as function names declared in any other classes or in procedural PHP code.

See also

- The *Creating a new enclosing shortcode* recipe

3
User Settings and Administration Pages

This chapter is focused on setting up pages that enable users to configure plugin settings. It covers the following topics:

- Creating default user settings on plugin initialization
- Storing user settings using arrays
- Removing plugin data on deletion
- Creating an administration page menu item in the settings menu
- Creating a multi-level administration menu
- Adding menu items leading to external pages
- Hiding items that users should not access from the default menu
- Rendering the admin page content using HTML
- Processing and storing plugin configuration data
- Displaying a confirmation message when options are saved
- Adding custom help pages
- Rendering the admin page contents using the Settings API
- Accessing user settings from action and filter hooks
- Formatting admin pages using meta boxes
- Splitting admin code from the main plugin file to optimize site performance
- Storing style sheet data in user settings
- Managing multiple sets of user settings from a single admin page
- Creating a network level plugin with admin pages

Introduction

As we saw in Chapter 2, *Plugin Framework Basics,* it is very easy for a plugin to register custom functions with action and filter hooks to change or augment the way WordPress renders web pages. That being said, some of the examples covered in Chapter 2, *Plugin Framework Basics,* have limitations when it comes to dealing with custom user information, such as the inability to easily specify a Google Analytics account number.

To make plugins easy to use for a wide audience, it is usually important to create one or more administration pages where users will be able to provide details that are specific to their installation, enter information on external accounts, and customize some of the aspects of the plugin's functionality. As an example, the Akismet plugin, provided in default WordPress installations, offers a configuration page that can be found under the **Settings** | **Akismet** configuration menu. Thankfully, WordPress has a rich set of functions that allows plugin developers to easily put together configuration pages that will seamlessly blend with the rest of the administrative panels.

This chapter covers how to use the WordPress Options **Application Programming Interface (API)** functions to store and access user options in the site database. It then goes on to explain how to create custom dialogs to provide users with complete control over the configuration of the plugins that you create.

Creating default user settings on plugin initialization

A typical first step of most user-configurable plugins is to create a default set of values for all options when the plugin is activated. These default options will subsequently be used to populate the plugin's settings page when it is visited by the site administrator. This recipe shows how to register a function that is called when a plugin is activated, and how to store option data in the site database.

How to do it...

1. Navigate to the WordPress plugin directory of your development installation.
2. Create a new directory called `ch3-individual-options`.
3. Navigate to this directory and create a new text file called `ch3-individual-options.php`.
4. Open the new file in a code editor and add an appropriate header at the top of the plugin file, naming the plugin `Chapter 3 - Individual Options`.
5. Add the following line of code to register a function that will be executed when the plugin is activated, after its initial installation or following an upgrade:

```
register_activation_hook( __FILE__, 'ch3io_set_default_options' );
```

6. Add the following code section to provide an implementation for the `ch3io_set_default_options` function:

```
function ch3io_set_default_options() {
    if ( false === get_option( 'ch3io_ga_account_name' ) ) {
        add_option( 'ch3io_ga_account_name', 'UA-0000000-0' );
    }
}
```

7. Save and close the plugin file. Execute the activation function that was just added by clicking on the **Activate** option of this `chapter 3 - Individual Options` plugin.
8. In your web server's MySQL database administration tool, select your WordPress database (`wordpressdev` if you followed the recipe in `Chapter 1`, *Preparing a Local Development Environment*), then select the `wpdev_options` table. Click on the **SQL** tab, replace the default query with the following statement, and click on **Go**:

```
select * from wpdev_options where option_name =
'ch3io_ga_account_name'
```

9. Your query should return a single row with the default value assigned to the new option:

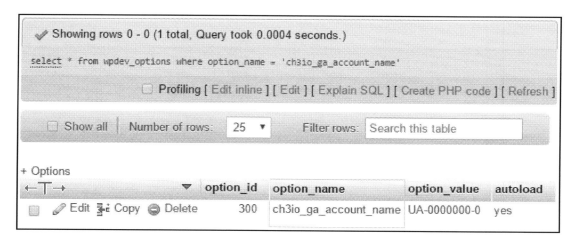

How it works...

The `register_activation_hook` function is used to indicate to WordPress the name of the function that should be called when it activates the plugin. Unlike other hooks, this function requires the name of the main plugin code file to be sent as its first argument, along with the name of the associated function. To do this easily, we can leverage the PHP `__FILE__` constant as the first argument, which will resolve to the filename.

When the callback function is called, we can use the Options API to create, update, or, delete settings in the options table of the site's MySQL database. In this specific example, we are using the `add_option` function to easily create an option called `ch3io_ga_account_name` with a default value of `UA-0000000-0`.

Just like function names, you should be careful when naming plugin options, to avoid conflicts with other plugins. A good practice is to add a unique prefix to the beginning of each variable name.

Before making a call to create the new option, the activation function checks whether the option is present in the WordPress options table using the `get_option` function. If the return value is false, indicating that the option was not found, a new default option can be created. Any other result would show that the plugin has been activated on the site previously and that options may have been changed from their default values. It is important to keep in mind when writing this code that plugins get deactivated and reactivated each time they are updated using the WordPress update tool, resulting in a call to their activation function. It is also possible that a user might have deactivated a plugin temporarily to debug site issues and brought it back at a later time, also resulting in the activation function being called.

Finally, it should be noted that it is possible to call the `add_option` function multiple times if more than one option is needed to implement a plugin's desired functionality. That being said, it is not necessary to verify the presence of all the options, as checking for a single one would indicate that they were all previously set.

There's more...

Beyond the creation of default values for a plugin, the activation hook can also be used to perform more advanced tasks, such as interacting with custom database tables or doing data initialization, as will be seen in later chapters. In contrast, the similar deactivation function hook does not have any real use within the creation of most plugins.

Deactivation function

Similar to the activation function that we used in this recipe, WordPress provides a way to register a deactivation function (using `register_deactivation_hook`). While it may be tempting to use this function to remove options created by the plugin, it is not possible to know why the activation function was called. The three situations that could trigger this call are a plugin upgrade, a temporary deactivation to debug a site problem, or just before the plugin gets deleted. Since it is best to keep user options in the first two situations, any cleanup and data removal code should be placed in a plugin's uninstallation file instead, as described in a later recipe.

See also

- The *Removing plugin data on deletion* recipe

Storing user settings using arrays

While the previous recipe worked quite well in creating entries in the site's options table for each individual plugin option, another way to manage user settings is to store them as arrays in the database.

This recipe creates the same option as the previous one, but also adds a second option and uses an array instead of individual options to store them. It also incorporates an upgrade strategy to deal with the creation of additional options as a plugin evolves over time.

Getting ready

You should have already followed the recipe entitled *Inserting link statistics tracking code in page body using plugin filters* in Chapter 2, *Plugin Framework Basics*, to have a starting point for this recipe. Alternatively, you can get the resulting code (Chapter 2/ch2-page-header-output/ch2-page-header-output-v2.php) from the code bundle downloaded from the Packt website (https://www.packtpub.com/support) and rename the file ch2-page-header-output.php.

How to do it...

1. Navigate to the ch2-page-header-output folder of the WordPress plugin directory of your development installation.
2. Open the file ch2-page-header-output.php in a code editor.
3. Add the following line of code to register a function to be called when the plugin is activated:

```
register_activation_hook( __FILE__,
                        'ch2pho_set_default_options_array' );
```

4. Add the following code section to provide an implementation for the `ch2pho_set_default_options_array` **function:**

```
function ch2pho_set_default_options_array() {
    ch2pho_get_options();
}
```

5. Add the following code to provide an implementation for the `ch2pho_get_options` **function:**

```
function ch2pho_get_options() {
    $options = get_option( 'ch2pho_options', array() );

    $new_options['ga_account_name'] = 'UA-0000000-0';
    $new_options['track_outgoing_links'] = false;

    $merged_options = wp_parse_args( $options, $new_options );

    $compare_options = array_diff_key( $new_options, $options );
    if ( empty( $options ) || !empty( $compare_options ) ) {
        update_option( 'ch2pho_options', $merged_options );
    }
    return $merged_options;
}
```

6. Save and close the plugin file.
7. Go to the Plugins section of the administration interface.
8. Click on the **Deactivate** link for the `Chapter 2 - Page Header Output` plugin, followed by a click on the **Activate** link to execute the activation function that was just added.
9. Using your web server's MySQL database administration tool, query the `wpdev_options` table of your WordPress installation for an option with the name `ch2pho_options`:

```
select * from wpdev_options where option_name = 'ch2pho_options'
```

10. Your query should return a single row with a serialized set of data representing all of the fields in the array:

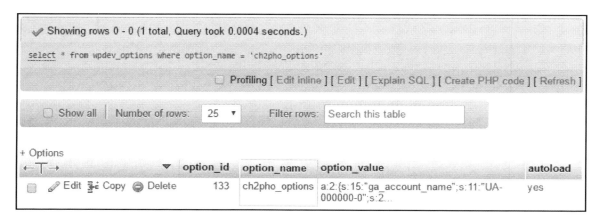

How it works...

The `add_option`, `get_option`, and `update_option` functions accept values as single variables or arrays of data. When given an array, they transform the information received to a serialized array that gets stored in the site database. The main advantage of using arrays over multiple options is that all of the information can be retrieved with a single function call, optimizing the access to the MySQL database and simplifying your plugin's code. This is especially important when your plugin options need to be queried every time a site page needs to be rendered.

Of course, this advantage is only true if you need to use most plugin options at the same time. Otherwise, your code will be managing large amounts of data for no reason.

Another benefit of using arrays instead of individual options is that the names of each option can be much shorter and simpler, since you only need to worry about avoiding naming conflicts at the top option name level, as opposed to each key in the array. Finally, having all the options stored in a single array makes the bulk removal of these options much easier than if they were all stored separately, as we will see in the next recipe.

The bulk of this recipe's code defines a utility function called `ch2pho_get_options`, which is used to make sure that we always get good values when retrieving options, even when our plugin runs for the first time or new options are introduced by an upgrade. As part of this utility function, we use the `wp_parse_args` function to quickly compare an existing set of options retrieved by the `get_option` function with the current set of default plugin options, specified by the `$new_options` array. For each array element that is not found in the existing options, `wp_parse_args` will simply merge it into the resulting array, which is returned at the end of the function. The last part of our option-retrieval function checks whether the previous option array was empty or whether any new keys were added to the new array, using the PHP `array_diff_key` function. In either of these cases, it will save the updated options array back to the site database.

It should finally be noted that, while the `ch2pho_get_options` function returns an array of all the site options, we are not actually using this return value in this recipe; we will use it in later recipes in this chapter.

See also

- The *Adding output content to page headers using plugin actions* recipe in `Chapter 2`, *Plugin Framework Basics*
- The *Inserting link statistics tracking code in page body using plugin filters* recipe in `Chapter 2`, *Plugin Framework Basics*
- The *Removing plugin data on deletion* recipe

Removing plugin data on deletion

As with any piece of software, it is quite possible that users might decide to remove a plugin from their WordPress installation if they no longer require the functionality that it provides or they have found an alternative that they prefer.

When this happens, the plugin author must decide if all of the configuration data stored in the site's database should be left in place, making it easier to re-install the plugin down the road, or to remove all of this information, leaving a clean database behind.

This recipe shows how to create a de-installation function that will remove options data from a site's database.

Getting ready

You should have already followed the *Storing user settings using arrays* recipe to have options data ready for deletion, and the resulting plugin should still be active in your development site. Alternatively, you can get the resulting code (Chapter 3/ch2-page-header-output/ch2-page-header-output-v3.php) from the downloaded code bundle. You should rename the file ch2-page-header-output-v3.php as ch2-page-header-output.php, and have activated the plugin once before starting this recipe.

How to do it...

1. Navigate to the ch2-page-header-output folder of the WordPress plugin directory of your development installation.
2. Create a new file called uninstall.php.
3. Open the new file in a text editor and add the following code to it:

```php
<?php
// Check that code was called from WordPress with
// uninstallation constant declared
if ( !defined( 'WP_UNINSTALL_PLUGIN' ) ) {
    exit;
}

// Check if options exist and delete them if present
if ( false != get_option( 'ch2pho_options' ) ) {
    delete_option( 'ch2pho_options' );
}
```

4. Save and close the plugin file.
5. Navigate to the administration page of your development WordPress installation.
6. Click on **Plugins** on the left-hand navigation menu.
7. Deactivate the Chapter 2 - Page Header Output plugin.
8. Make a copy of your plugin and uninstallation files to avoid losing them upon deletion of the plugin in the following steps. The copy should be moved outside of the plugins folder to avoid WordPress seeing two copies of the plugin.

9. Click on the **Delete** link under the `Chapter 2 - Page Header Output` plugin.
10. Click on the **OK** button to delete all the plugin files.

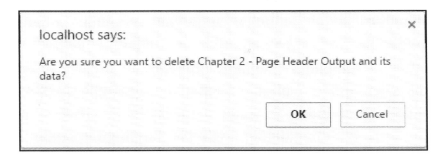

 Depending on the configuration of your development site, you may be prompted to provide FTP credentials before WordPress is able to delete the plugin files.

11. Using your web server's MySQL database administration tool, query the `wpdev_options` table of your WordPress installation for an option with the name `ch2pho_options` to see that the option has been deleted:

    ```
    select * from wpdev_options where option_name = 'ch2pho_options'
    ```

How it works...

When a plugin is inactive and a site administrator clicks on its deletion link, WordPress checks for the presence of a file called `uninstall.php` in the plugin directory. If the file exists and the user clicks the OK button to delete, WordPress proceeds with the deletion of all the plugin files and executes the content of the `uninstall.php` file. This file should contain straight PHP code that deletes all the plugin options and any other content created by the plugin's code. Once executed, the uninstall script will be deleted with the rest of the files.

Looking at the content of the uninstall script, the first few lines of code check for the presence of a constant that WordPress should have set before calling the script. If it is not present, the script will abort immediately for security purposes. This ensures that an external visitor knowing that a certain plugin is installed won't be able to try to delete it. Once the intent has been verified, the rest of the code checks for the existence of the `ch2pho_options` array that was created in the previous recipe and deletes it. If you created more than one option to store your configuration data, you will need to delete each option with individual calls to the `delete_option` function.

See also

- The *Storing user settings using arrays* recipe

Creating an administration page menu item in the settings menu

After defining default values for plugin configuration options, the next step is to create a place where users will be able to view and change these values. By using the WordPress API, we are able to create new items in the administration menu that will later allow us to create custom plugin configuration pages. This recipe shows how to create a new menu item that will appear under the **Settings** subsection of the administration menu.

Getting ready

You should have already followed the *Storing user settings using arrays* recipe to have options data available to manage. Alternatively, you can get the resulting code (`Chapter 3/ch2-page-header-output/ch2-page-header-output-v3.php`) from the downloaded code bundle. You should rename the file `ch2-page-header-output-v3.php` as `ch2-page-header-output.php` before starting this recipe.

How to do it...

1. Navigate to the root directory of your WordPress development installation.
2. Open the `wp-config.php` file in a text editor.
3. Set the `WP_DEBUG` variable to be `true`:

   ```
   define('WP_DEBUG', true);
   ```

4. Save the configuration file.
5. Navigate to the `ch2-page-header-output` folder of the WordPress plugin directory of your development installation.
6. Open the `ch2-page-header-output.php` file in a text editor.
7. Add the following line of code to register a function to be called when WordPress is building the administration pages menu:

   ```
   add_action( 'admin_menu', 'ch2pho_settings_menu' );
   ```

8. Add the following code section to provide an implementation for the `ch2pho_settings_menu` function:

   ```
   function ch2pho_settings_menu() {
       add_options_page( 'My Google Analytics Configuration',
                         'My Google Analytics', 'manage_options',
                         'ch2pho-my-google-analytics',
                         'ch2pho_config_page' );
   }
   ```

9. Save and close the plugin file.
10. Navigate to the administration page of your development WordPress installation.
11. **Activate** the `Chapter 2 - Page Header Output` plugin if you left it deactivated after following the previous recipe.

12. Click on the **Settings** section on the left-hand navigation menu to expand it. You will see a new menu item called **My Google Analytics** in the tree, created from the code that was just added to the plugin.

13. Click on the **My Google Analytics** menu item. You will see an error message displayed, since WordPress cannot find the function intended to populate the configuration page. This error will go away once you perform the recipe titled *Rendering the admin page contents using HTML*.

14. Back in the `wp-config.php` file, return the `WP_DEBUG` variable to its default value of `false`:

    ```
    define('WP_DEBUG', false);
    ```

15. Save and close the configuration file.

 If you had not set the `WP_DEBUG` variable to be `true` at the beginning of this recipe, WordPress would only display a blank page after performing step 13, instead of displaying an error message.

How it works...

The first line of code of this recipe registers a function to be called when WordPress is building the administration menu. When it is executed, the custom function that we created makes a call to the `add_options_page` function to add an item to the **Settings** menu. This function has a number of parameters that we will look at, as follows:

```
add_options_page( $page_title, $menu_title, $capability,
                  $menu_slug, $function );
```

The first two parameters are text strings that will be visible to site administrators, with the first one appearing in the browser title bar or tab title, and the second being the text of the submenu item that will appear under the **Settings** menu.

The third parameter is a bit more complicated and refers to the **user capability** required to be able to see and access this menu item. When creating users in a WordPress installation, each user is assigned one of the five default user roles (Subscriber, Administrator, Editor, Author, or Contributor). Each of these roles is mapped to a number of permissions that determine the actions that users with this role can perform. For a full list of roles and their associated capabilities, please refer to the WordPress Codex page on the topic (`https://codex.wordpress.org/Roles_and_Capabilities`). In this example, we used the user capability `manage_options`, which is assigned to users who have administrative rights on the site and to super admins when working in a network WordPress installation.

The fourth menu item, `menu_slug`, is a text string that will be used internally by WordPress to identify the menu item. This string should be unique to avoid conflicts with other plugins.

 The `menu_slug` name should be all lowercase to ensure that more advanced functionalities, such as WordPress meta boxes, work correctly.

The last parameter specifies the name of the function to be called to display the contents of the configuration page when the submenu item is clicked.

The **Settings** menu is a perfect location for plugins that only require a single configuration page, as you may have seen when installing other plugins, while more complex plugins that require multiple menu sections should use the technique shown in the next recipe.

There's more...

While new items will always be located under the default **Settings** menu items created by WordPress (General, Writing, Reading, and so on), plugin developers do have some control over the location of their plugin in the list.

Settings hook priority to determine menu order

As mentioned in the previous chapter, when action hooks were first introduced, the `add_action` function's third parameter is used to indicate the priority of a registered callback over other functions registered for the same hook (in this case, the `admin_menu` hook). To ensure that the newly created menu item is as high as possible in the menu, the priority of the registered function can be set to a value of 1:

```
add_action( 'admin_menu', 'ch2pho_settings_menu', 1 );
```

 It should be noted that other plugins can also set their callback to this priority. In such cases, alphabetical priority and activation sequence are other factors to determine which menu item will be displayed first after **Permalinks**.

See also

- The *Storing user settings using arrays* recipe

Creating a multi-level administration menu

When plugins grow in complexity, their configuration options often grow in numbers, giving users a high level of flexibility in choosing how the plugin behaves on their site. While it is possible to display all the plugin options on a single lengthy configuration page, creating a new top-level menu item with multiple sections can help organize parameters in logical groupings that will allow users to find what they are looking for more quickly.

This recipe shows how to create a new top-level menu item in the administration menu with an accompanying submenu item.

How to do it...

1. Navigate to the WordPress plugin directory of your development installation.

2. Create a new directory called `ch3-multi-level-menu`.

3. Navigate to this directory and create a new text file called `ch3-multi-level-menu.php`.

4. Open the new file in a code editor and add an appropriate header at the top of the plugin file, naming the plugin `Chapter 3 - Multi-level menu`.

5. Add the following line of code to register a function that will be called when WordPress is preparing data to display the site's administration menu:

    ```
    add_action( 'admin_menu', 'ch3mlm_admin_menu' );
    ```

6. Add the following code section to provide an implementation for the `ch3mlm_admin_menu` function:

    ```
    function ch3mlm_admin_menu() {
        // Create top-level menu item
        add_menu_page( 'My Complex Plugin Configuration Page',
                       'My Complex Plugin', 'manage_options',
                       'ch3mlm-main-menu', 'ch3mlm_my_complex_main',
                       plugins_url( 'myplugin.png', __FILE__ ) );

        // Create a sub-menu under the top-level menu
        add_submenu_page( 'ch3mlm-main-menu',
                          'My Complex Menu Sub-Config Page',
                          'Sub-Config Page',
                          'manage_options', 'ch3mlm-sub-menu',
                          'ch3mlm_my_complex_submenu' );
    }
    ```

7. Save and close the plugin file.

8. Find and download a PNG format 24 x 24 pixel icon from a site, such as IconArchive (`http://www.iconarchive.com`), resize it to 20 x 20 pixels, and save it as `myplugin.png` in the plugin directory.

9. Navigate to the **Plugins** section of your site's administration area.

10. **Activate** your new plugin.

11. You will now see a new menu item in the administration menu.

12. Expand the top-level new menu item to see the submenu item.

As with the previous recipe, clicking on the menu items will display an error, since we have not implemented a function to generate actual content for these menu items. We will not be implementing pages for these two menu items, but you can use a technique similar to what is shown in the *Rendering the admin page contents using HTML* recipe to create your own ch3mlm_my_complex_main and ch3mlm_my_complex_submenu functions.

How it works...

The add_menu_page function is very similar to the add_options_page function seen in the previous recipe, with its first five parameters being identical:

```
add_menu_page( $page_title, $menu_title, $capability,
               $menu_slug, $function, $icon_url, $position );
```

The last two items are specific to this function, with the first allowing us to display a custom icon in the menu next to our new top-level item, and the second specifying where the new menu should be positioned within the administration menu.

While it might seem interesting to use the position argument of the add_menu_page function to specify an exact position for a new menu item, doing so is risky, since only one menu item will be displayed if two plugins create entries with the same position value. If the position parameter is not specified, the new menu item will appear at the bottom of the menu structure, which should be fine in most cases.

Once the first menu item has been created, the `add_submenu_page` function can be used to attach a submenu item. The following are its parameters, which are virtually identical to the `add_options_page` function, except for the first parameter, which should be the unique string identifier of the top-level menu item to which the submenu should be attached:

```
add_submenu_page( $parent_slug, $page_title, $menu_title,
                  $capability, $menu_slug, $function );
```

While it is possible to use this technique to create top-level menu items for plugins with a single configuration page, these simpler extensions should create a single entry under the Settings menu, as shown in the previous recipe.

See also

- The *Creating an administration page menu item in the Settings menu* recipe

Adding menu items leading to external pages

While the WordPress plugin repository offers a number of useful sections under each plugin's page to host important information, including its description, FAQs, screenshots and support forums, a number of developers prefer to move documentation, FAQs, and even support to their own website. This allows them to create more feature-rich content for these sections and to create a more customized brand experience, especially in the case of plugins that offer free and premium versions.

This recipe shows how to add menu items that will lead users to external web pages.

Getting ready

You should have already followed the *Creating a multi-level administration menu* recipe to have a multi-level menu in place in your administration interface and the resulting plugin should still be active. Alternatively, you can get the resulting code (`Chapter 3/ch3-multi-level-menu/ch3-multi-level-menu.php`) from the downloaded code bundle.

How to do it...

1. Navigate to the `ch3-multi-level-menu` folder of the WordPress plugin directory of your development installation.
2. Open the `ch3-multi-level-menu.php` file in a text editor.
3. Add the following lines of code at the end of the `ch3mlm_admin_menu` function after the two calls to `add_submenu_page`:

```
global $submenu;
$url = 'https://www.packtpub.com/books/info/packt/faq';
$submenu['ch3mlm-main-menu'][] = array( 'FAQ', 'manage_options', $url );
```

4. Save and close the plugin file.
5. Refresh the administration page of your development WordPress installation to see the new submenu item under the **My Complex Plugin** menu:

How it works...

As calls to the menu creation functions are made by the core WordPress code and all active plugins, the system builds an array containing all the items that will be displayed to the current user based on their access level. This recipe's code accesses the WordPress global variable containing this array and simply inserts an extra element under the `ch3mlm-main-menu` parent menu that was created in the previous recipe. The data that gets added is an array containing three elements: the label of the menu item, the permissions required to see the item, and the URL that will be assigned to the new menu link.

While this code works in current versions of WordPress, and has worked for many versions, there is a chance that it might no longer work at some point if WordPress changes the way it builds its menus. That being said, if changes are made to the way that menus are constructed, there will likely be new APIs introduced to reproduce this functionality, as it is widely used.

See also

- The *Creating a multi-level administration menu* recipe

Hiding items which users should not access from the default menu

Many users praise WordPress for its ease of use and streamlined administration interface. That being said, almost everyone who has deployed it to new users has instructed them to avoid certain menu items, as they do not need to enter these sections and could potentially introduce site malfunctions if they modify settings in these areas.

A better solution than prevention through training is to use a few simple API functions to hide the undesired menu items. This recipe shows how to use these functions to remove the Comments editor and Permalinks settings menu items.

How to do it...

1. Navigate to the WordPress plugin directory of your development installation.
2. Create a new directory called ch3-hide-menu-item.
3. Navigate to this directory and create a new text file called ch3-hide-menu-item.php.
4. Open the new file in a code editor and add an appropriate header at the top of the plugin file, naming the plugin Chapter 3 - Hide Menu Item.
5. Add the following line of code to register a function that will be called when WordPress is preparing data to display the site's navigation menu:

```
add_action( 'admin_menu', 'ch3hmi_hide_menu_item' );
```

6. Add the following code section to provide an implementation for the ch3hmi_hide_menu_item function, hiding the **Comments** menu item:

```
function ch3hmi_hide_menu_item() {
    remove_menu_page( 'edit-comments.php' );
}
```

7. Add an extra function call to the ch3hmi_hide_menu_item function to hide the Permalinks submenu item found under the Settings menu:

```
remove_submenu_page( 'options-general.php',
                     'options-permalink.php' );
```

8. Save and close the plugin file.
9. Navigate to the **Plugins** section of the administration interface.
10. **Activate** your new plugin.
11. Look at the administration menu to see that the **Comments** menu is no longer visible:

12. Expand the **Settings** menu to see that the **Permalinks** submenu item is not visible either.

How it works...

The default WordPress administration menu uses the names of the PHP code files used to render each section as their unique identifiers. One way to quickly find out the identifier for a menu item is to hover the mouse cursor over it in a web browser and to look at the address that the link points to. In the case of the **Comments** menu item, the URL is http://localhost/wp-admin/edit-comments.php; thus the use of edit-comments.php in the call to remove_menu_page.

A similar technique was used to determine the arguments to pass to the `remove_submenu_page` function, identifying that the **Settings** section has a URL of `http://localhost/wp-admin/options-general.php`, while the **Permalinks** section has the address `http://localhost/wp-admin/options-permalink.php`.

Rendering the admin page contents using HTML

Once a custom menu item has been created, WordPress will call the function associated with it when it gets visited. The assigned function's main purpose is to render a configuration page containing a form with all the options available to the user and to send the captured data back to WordPress for processing.

There are two main methods that can be used to render plugin configuration pages: straight HTML and the Settings API. This recipe explores the use of HTML to create a configuration panel, while a later recipe will show how to use the Settings API to prepare the page output.

Getting ready

You should have already followed the *Creating an administration page menu item in the Settings menu* recipe and the resulting plugin should still be active in your development site. Alternatively, you can get the resulting code (`Chapter 3/ch2-page-header-output/ch2-page-header-output-v4.php`) from the downloaded code bundle. You should rename the file `ch2-page-header-output-v4.php` as `ch2-page-header-output.php` before starting this recipe.

How to do it...

1. Navigate to the `ch2-page-header-output` folder of the WordPress plugin directory of your development installation.
2. Open the `ch2-page-header-output.php` file in a text editor.

3. Add the following lines of code to implement the rendering code for the plugin options page:

```php
function ch2pho_config_page() {
    // Retrieve plugin configuration options from database
    $options = ch2pho_get_options();
    ?>

    <div id="ch2pho-general" class="wrap">
    <h2>My Google Analytics</h2><br />

    <form method="post" action="admin-post.php">
    <input type="hidden" name="action"
           value="save_ch2pho_options" />

    <!-- Adding security through hidden referrer field -->
    <?php wp_nonce_field( 'ch2pho' ); ?>
    Account Name: <input type="text" name="ga_account_name"
     value="<?php echo esc_html( $options['ga_account_name'] );
     ?>"/><br />
    Track Outgoing Links: <input type="checkbox"
     name="track_outgoing_links"
     <?php checked( $options['track_outgoing_links'] ); ?>/>
    <br /><br />
    <input type="submit" value="Submit" class="button-primary"/>
    </form>
    </div>
<?php }
```

4. Save and close the plugin file.
5. Click on the **Settings** section in the administration pages.
6. Click on the **My Google Analytics** menu item to display the plugin configuration page.

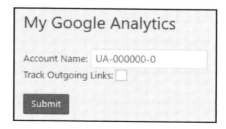

How it works...

Any output generated within the configuration page implementation function will be sent to the browser, enclosed within the WordPress administration interface layout. In this recipe's code, we first start by using the ch2pho_get_options function that we defined earlier in this chapter to retrieve all options for the plugin, conveniently organized in an array that we can store in a single variable.

We then use a closing PHP bracket to be able to write direct HTML code for the rest of the function's body, sending this content directly to the browser. The HTML code takes care of creating a standard form, rendering a text field to display and accepting new values for the Google Analytics Account Number, and a checkbox for the user to specify whether or not outgoing links should be tracked. Finally, the HTML code adds a Submit button to allow users to submit any changes made to the plugin's configuration.

Taking a closer look at the code, it also contains small snippets of PHP code that display the current configuration values when the options page is displayed and uses the checked WordPress utility function to output the correct HTML code when the passed argument is true.

The biggest advantage of using straight HTML to render a plugin's configuration page is that it allows for the creation of intricate layouts to present all of the options to the end user. This is in sharp contrast to using the Settings API, as we will see in a later recipe. HTML is also easier to understand for many web designers than working with intricate functions.

 It should be noted that any changes submitted from this form in its current state won't be saved, since we have not implemented the code necessary to process the submitted data and store it back in the options database table. This will be covered in the next recipe.

There's more...

As soon as user submission processing comes into play, it is important to think about security, to be sure to avoid the most common application security risks (https://www.owasp.org/index.php/Top_10_2017-Top_10). The form that was created in this recipe is no exception.

wp_nonce_field

The `wp_nonce_field` function that was used in this recipe is part of a security measure to ensure that the data being sent for submission comes from the WordPress administration pages and not an external source. By adding this function call, a hidden text field is added to the plugin configuration form with information that will be checked when the post data is received.

While it is optional, the first argument of the function is a unique identifier that should always be set to ensure better security. If it is not set, default values will be used, facilitating security breaches. The function also has a number of other optional parameters, as follows:

```
wp_nonce_field( [$action], [$name], [$referer], [$echo] );
```

The other three arguments are used to specify a name for the nonce, which would need to be matched on the receiving end, a Boolean variable to indicate if the referer field should be set for validation, and another Boolean parameter to determine whether the hidden form field should be displayed immediately or returned.

See also

- The *Creating an administration page menu item in the Settings menu* recipe
- The *Storing user settings using arrays* recipe

Processing and storing plugin configuration data

With the configuration page in place, plugin users will be able to modify configuration options and submit them to be stored in the WordPress database. The missing link at this time is the creation of a data processing function that will receive the data posted by the user and store it in the site's `options` table.

This recipe describes how to implement a data processing function to validate that the information being sent for storage is legitimate and to store the information in an options array.

Getting ready

You should have already followed the *Rendering the admin page contents using HTML* recipe and the resulting plugin should still be active in your development site. Alternatively, you can get the resulting code (`Chapter 3/ch2-page-header-output/ch2-page-header-output-v5.php`) from the downloaded code bundle. You should rename the file `ch2-page-header-output-v5.php` as `ch2-page-header-output.php` before starting this recipe.

How to do it...

1. Navigate to the `ch2-page-header-output` folder of the WordPress plugin directory of your development installation.
2. Open the `ch2-page-header-output.php` file in a text editor.
3. Add the following line of code to register a function to be called when WordPress first identifies that the requested page is an administration page:

```
add_action( 'admin_init', 'ch2pho_admin_init' );
```

4. Add the following code section to provide an implementation for the `ch2pho_admin_init` function:

```
function ch2pho_admin_init() {
    add_action( 'admin_post_save_ch2pho_options',
                'process_ch2pho_options' );
}
```

5. Add the following code section to provide an implementation for the `process_ch2pho_options` function that was declared in the previous step:

```
function process_ch2pho_options() {
    // Check that user has proper security level
    if ( !current_user_can( 'manage_options' ) ) {
        wp_die( 'Not allowed' );
    }

    // Check if nonce field configuration form is present
    check_admin_referer( 'ch2pho' );

    // Retrieve original plugin options array
    $options = ch2pho_get_options();
```

```
// Cycle through all text form fields and store their values
// in the options array
foreach ( array( 'ga_account_name' ) as $option_name ) {
    if ( isset( $_POST[$option_name] ) ) {
        $options[$option_name] =
            sanitize_text_field( $_POST[$option_name] );
    }
}

// Cycle through all check box form fields and set the options
// array to true or false values based on presence of variables
foreach ( array( 'track_outgoing_links' ) as $option_name ) {
    if ( isset( $_POST[$option_name] ) ) {
        $options[$option_name] = true;
    } else {
        $options[$option_name] = false;
    }
}

// Store updated options array to database
update_option( 'ch2pho_options', $options );

// Redirect the page to the configuration form
wp_redirect( add_query_arg( 'page',
                            'ch2pho-my-google-analytics',
                    admin_url( 'options-general.php' ) ) );
exit;
}
```

6. Save and close the plugin file.
7. Click on the **Settings** section of the administration menu.
8. Click on the **My Google Analytics** menu item to display the configuration page.
9. Change the value of one of the fields and click on the **Submit** button.
10. When the page refreshes, you will see that the values displayed reflect the values submitted.

How it works...

This recipe is the first to introduce an action hook that has a variable name. Instead of writing a specific action hook name when calling add_action, this hook name starts with the words admin_post_ and is followed by the name of an action that it expects to match with a hidden form field. In this case, the action name is save_ch2pho_options. Going back to the previous recipe, you can see that this text is the same as the one that was placed in the hidden form field called action:

```
<input type="hidden" name="action" value="save_ch2pho_options" />
```

When the configuration page form is submitted, it sends all data to the admin-post.php script, which checks for an action field and then sends the data that it received to the associated function, if present.

Once the processing function is executed, the calls to current_user_can and check_admin_referer are security measures where we check to see whether the user who is currently logged in has administrative rights and whether the nonce field that was part of the form is present. An error in these permission checks will result in a specific error message, letting the user know that he does not have the rights to perform this action, while the nonce check will display a vague error message to throw off potential hackers:

Are you sure you want to do this?

Please try again.

The rest of the function focuses on retrieving the current set of plugin options using the ch2pho_get_options function, processing the posted fields, and storing the updated values back in the site database. While using foreach loops might seem to be overkill to store two simple data fields, this approach can easily scale up to support large amounts of configuration fields.

The final step is a call to the `wp_redirect` function to send the browser back to the plugin options page after all the data has been stored. It is important to always call the `exit` PHP function after a call to `wp_redirect`, as shown in this recipe.

See also

- The *Rendering the admin page contents using HTML* recipe

Displaying a confirmation message when options are saved

An important usability aspect of any user interface is to display an acknowledgement message when users have completed a task successfully. As you may have noticed in the previous recipe, WordPress does not provide any user feedback by default after configuration data has been saved to the options table.

This recipe explains how to display an acknowledgement message on the configuration page after the user has updated the plugin's configuration options.

Getting ready

You should have already followed the *Processing and storing plugin configuration data* recipe and the resulting plugin should still be active in your development site. Alternatively, you can get the resulting code (`Chapter 3/ch2-page-header-output/ch2-page-header-output-v6.php`) from the downloaded code bundle. You should rename the file `ch2-page-header-output-v6.php` to `ch2-page-header-output.php` before starting this recipe.

How to do it...

1. Navigate to the `ch2-page-header-output` folder of the WordPress plugin directory of your development installation.
2. Open the `ch2-page-header-output.php` file in a text editor.

3. Modify the call to `wp_redirect` at the end of the `process_ch2pho_options` function, as follows, with modifications shown in bold:

```
wp_redirect( add_query_arg(
                  array( 'page' => 'ch2pho-my-google-analytics',
                         'message' => '1' ),
                  admin_url( 'options-general.php' ) ) );
```

4. Add the following code (in bold) after the configuration page title within the `ch2pho_config_page` function:

```
<h2>My Google Analytics</h2><br />

<?php if ( isset( $_GET['message'] ) &&
            $_GET['message'] == '1' ) { ?>
    <div id='message' class='updated fade'>
    <p><strong>Settings Saved</strong></p></div>
<?php } ?>
```

5. Save and close the plugin file.
6. Click on the Settings section of the administration menu.
7. Click on the **My Google Analytics** menu item.
8. Change the value of one of the fields and click on the **Submit** button to see the newly created message indicating that the settings have been saved.

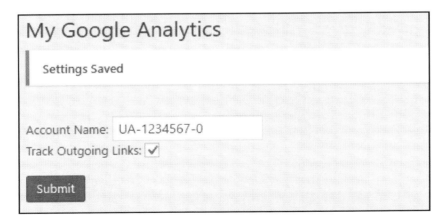

How it works...

When a redirection call is made, user-submitted fields and PHP variables do not carry forward to the target page. Therefore, we need to use another method, query arguments, to determine that a confirmation message should be displayed.

The first part of the recipe modifies the existing call to `wp_redirect` slightly to add a new query variable called `message`, set to a value of `1`.

Once it receives this variable, the code responsible for rendering the options page can display a message, following the standard WordPress styling.

The same mechanism could be used to display different messages based on the outcome of the options storage. For example, if some fields need to receive data formatted a certain way, the `process_ch2pho_options` function could set the message value differently depending on the success or failure of the data processing operation.

See also

- The *Processing and storing plugin configuration data* recipe

Adding custom help pages

As descriptive as field labels can be, a good plugin always needs to be accompanied by a set of documentation to allow users to quickly understand how to activate the plugin and perform the right steps to get the expected results. While a `ReadMe` file is often what developers first think of producing, users almost never read an external file or instructions on the official WordPress plugin page, they just install the plugin and try to figure it out by themselves.

To address this concern, WordPress introduced the ability to create elaborate multi-section help pages right in the plugin's administration pages to enable users to quickly get answers to their questions. This recipe shows you how to register the appropriate callback function to add a help section to your plugin configuration page, containing multiple tabs of information.

Getting ready

You should have already followed the *Displaying a confirmation message when options are saved* recipe, and the resulting plugin should still be active in your development site. Alternatively, you can get the resulting code (`Chapter 3/ch2-page-header-output/ch2-page-header-output-v7.php`) from the downloaded code bundle. You should rename the file `ch2-page-header-output-v7.php` as `ch2-page-header-output.php` before starting this recipe.

How to do it...

1. Navigate to the `ch2-page-header-output` folder of the WordPress plugin directory of your development installation.
2. Open the `ch2-page-header-output.php` file in a text editor.
3. Find the `ch2pho_settings_menu` function in the existing code.
4. Modify the code to store the return value of the `add_options_page` function call to a variable:

    ```
    $options_page =
        add_options_page( 'My Google Analytics Configuration',
                          'My Google Analytics',
                          'manage_options',
                          'ch2pho-my-google-analytics',
                          'ch2pho_config_page' );
    ```

5. Add the following block of code to the `ch2pho_settings_menu` function to register an action that will be called when the plugin's options page is loaded:

    ```
    if ( !empty( $options_page ) ) {
        add_action( 'load-' . $options_page, 'ch2pho_help_tabs' );
    }
    ```

6. Add the following code at the end of the plugin file to implement the newly declared `ch2pho_help_tabs` function:

```
function ch2pho_help_tabs() {
    $screen = get_current_screen();
    $screen->add_help_tab( array(
            'id'       => 'ch2pho-plugin-help-instructions',
            'title'    => 'Instructions',
            'callback' => 'ch2pho_plugin_help_instructions',
        ) );
    $screen->add_help_tab( array(
            'id'       => 'ch2pho-plugin-help-faq',
            'title'    => 'FAQ',
            'callback' => 'ch2pho_plugin_help_faq',
        ) );
    $screen->set_help_sidebar( '<p>This is the sidebar
        content</p>' );
}
```

7. Add the following code section to provide an implementation for the `ch2pho_plugin_help_instructions` function:

```
function ch2pho_plugin_help_instructions() { ?>
    <p>These are instructions explaining how to use this
        plugin.</p>
<?php }
```

8. Add the following code section to provide an implementation for the `ch2pho_plugin_help_faq` function:

```
function ch2pho_plugin_help_faq() { ?>
    <p>These are the most frequently asked questions on the use of
        this plugin.</p>
<?php }
```

9. Save and close the plugin file.
10. Click on the **Settings** section of the administration menu.
11. Click on the **My Google Analytics** menu to display the plugin configuration page. You will now see a **Help** tab appear in the top-right corner of the page.
12. Click on the **Help** tab to see all of the help content that has been added to the plugin.

Instructions	These are the most frequently asked questions on the use of this plugin.	This is the sidebar content
FAQ		

Help ▲

My Google Analytics

Account Name: UA-1234567-0

Track Outgoing Links: ✔

Submit

How it works...

As first discussed in the *Processing and storing plugin configuration data* recipe, some WordPress action hooks have names that contain a variable element that allows the plugin developer to get code executed when a specific page is rendered, or when data from a specific form is submitted. In this example, the load-<pagename> hook is used to register a function that gets executed when a specific administration page is accessed by the user.

Once the callback occurs, the function's code retrieves a reference to the WordPress screen object, which contains data about the screen that is currently displayed, along with a number of utility functions to manipulate and add content to the page. The code from the recipe then proceeds to register functions to render the content of two sections in the **Help** tab using the add_help_tab function.

The add_help_tab function is a little different from the functions that we have seen before, expecting a single array of options as its parameter. These options indicate a unique identifier for the menu section, a title to be displayed on each tab, and the name of the function that will render the tab contents. It is also possible to replace the callback argument with a parameter called content, which would directly contain the HTML code intended to be displayed in the **Help** tab. With this information, WordPress is able to integrate the provided HTML code when rendering the options page interface, including all of the necessary wrapper code to make the **Help** tab open and close, as well as allowing the user to switch between the different sections.

The other function used in this recipe, set_help_sidebar, is even simpler than add_help_tab, with a single argument indicating the HTML content to be displayed on the right-hand side of the help section.

See also

- The *Rendering the admin page contents using HTML* recipe

Rendering the admin page contents using the Settings API

In addition to creating administration pages through HTML code, WordPress also offers a set of functions referred to as the Settings API that can be used to automate the creation of complex configuration pages. While the work required to put this rendering technique in place is a bit overkill for plugins that only have a handful of options, it is definitely useful if you are dealing with tens or hundreds of configuration fields, simplifying the task of writing out HTML code for every single item to calling a single function for each of them. It also provides some automation around the processing and storing of plugin configuration data.

This recipe explains how to specify the contents of a configuration page using the Settings API and how to provide rendering functions for the most commonly used types of form field used in configuration pages. It uses the same set of configuration options as the other recipes in this chapter to show how the two techniques compare.

How to do it...

1. Navigate to the WordPress plugin directory of your development installation.
2. Create a new directory called ch3-settings-api.
3. Navigate to this directory and create a new text file called ch3-settings-api.php.
4. Open the new file in a code editor and add an appropriate header at the top of the plugin file, naming the plugin Chapter 3 - Settings API.

5. Add the following line of code to register a function that will be called when WordPress activates the plugin:

```
register_activation_hook( __FILE__,
                          'ch3sapi_set_default_options' );
```

6. Add the following code section to provide an implementation for the ch3sapi_set_default_options function to set default plugin options:

```
function ch3sapi_set_default_options() {
    ch3sapi_get_options();
}
```

7. Add the following code to provide an implementation for the ch3sapi_get_options function:

```
function ch3sapi_get_options() {
    $options = get_option( 'ch3sapi_options', array() );

    $new_options['ga_account_name'] = 'UA-0000000-0';
    $new_options['track_outgoing_links'] = false;

    $merged_options = wp_parse_args( $options, $new_options );

    $compare_options = array_diff_key( $new_options, $options );
    if ( empty( $options ) || !empty( $compare_options ) ) {
        update_option( 'ch3sapi_options', $merged_options );
    }
    return $merged_options;
}
```

8. Add the following registration function to associate a callback with the admin_init action hook:

```
add_action( 'admin_init', 'ch3sapi_admin_init' );
```

9. Add an implementation for the ch3sapi_admin_init function, creating the settings group for the plugin and defining its contents:

```
function ch3sapi_admin_init() {
    // Register a setting group with a validation function
    // so that post data handling is done automatically for us
    register_setting( 'ch3sapi_settings',
        'ch3sapi_options', 'ch3sapi_validate_options' );

    // Add a new settings section within the group
    add_settings_section( 'ch3sapi_main_section', 'Main Settings',
```

```
                   'ch3sapi_main_setting_section_callback',
                   'ch3sapi_settings_section' );

        // Add each field with its name and function to use for
        // our new settings, put them in our new section
        add_settings_field( 'ga_account_name', 'Account Name',
            'ch3sapi_display_text_field', 'ch3sapi_settings_section',
            'ch3sapi_main_section',
            array( 'name' => 'ga_account_name' ) );

        add_settings_field( 'track_outgoing_links',
            'Track Outgoing Links', 'ch3sapi_display_check_box',
            'ch3sapi_settings_section', 'ch3sapi_main_section',
            array( 'name' => 'track_outgoing_links' ) );
    }
```

10. Declare a body for the ch3sapi_validate_options function, which was declared when registering the settings in the previous section:

```
function ch3sapi_validate_options( $input ) {
    foreach ( array( 'ga_account_name' ) as $option_name ) {
        if ( isset( $input[$option_name] ) ) {
            $input[$option_name] =
                sanitize_text_field( $input[$option_name] );
        }
    }

    foreach ( array( 'track_outgoing_links' ) as $option_name ) {
        if ( isset( $input[$option_name] ) ) {
            $input[$option_name] = true;
        } else {
            $input[$option_name] = false;
        }
    }
    return $input;
}
```

11. Declare a body for the ch3sapi_main_setting_section_callback function, declared when the settings section was created:

```
function ch3sapi_main_setting_section_callback() { ?>
    <p>This is the main configuration section.</p>
<?php }
```

12. Provide an implementation for the `ch3sapi_display_text_field` function, declared when a text field was added to the settings section:

```php
function ch3sapi_display_text_field( $data = array() ) {
    extract( $data );
    $options = ch3sapi_get_options();
    ?>
    <input type="text" name="ch3sapi_options[<?php echo $name; ?>]"
            value="<?php echo esc_html( $options[$name] ); ?>"/>
    <br />
<?php }
```

13. Declare and define the `ch3sapi_display_check_box` function, declared when a checkbox was added to the settings section:

```php
function ch3sapi_display_check_box( $data = array() ) {
    extract ( $data );
    $options = ch3sapi_get_options();
    ?>
    <input type="checkbox"
            name="ch3sapi_options[<?php echo $name;   ?>]"
            <?php checked( $options[$name] ); ?>/>
<?php }
```

14. Add the following line of code to register a function that will be called when WordPress is preparing data to display the site's administration menu:

```php
add_action( 'admin_menu', 'ch3sapi_settings_menu' );
```

15. Provide code for the implementation of the `ch3sapi_settings_menu` function:

```php
function ch3sapi_settings_menu() {
    add_options_page( 'My Google Analytics Configuration',
        'My Google Analytics - Settings API', 'manage_options',
        'ch3sapi-my-google-analytics', 'ch3sapi_config_page' );
}
```

16. Add a definition for the `ch3sapi_config_page` function, defined when the new options page was declared:

```php
function ch3sapi_config_page() { ?>
    <div id="ch3sapi-general" class="wrap">
    <h2>My Google Analytics - Settings API</h2>

    <form name="ch3sapi_options_form_settings_api" method="post"
            action="options.php">
```

```php
<?php settings_fields( 'ch3sapi_settings' ); ?>
<?php do_settings_sections( 'ch3sapi_settings_section' ); ?>

<input type="submit" value="Submit" class="button-primary" />
</form></div>
<?php }
```

17. Save and close the plugin file.
18. Navigate to the **Plugins** menu of the administration area.
19. **Activate** your new plugin.
20. Navigate to the **Settings** menu and click on the **My Google Analytics - Settings API** menu item to see the configuration page for this plugin.

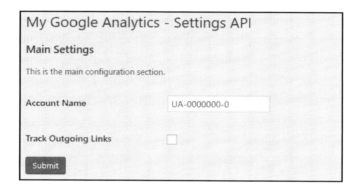

21. Make a change to the options and submit them to see that they are automatically handled by WordPress without having written express code to save options.

How it works...

The Settings API is an intricate series of callbacks that allow plugin developers to streamline the creation of administration pages and to automatically store user options.

This self-contained plugin recipe starts with the creation of a new set of default options, to avoid inadvertently deleting options from previous recipes.

The code continues with registering a function to be called whenever admin pages are prepared for display using the `admin_init` action hook. Upon getting called, the callback function takes care of registering a new setting group, a setting section belonging to this group, and two fields that will display the desired options within the section. As can be seen throughout this code, additional functions are registered to validate the user-submitted data, to display custom text at the beginning of the section, and to display the two different types of fields required to capture and display user input.

Taking a closer look at each of the functions that were just used, the first function has three parameters, which are as follows:

```
register_setting( $option_group, $option_name, $sanitize_callback );
```

Within these parameters, the first option is a unique identifier for the settings group, the second is the name of the options array that will be used to store configuration data in the site database, while the third is the name of a callback function that will receive user input for validation.

Moving on to the second function used in this example, `add_settings_section`, the four parameters that it requires respectively indicate a unique identifier for the section, the title string that will be displayed when the section is rendered, a callback function that will be used to display a description for the section, and finally a page identifier that will be used to render all similar functions later within the plugin code:

```
add_settings_section( $id, $title, $callback, $page );
```

The third function of the Settings API used in this recipe, `add_settings_field`, is called multiple times to define the fields that make up each section:

```
add_settings_field( $id, $title, $callback, $page, $section, [$args] );
```

Similar to the other functions, the first parameter is a unique identifier for the field, the second parameter is a label that will be displayed next to the field, and the third parameter is a callback function that will be executed to output the necessary HTML code to display the field. The next three parameters indicate the page that the field belongs to, the section that it is contained in, and an optional array of additional data to be sent to the callback function. As can be seen in the rest of this recipe, we are leveraging this optional additional data argument to send data to the field processing function to make them more generic.

When the configuration page is visited, the top-level form is created using regular HTML code, setting the action to `options.php`. This script is responsible for automating the processing of user data. The rest of the form is quite simple, since it gets generated by the `settings_fields` and `do_settings_sections` functions.

When they are called, the setting group created earlier is rendered, followed by calls to the functions designed to draw all the sections that it contains and all the registered fields within these sections.

While the Settings API provides full control over the layout of the form fields themselves, its use dictates the general layout of the configuration page, creating a two-column table that contains the labels for each field in the first column and the code produced by the plugin's callback functions in the second one. As the functions for each type of field are called, they receive the array data that was associated with each of them and use it to retrieve the current field values and to specify the name of each field to be stored back upon user input.

The last piece of the puzzle is the validation function that was registered when the setting group was first created. The purpose of this function is to allow plugin developers to perform data type or content validation as user data is submitted through the form, similar to the way we validate user-submitted data in the *Processing and storing plugin configuration data* recipe.

There's more...

While this recipe shows how to create rendering functions for two types of data fields, you may require other types of options for your plugin. The following are code examples that show how to handle most typical data types used in plugin options.

Rendering a drop-down list settings field

Before adding the select list itself, we would first add a line to initialize the `select_list` option in the `ch3sapi_get_options` function, if not found in the options retrieved from the database: `$new_options['select_list'] = 'First';`

The next step to rendering a drop-down list is to provide the list of all possible options, along with the option name, in the optional field data array. Here is an example of a call to the `add_settings_field` function call with such a list:

```
add_settings_field( 'select_list', 'Select List',
    'ch3sapi_select_list', 'ch3sapi_settings_section',
    'ch3sapi_main_section',
    array( 'name' => 'select_list',
           'choices' => array( 'First', 'Second', 'Third' ) ) );
```

With this information, we can provide an implementation for the `ch3sapi_select_list` function that will be able to render an HTML select element using the `choices` array to populate it:

```php
function ch3sapi_select_list( $data = array() ) {
    extract ( $data );
    $options = ch3sapi_get_options();
    ?>
    <select name="ch3sapi_options[<?php echo $name; ?>]">
        <?php foreach( $choices as $item ) { ?>
        <option value="<?php echo $item; ?>"
        <?php selected( $options[$name] == $item ); ?>>
        <?php echo $item; ?></option>;
    <?php } ?>
    </select>
<?php }
```

Rendering a text area settings field

Another common field type used in configuration pages is a multi-line text area. Once again, we would need to update the `ch3sapi_get_options` function to specify a default value for this new option if not found. Once this is done, the `add_settings_field` function is identical to the text and checkbox examples shown in the recipe, while the field rendering code is as follows:

```php
function ch3sapi_display_text_area( $data = array() ) {
    extract ( $data );
    $options = ch3sapi_get_options();
    ?>
    <textarea type="text" name="ch3sapi_options[<?php echo $name; ?>]"
            rows="5" cols="30">
        <?php echo esc_html ( $options[$name] ); ?></textarea>
<?php }
```

See also

- The *Rendering the admin page contents using HTML* recipe
- The *Processing and storing plugin configuration data* recipe

Accessing user settings from action and filter hooks

After creating a default set of values for our plugin's configuration and creating an interface to allow users to modify and update those values, we are now ready to start using these options when pages are rendered using our additional plugin functionality. Going back to the Google Analytics example created in `Chapter 2`, *Plugin Framework Basics*, this recipe shows how to access the plugin options data using a familiar function to make the existing code much more flexible.

Getting ready

You should have already followed the *Adding custom help pages* recipe, and the resulting plugin should be active in your development site. Alternatively, you can get the resulting code (`Chapter 3/ch2-page-header-output/ch2-page-header-output-v8.php`) from the downloaded code bundle. You should rename the file `ch2-page-header-output-v8.php` as `ch2-page-header-output.php` before starting this recipe.

How to do it...

1. Navigate to the `ch2-page-header-output` folder of the WordPress plugin directory of your development installation.
2. Open the `ch2-page-header-output.php` file in a text editor.
3. Modify the implementation of the `ch2pho_page_header_output` function to retrieve the plugin options array and use the stored value for the account number to embed it in the page header code. The new sections are identified in bold:

```
function ch2pho_page_header_output() {
    $options = ch2pho_get_options();
    ?>
    <script>
        (function(i,s,o,g,r,a,m){i['GoogleAnalyticsObject']=r;
        i[r]=i[r]||function(){
        (i[r].q=i[r].q||[]).push(arguments)},i[r].l=1*new Date();
        a=s.createElement(o),
        m=s.getElementsByTagName(o)[0];a.async=1;a.src=g;
        m.parentNode.insertBefore(a,m)})(window,document,'script',
        'https://www.google-analytics.com/analytics.js','ga');
```

```
            ga( 'create', '<?php echo $options['ga_account_name']; ?>',
                'auto' );
            ga('send', 'pageview');
        </script>
    <?php }
```

4. Add code to check whether outgoing code tracking should be done before registering an action hook to filter all post and page content, with the changes made identified in bold:

```
$options = ch2pho_get_options();

if ( true == $options['track_outgoing_links'] ) {
    add_filter( 'the_content','ch2lfa_link_filter_analytics' );
}
```

5. Use the same check to determine whether page footer code should be added to provide the JavaScript necessary for outgoing link tracking to occur with the changes made identified in bold:

```
if ( true == $options['track_outgoing_links'] ) {
    add_action( 'wp_footer', 'ch2lfa_footer_analytics_code' );
}
```

6. Save and close the plugin file.
7. Visit the site and look at the page source to see that the previous UA-0000000-0 has been replaced by the last value saved in the plugin's configuration page. You can also set the link tracking code to be displayed or not by changing the track outgoing links option.

How it works...

As we saw earlier in this chapter, when creating administrative pages, our custom ch2pho_get_options function can query the site's database and return the plugin configuration data that it contains. This data can be in the form of a single variable or an array of information. In this case, following the *Storing user settings using arrays* recipe found earlier in this chapter, an array was used and accessed to inject values in the page output when header and footer action hooks are called and when page content is being filtered.

See also

- The *Storing user settings using arrays* recipe

Formatting admin pages using meta boxes

As a plugin's administration page becomes longer and more complex, it becomes important to divide its content into multiple sections. While standard HTML headers or fieldset tags could be used for this task, they lack the usefulness and nice visual appearance of meta boxes. Meta boxes are the containers that show up in most default WordPress content editors, as well as on the main administration Dashboard page.

Beyond visually organizing content, meta boxes are very powerful, since they allow site administrators to collapse configuration sections that they don't use, re-order sections based on their needs, and even hide elements that they don't use.

This recipe explains how to convert the HTML-based configuration page that was created earlier in this chapter to use the built-in meta box system.

Getting ready

You should have already followed the *Accessing user settings from action and filter hooks* recipe. Alternatively, you can get the resulting code (`Chapter 3/ch2-page-header-output/ch2-page-header-output-v9.php`) from the downloaded code bundle. You should rename the file `ch2-page-header-output-v9.php` as `ch2-page-header-output.php` before starting the recipe.

How to do it...

1. Browse to the **Plugins** section of the administration section of your site and deactivate the `Chapter 2 - Page Header Output` plugin.
2. Navigate to the `ch2-page-header-output` folder of the WordPress plugin directory of your development installation.
3. Copy the file `ch2-page-header-output.php` to `ch2-page-header-output-metaboxes.php`.
4. Open the `ch2-page-header-output-metaboxes.php` file in a text editor.

5. Change the plugin name in the header from `Chapter 2 - Page Header Output` to `Chapter 2 - Page Header Output Meta Boxes`.

6. Right under the top plugin header comment, add a line of code to declare a global variable to hold the identifier for the options page:

```
global $options_page;
```

7. Find the `ch2pho_settings_menu` function in the existing code.

8. Add a line at the top of the function to point to the global options page variable:

```
global $options_page;
```

9. Find the `ch2pho_help_tabs` function within the plugin code.

10. Add the following block of code at the end of the function body to create meta boxes to be drawn on the screen and specify functions to be called to populate these boxes:

```
global $options_page;

add_meta_box( 'ch2pho_general_meta_box', 'General Settings',
              'ch2pho_plugin_meta_box', $options_page,
              'normal', 'core' );

add_meta_box( 'ch2pho_second_meta_box', 'Second Settings Section',
              'ch2pho_second_meta_box', $options_page,
              'normal', 'core' );
```

11. Add a line of code at the end of the plugin code file to register a function to be called when administration page styles are placed in a queue:

```
add_action( 'admin_enqueue_scripts', 'ch2pho_load_admin_scripts' );
```

12. Insert the following code segment to provide an implementation for the `ch2pho_load_admin_scripts` function:

```
function ch2pho_load_admin_scripts() {
    global $current_screen;
    global $options_page;

    if ( $current_screen->id == $options_page ) {
        wp_enqueue_script( 'common' );
        wp_enqueue_script( 'wp-lists' );
        wp_enqueue_script( 'postbox' );
    }
}
```

13. Create a new function to implement the `ch2pho_plugin_meta_box` function that was declared a few steps back. Notice that the body of the function is a direct copy and paste of the previous form code that was used to render the Account Name and Track Outgoing Links field:

```
function ch2pho_plugin_meta_box( $options ) { ?>
    Account Name: <input type="text" name="ga_account_name"
        value="<?php echo esc_html( $options['ga_account_name'] );
        ?>"/><br />

    Track Outgoing Links <input type="checkbox"
        name="track_outgoing_links"
        <?php checked( $options['track_outgoing_links'] ); ?>/>
        <br />
<?php }
```

14. Add the following code to provide an implementation for the `ch2pho_second_meta_box` function to display a second meta box. This second box will not have any real content. It will only be used to illustrate some of the meta box functionality:

```
function ch2pho_second_meta_box( $options ) { ?>
    <p>This is the content of the second metabox.</p>
<?php }
```

15. Find the code for the `ch2pho_config_page` function in your code and modify it as shown in the following code, where all the new code segments are in bold. Delete the original code that rendered the `ga_account_name` and `track_outgoing_links` fields:

```
function ch2pho_config_page() {
    // Retrieve plugin configuration options from database
    $options = ch2pho_get_options();
    global $options_page;
    ?>

    <div id="ch2pho-general" class="wrap">
    <h2>My Google Analytics</h2><br />

    <?php if ( isset( $_GET['message'] ) &&
            $_GET['message'] == '1' ) { ?>
        <div id='message' class='updated fade'>
        <p><strong>Settings Saved</strong></p>
        </div>
    <?php } ?>
```

```
<form action="admin-post.php" method="post">
<input type="hidden" name="action"
       value="save_ch2pho_options" />

<!-- Adding security through hidden referrer field -->
<?php wp_nonce_field( 'ch2pho' ); ?>

<!-- Security fields for meta box save processing -->
<?php wp_nonce_field( 'closedpostboxes',
                      'closedpostboxesnonce', false ); ?>
<?php wp_nonce_field( 'meta-box-order',
                      'meta-box-order-nonce', false ); ?>

<div id="poststuff" class="metabox-holder">
    <div id="post-body">
        <div id="post-body-content">
        <?php do_meta_boxes( $options_page, 'normal',
                                          $options ); ?>
            <input type="submit" value="Submit"
                   class="button-primary"/>
        </div>
    </div>
    <br class="clear"/>
</div>
</form>
</div>

<script type="text/javascript">
//<![CDATA[
jQuery( document ).ready( function( $ ) {
    // close postboxes that should be closed
    $( '.if-js-closed' ) .removeClass( 'if-js-closed' ).
        addClass( 'closed' );

    // postboxes setup
    postboxes.add_postbox_toggles(
        '<?php echo $options_page; ?>' );
});

//]]>
</script>
<?php }
```

16. Save and close the plugin file.
17. **Activate** your new plugin.
18. Click on the **Settings** section on the left-hand navigation menu to expand it.

19. Click on the **My Google Analytics** in the tree to display the re-designed administration page.

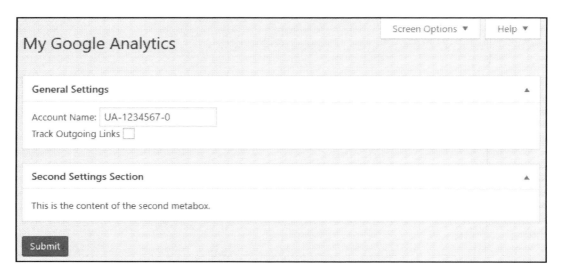

20. Drag and drop one of the meta boxes to re-order them.
21. Click on one of the meta box titles to collapse that section.
22. Click on the **Screen Options** menu in the top-right corner to open a menu to control the visibility of all the meta boxes.
23. Move to another section of the administration menu and come back to the **My Google Analytics** section to see that all the changes made to the layout of the configuration page have been retained.

How it works...

The setup of the meta box functionality is done in the `load-<pagename>` callback function by calling the `add_meta_box` function multiple times based on the desired number of boxes to be displayed on the screen.

The function takes a number of arguments, as shown:

```
add_meta_box( $id, $title, $callback, [$page], [$context], [$priority],
              [$callback_args] );
```

Going over the parameters in this function, the first is a unique identifier for the meta box, while the second is the string that will be displayed as the title of the box itself and is also the name that will show up in the Screen Options configuration tab. The third parameter is the name of the function to be called to render the contents of the meta box. The fourth argument identifies the page where the meta boxes will be rendered. In this case, we use the value of the global variable $options_page for this parameter, to be sure that it will be assigned the correct page identifier. Global PHP variables are powerful tools that can help us share data between functions in a plugin. By using the keyword global in front of the name of a variable, a website's PHP interpreter will know that it has to access a common memory space to store and access information.

The fifth parameter is an arbitrary name that indicates the name of a section where the box should be displayed. This name will be used when making a request to WordPress to render all the meta boxes belonging to a specific section. The only requirement for this to work correctly is to use the same name when calling the do_meta_boxes function.

The sixth argument indicates the priority of the registered meta box within the section it belongs to, relative to other meta boxes. If all the boxes have the same priority, the order in which the calls to the add_meta_box function were made will determine their original drawing order. Of course, as was seen in this recipe, this order can be overridden by the user through a simple drag-and-drop operation. The final parameter is optional and can be used to send information to the function that will render the meta box contents.

While it is actually possible to call add_meta_box from other action hook callbacks, only meta boxes registered during a load-<pagename> callback will show up in the Screen Options list to allow the user to control their visibility. You may want to create meta boxes outside of this action hook on purpose, to be sure that important boxes are always shown and to provide a standard user experience for all users.

In addition to the calls to add_meta_box, we must make multiple calls to wp_enqueue_script in the page load function to request for three JavaScript scripts to be loaded when our configuration page is rendered. These scripts provide the drag-and-drop, minimize, and hiding functionalities that were demonstrated at the end of the recipe, with only a few initialization calls needed to be done from our code through JavaScript functions.

Once the meta boxes have been created, the bulk of the work is done within the options page rendering function. As we can see in the modified code, the first thing that is done is to create new nonce fields. These unique numbers will be generated as hidden data in the page and will be used for authentication to save layout changes within the configuration page. Next, we create a number of `div` sections with specific `id` names that contain a nested call to the `do_meta_boxes` function. These div tags are used to ensure that the meta boxes are styled using the WordPress administration pages style sheet.

Once called, the `do_meta_boxes` function takes care of drawing all of the meta boxes that were created for the given page (specified in the first argument) and given section (second argument). It also passes along any data specified in the third function argument to the functions associated with each box.

The remaining changes to the page rendering function is a block of JavaScript code that takes care of closing down any meta box section that was closed by the user during a previous visit to the page. It also assigns jQuery callbacks to the meta boxes so that any user interaction with them is saved to the site database by sending AJAX requests to the web server.

Last, but not least, the meta box rendering functions are responsible for rendering the content inside each meta box. They can do this by outputting straight HTML. By passing along the complete options array to these functions, the code that is contained within them can be exactly the same as before to render the various options fields.

See also

- The *Rendering the admin page contents using HTML* recipe

Splitting admin code from the main plugin file to optimize site performance

As mentioned in Chapter 2, *Plugin Framework Basics*, the entire content of the main code file of a WordPress plugin gets evaluated every time any page is rendered on the site, whether it's a visitor-facing page or a backend administration page. This means that large amounts of PHP code can potentially be parsed on every iteration, wasting processing power on the site's server, even though some of this code will never be active when regular visitors are browsing the site.

A prime example of this waste is all of the code samples that we have been building in this chapter. While this code is extremely useful for site administrators, there is no sense in having the web server parse and validate that code when regular pages are displayed. For this reason, it is better to isolate this code in a separate file which will only be loaded and parsed when someone is visiting the site's dashboard. The following recipe shows how to isolate the less frequently required code to a separate file and only load it when a user is visiting the site administration section.

Getting ready

You should have already followed the *Hiding items which users should not access from the default menu* recipe to have a starting point for this recipe, and the resulting plugin should still be active in your development site. Alternatively, you can get the resulting code (Chapter 3/ch3-hide-menu-item/ch3-hide-menu-item.php) from the downloaded code bundle.

How to do it...

1. Navigate to the ch3-hide-menu-item folder of the WordPress plugin directory of your development installation.
2. Open the ch3-hide-menu-item.php file in a text editor.
3. Create a new PHP code file called ch3-hide-menu-item-admin-functions.php in the same directory and open it in a text editor.
4. Move the calls to the add_action function and the definition of the ch3hmi_hide_menu_item function to the new file, preceded by a standard PHP open tag and checking for the definition of a constant:

```php
<?php

if ( !defined( 'ch3hmi' ) ) {
    exit;
}
```

5. Back in the main plugin code file (`ch3-hide-menu-item.php`), add code that will define a constant and check whether the current page being rendered is an administration page and proceed to load the administration functions if it is:

```
define( 'ch3hmi', 1 );

if ( is_admin() ) {
    require plugin_dir_path( __FILE__ ) .
        'ch3-hide-menu-item-admin-functions.php';
}
```

6. Save and close the plugin file.
7. While the plugin will continue to work as it did before, the action hook registration code will only be processed when an administration page is displayed.

How it works...

The `is_admin` function is used to quickly tell if the page currently being rendered is an administration page. If it is, our plugin code uses the standard PHP `include` function to load and execute the contents of a separate file. In this case, the file is a second PHP file located in the plugin directory. To be flexible with regards to the location of the plugin files, we build a path to the file containing the administration functions using the WordPress `plugin_dir_path` function.

While the benefit of placing so little code in a separate file is minimal, this technique has a larger impact on performance when dealing with larger administration panels. In addition to not having to register an action hook on every page load, the PHP interpreter does not have to make sure that the syntax for the entire contents of that second file is valid when rendering front-facing pages.

See also

- The *Hiding items which users should not access from the default menu* recipe

Storing style sheet data in user settings

While most common plugin options are typically presented to users as simple textboxes, checkboxes, or drop-down lists, there are instances where more text needs to be stored for user settings. A good example of this are plugin-specific style sheets, which allow users to change the visual appearance of plugin output. While loading a separate style sheet file worked well in the *Loading a style sheet to format plugin output* recipe in Chapter 2, *Plugin Framework Basics*, this approach did not give users a lot of liberty in changing these styling rules to work better with their site design, since any changes that users make to the style sheet will get overwritten when the plugin is updated using the WordPress plugin upgrade process.

A solution to this problem is to store style sheet data with the rest of the configuration options in the site database. This way, the information will remain intact when upgrades are performed. This recipe shows how to change the plugin created in the previous chapter to initialize the plugin options using an external file, how to create an administration panel to allow users to modify or reset the style sheet, and how to use the new data to output the style information to the page header. Many of the lessons learned in this chapter will be put to use to create the final result.

Getting ready

You should have already followed the *Loading a style sheet to format plugin output* recipe in the previous chapter to have a starting point for this recipe. Alternatively, you can get the resulting code (Chapter 2/ch2-private-item-text/ch2-private-item-text-v2.php) from the downloaded code bundle and rename the file to ch2-private-item-text.php before starting the recipe.

How to do it...

1. Navigate to the ch2-private-item-text folder of the WordPress plugin directory of your development installation.
2. Open the ch2-private-item-text.php file in a text editor.
3. Add the following lines of code to implement an activation callback to initialize plugin options when it is installed or upgraded:

```
register_activation_hook( __FILE__, 'ch2pit_get_options' );

function ch2pit_get_options() {
```

```
$options = get_option( 'ch2pit_options', array() );

$stylesheet_location = plugin_dir_path( __FILE__ ) .
                           'stylesheet.css';
$new_options['stylesheet'] =
    file_get_contents( $stylesheet_location );

$merged_options = wp_parse_args( $options, $new_options );
$compare_options = array_diff_key( $new_options, $options );
if ( empty( $options ) || !empty( $compare_options ) ) {
    update_option( 'ch2pit_options', $merged_options );
}
return $merged_options;
}
```

4. Add the following code segment to register a function to be called when the menu is built to add an additional item under the Settings menu:

```
add_action( 'admin_menu', 'ch2pit_settings_menu' );

function ch2pit_settings_menu() {
    add_options_page( 'Private Item Text Configuration',
        'Private Item Text', 'manage_options',
        'ch2pit-private-item-text', 'ch2pit_config_page' );
}
```

5. Insert the following code to render the options page.

 The line that prints the style sheet in the text area should start at the beginning of a new line to avoid having extra spaces at the beginning of the style sheet editor. Also, make sure you do not lose the hyphen in `font-family` if you are copying the code from a digital copy of this book.

```
function ch2pit_config_page() {
    // Retrieve plugin configuration options from database
    $options = ch2pit_get_options(); ?>

    <div id="ch2pit-general" class="wrap">
    <h2>Private Item Text</h2>

    <!-- Code to display confirmation messages when settings
        are saved or reset -->
    <?php if ( isset( $_GET['message'] ) &&
            $_GET['message'] == '1' ) { ?>
        <div id='message' class='updated fade'><p>
            <strong>Settings Saved</strong></p></div>
    <?php } elseif ( isset( $_GET['message'] )
```

```
                            && $_GET['message'] == '2' ) { ?>
        <div id='message' class='updated fade'><p>
        <strong>Stylesheet reverted to original</strong></p></div>
    <?php } ?>

    <form name="ch2pit_options_form" method="post"
        action="admin-post.php">
    <input type="hidden" name="action"
        value="save_ch2pit_options" />
    <?php wp_nonce_field( 'ch2pit' ); ?>

    Stylesheet<br />
<textarea name="stylesheet" rows="10" cols="40" style="font-
family:Consolas,Monaco,monospace"><?php echo esc_html (
$options['stylesheet'] ); ?></textarea><br />
    <input type="submit" value="Submit" class="button-primary" />
    <input type="submit" value="Reset" name="resetstyle"
        class="button-primary" />
    </form>
    </div>
<?php }
```

6. Add the following block of code to register a function to be called when user options are saved and to provide an implementation for this function:

```
add_action( 'admin_init', 'ch2pit_admin_init' );

function ch2pit_admin_init() {
    add_action( 'admin_post_save_ch2pit_options',
                'process_ch2pit_options' );
}

function process_ch2pit_options() {
    // Check that user has proper security level
    if ( !current_user_can( 'manage_options' ) ) {
        wp_die( 'Not allowed' );
    }

    // Check if nonce field is present
    check_admin_referer( 'ch2pit' );

    // Retrieve original plugin options array
    $options = ch2pit_get_options();

    if ( isset( $_POST['resetstyle'] ) ) {
        $stylesheet_location = plugin_dir_path( __FILE__ ) .
                                    'stylesheet.css';
        $options['stylesheet'] =
```

```
                            file_get_contents( $stylesheet_location );
            $message = 2;
        } else {
            // Cycle through all fields and store their values
            // in the options array
            foreach ( array( 'stylesheet' ) as $option_name ) {
                if ( isset( $_POST[$option_name] ) ) {
                    $options[$option_name] = $_POST[$option_name];
                }
            }
            $message = 1;
        }

        // Store updated options array to database
        update_option( 'ch2pit_options', $options );

        // Redirect the page to the configuration form
        wp_redirect( add_query_arg(
                        array(
                            'page' => 'ch2pit-private-item-text',
                            'message' => $message ),
                            admin_url( 'options-general.php' ) ) );
        exit;
    }
```

7. Delete the call to the `add_action` function, which associated the function `ch2pit_queue_stylesheet` with the `wp_enqueue_scripts` action hook, along with the `ch2pit_queue_stylesheet` function itself.

8. Add the following code to add the user-modifiable style sheet code to the page header:

```
add_action( 'wp_head', 'ch2pit_page_header_output' );

function ch2pit_page_header_output() { ?>
    <style type='text/css'>
    <?php
        $options = ch2pit_get_options();
        echo $options['stylesheet'];
    ?>
    </style>
<?php }
```

9. Save and close the plugin file.

10. Deactivate and then **Activate** the `Chapter 2 - Private Item Text` plugin from the administration interface.

11. Navigate to the **Settings** menu and select the **Private Item Text** submenu item to see the newly created configuration panel, with options to submit changes to the style sheet or reset it to its initial state, as shown in the following screenshot:

12. Visit the website and look at the page source to see that the style sheet data entered in the configuration page shows up in the HTML header:

```
<style type='text/css'>
.private {
    color: #6E6A6B;
}

.register {
    background-color: #ff4d4d;
    color: #fff;
    padding-left: 10px;
}
</style>
```

How it works...

Re-using many of the elements covered in this chapter, this recipe creates a simple yet effective configuration interface to allow users to make changes to the color that is used to highlight private text in posts, instead of this color being hardcoded in a plugin file.

That being said, this recipe does introduce two new concepts. The first is the initialization of the plugin options by reading data from a file instead of having all of that information stored in the PHP code. This technique is useful when dealing with an option that has a lot of content, such as a style sheet.

The next element of interest is within the data processing function, where the code checks to see which button was pressed between the one to reset the style sheet and the one to submit user changes to be stored in the site database. Based on the result, the processing code will either read back the initial style sheet from the file or use the user-posted data to update the configuration data.

Beyond these two new concepts, the other main change is to the code that was outputting header code referencing an external style sheet file. In this new version, a change was made to echo the content of the style sheet that is stored in the options table directly to the browser.

 It should be noted that this recipe does not check to see if the user enters valid CSS code in the field before adding it to the page header, since verifying this would be too complex for now. A library such as CSSTidy (`http://csstidy.sourceforge.net/`) could be used to perform this task, as desired.

See also

- The *Creating a new enclosing shortcode* recipe in Chapter 2, *Plugin Framework Basics*
- The *Loading a style sheet to format plugin output* recipe in Chapter 2, *Plugin Framework Basics*

Managing multiple sets of user settings from a single admin page

Throughout this chapter, you have learned how to create configuration pages to manage single sets of configuration options for our plugins. In some cases, only being able to specify a single set of options will not be enough. For example, looking back at the Twitter embed shortcode plugin that was created in the previous chapter, a single configuration panel would only allow users to specify one set of options, such as the desired Twitter feed dimensions or the number of tweets to display.

A more flexible solution would be to allow users to specify multiple sets of configuration options, which could then be called up by using an extra shortcode parameter (for example, [twitterfeed user_name="WordPress" option_id="2"]).

While the first thought that might cross your mind to configure such a plugin is to create a multi-level menu item with submenus to store a number of different settings, this method would produce a very awkward interface for users to navigate. A better way is to use a single panel but give the user a way to select between multiple sets of options to be modified.

In this recipe, you will learn how to enhance the previously created Twitter feed shortcode plugin to be able to control the embedded feed width and number of tweets to display from the plugin configuration panel and to give users the ability to specify multiple display sizes.

Getting ready

You should have already followed the *Creating a new shortcode with parameters* recipe in the previous chapter to have a starting point for this recipe. Alternatively, you can get the resulting code (Chapter 2/ch2-twitter-embed/ch2-twitter-embed.php) from the downloaded code bundle.

How to do it...

1. Navigate to the ch2-twitter-embed folder of the WordPress plugin directory of your development installation.
2. Open the ch2-twitter-embed.php file in a text editor.
3. Add the following lines of code to implement an activation callback to initialize plugin options when it is installed or upgraded:

```
register_activation_hook( __FILE__,
                          'ch2te_set_default_options_array' );

function ch2te_set_default_options_array() {
    ch2te_get_options();
}

function ch2te_get_options( $id = 1 ) {
    $options = get_option( 'ch2te_options_' . $id, array() );

    $new_options['setting_name'] = 'Default';
    $new_options['width'] = 560;
```

```
        $new_options['number_of_tweets'] = 3;

        $merged_options = wp_parse_args( $options, $new_options );
        $compare_options = array_diff_key( $new_options, $options );
        if ( empty( $options ) || !empty( $compare_options ) ) {
            update_option( 'ch2te_options_' . $id, $merged_options );
        }
        return $merged_options;
    }
```

4. Insert the following code segment to register a function to be called when the administration menu is put together. When this happens, the callback function adds an item to the **Settings** menu and specifies the function to be called to render the configuration page:

```
// Assign function to be called when admin menu is constructed
add_action( 'admin_menu', 'ch2te_settings_menu' );

// Function to add item to Settings menu and
// specify function to display options page content
function ch2te_settings_menu() {
    add_options_page( 'Twitter Embed Configuration',
                      'Twitter Embed', 'manage_options',
                      'ch2te-twitter-embed', 'ch2te_config_page' );
}
```

5. Add the following code to implement the configuration page rendering function:

```
// Function to display options page content
function ch2te_config_page() {
    // Retrieve plugin configuration options from database
    if ( isset( $_GET['option_id'] ) ) {
        $option_id = intval( $_GET['option_id'] );
    } elseif ( isset( $_POST['option_id'] ) ) {
        $option_id = intval( $_POST['option_id'] );
    } else {
        $option_id = 1;
    }

    $options = ch2te_get_options( $option_id ); ?>

    <div id="ch2te-general" class="wrap">
    <h2>Twitter Embed</h2>

    <!-- Display message when settings are saved -->
    <?php if ( isset( $_GET['message'] ) &&
               $_GET['message'] == '1' ) { ?>
```

```
            <div id='message' class='updated fade'>
                <p><strong>Settings Saved</strong></p></div>
    <?php } ?>

    <!-- Option selector -->
    <div id="icon-themes" class="icon32"><br></div>
    <h2 class="nav-tab-wrapper">
    <?php for ( $counter = 1; $counter <= 5; $counter++ ) {
        $temp_options = ch2te_get_options( $counter );
        $class = ( $counter == $option_id ) ?
                ' nav-tab-active' : ''; ?>

    <a class="nav-tab<?php echo $class; ?>" href="<?php echo
       add_query_arg( array( 'page' => 'ch2te-twitter-embed',
'option_id' => $counter ), admin_url( 'options-general.php' ) );
?>"><?php echo $counter; ?><?php if ( $temp_options !== false )
echo ' (' . $temp_options['setting_name'] . ')'; else echo '
(Empty)'; ?></a>
    <?php } ?>
    </h2><br />
    <!-- Main options form -->
    <form name="ch2te_options_form" method="post"
            action="admin-post.php">
    <input type="hidden" name="action"
            value="save_ch2te_options" />
    <input type="hidden" name="option_id"
                        value="<?php echo $option_id; ?>" />
    <?php wp_nonce_field( 'ch2te' ); ?>
    <table>
        <tr><td>Setting name</td>
            <td><input type="text" name="setting_name"
      value="<?php echo esc_html( $options['setting_name'] ); ?>"/>
            </td>
        </tr>
        <tr><td>Feed width</td>
            <td><input type="text" name="width"
      value="<?php echo esc_html( $options['width'] ); ?>"/></td>
        </tr>
        <tr><td>Number of Tweets to display</td>
            <td><input type="text" name="number_of_tweets" value=
      "<?php echo esc_html( $options['number_of_tweets'] ); ?>"
            /></td>
        </tr>
    </table><br />
    <input type="submit" value="Submit" class="button-primary" />
    </form>
    </div>
<?php }
```

6. Add the following block of code to register a function that will process user options when submitted to the site:

```
add_action( 'admin_init', 'ch2te_admin_init' );

function ch2te_admin_init() {
    add_action( 'admin_post_save_ch2te_options',
                'process_ch2te_options' );
}
```

7. Add the following code to implement the `process_ch2te_options` function, declared in the previous block of code:

```
// Function to process user data submission
function process_ch2te_options() {
    // Check that user has proper security level
    if ( !current_user_can( 'manage_options' ) ) {
        wp_die( 'Not allowed' );
    }

    // Check that nonce field is present
    check_admin_referer( 'ch2te' );

    // Check if option_id field was present
    if ( isset( $_POST['option_id'] ) ) {
        $option_id = intval( $_POST['option_id'] );
    } else {
        $option_id = 1;
    }

    // Build option name and retrieve options
    $options = ch2te_get_options( $option_id );
    // Cycle through all text fields and store their values
    foreach ( array( 'setting_name' ) as $param_name ) {
        if ( isset( $_POST[$param_name] ) ) {
            $options[$param_name] = sanitize_text_field(
                                    $_POST[$param_name] );
        }
    }

    // Cycle through all numeric fields, convert to int and store
    foreach( array( 'width',
                    'number_of_tweets' ) as $param_name ) {
        if ( isset( $_POST[$param_name] ) ) {
            $options[$param_name] = intval( $_POST[$param_name] );
        }
    }
```

```
// Store updated options array to database
$options_name = 'ch2te_options_' . $option_id;
update_option( $options_name, $options );

$clean_address = add_query_arg( array( 'message' => 1,
                    'option_id' => $option_id,
                    'page' => 'ch2te-twitter-embed' ),
                    admin_url( 'options-general.php' ) );
wp_redirect( $clean_address );
exit;
}
```

8. Find the ch2te_twitter_embed_shortcode function and modify it as follows to accept the new option_id parameter and load the plugin options to produce the desired output. The changes are identified in bold within the recipe:

```
function ch2te_twitter_embed_shortcode( $atts ) {
    extract( shortcode_atts( array(
            'user_name' => 'ylefebvre',
            'option_id' => '1'
        ), $atts ) );

    if ( intval( $option_id ) < 1 || intval( $option_id ) > 5 ) {
        $option_id = 1;
    }
    $options = ch2te_get_options( $option_id );

    if ( !empty( $user_name ) ) {
        $output = '<a class="twitter-timeline" href="';
        $output .= esc_url( 'https://twitter.com/' . $user_name );
        $output .= '" data-width="' . $options['width'] . '" ';
        $output .= 'data-tweet-limit="';
        $output .= $options['number_of_tweets'];
        $output .= '">Tweets by ' . esc_html( $user_name );
        $output .= '</a><script async ';
        $output .= 'src="//platform.twitter.com/widgets.js"';
        $output .= ' charset="utf-8"></script>';
    } else {
        $output = '';
    }
    return $output;
}
```

9. Save and close the plugin file.

10. Deactivate and then **Activate** the Chapter 2 - Twitter Embed plugin from the administration interface to execute its activation function and create default settings.

11. Navigate to the **Settings** menu and select the **Twitter Embed** submenu item to see the newly created configuration panel with the first set of options being displayed and more sets of options accessible through the drop-down list shown at the top of the page.

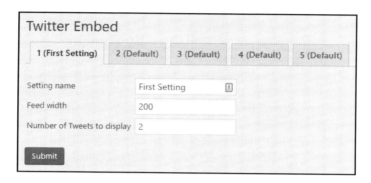

12. To select the set of options to be used, add the parameter option_id to the shortcode used to display a Twitter feed, as follows:

```
[twitterfeed user_name="WordPress" option_id="1"]
```

How it works...

This recipe shows how we can leverage options arrays to create multiple sets of options simply by creating the name of the options array on the fly. Instead of having a specific option name in the first parameter of the get_option function call, we create a string with an option ID. This ID is sent through as a URL parameter on the configuration page and as a hidden text field when processing the form data.

The rest of the code is very similar to the other examples that we have seen in this chapter, since the way to access the array elements remains the same.

See also

- The *Rendering the admin page contents using HTML* recipe

Creating network-level admin pages

A very powerful feature of WordPress is its ability to run multiple websites from a single installation of the platform. Each site can have its own content and its own visual identity, while administrators can manage all sites from one Dashboard. When you run WordPress as a multi-site network, it adds an additional section to the Dashboard, for network-level management. All of the plugins we have created so far in this chapter present configuration panels at the site level, allowing for the custom configuration of options on a per-site basis. While this will be the desired behavior for most plugins, it might be preferable for some configuration elements to be set in a single place by a network-level administrator and apply to all the sites in the network.

In this recipe, you will learn how to modify our Google Analytics plugin to be configured at the network level when running on a multi-site installation and at the site level on regular WordPress configurations.

Getting ready

You should have already followed the *Accessing user settings from action and filter hooks* recipe, and the resulting plugin should be active in your development site. Alternatively, you can get the resulting code (`Chapter 3/ch2-page-header-output/ch2-page-header-output-v9.php`) from the downloaded code bundle and rename the file `ch2-page-header-output-v9.php` as `ch2-page-header-output.php` before starting this recipe. You should also have access to a WordPress installation configured in Network mode. You can read more about the steps required to configure WordPress to run as a multisite at `https://codex.wordpress.org/Create_A_Network`.

How to do it...

1. Navigate to the `ch2-page-header-output` folder of the WordPress plugin directory of your development installation.
2. Open the `ch2-page-header-output.php` file in a text editor.

3. Modify the implementation of the ch2pho_get_options function to replace both option functions with network-level versions. The code section shows the two lines that need to be changed with modifications in bold:

```
$options = get_site_option( 'ch2pho_options', array() );

update_site_option( 'ch2pho_options', $merged_options );
```

4. Locate the add_action function call that adds a callback to populate the admin menu and add code to check whether the installation is a single site or multisite before registering callbacks. The following code shows new elements in bold:

```
if ( is_multisite() ) {
    add_action( 'network_admin_menu', 'ch2pho_settings_menu' );
} else {
    add_action( 'admin_menu', 'ch2pho_settings_menu' );
}
```

5. Modify the ch2pho_settings_menu function to add new items to different menus based on whether the site is a regular site or a multisite with the new sections identified in bold:

```
function ch2pho_settings_menu() {
    if ( is_multisite() ) {
        $options_page = add_submenu_page( 'settings.php',
            'My Google Analytics Configuration',
            'My Google Analytics',
            'manage_options', 'ch2pho-my-google-analytics',
            'ch2pho_config_page' );
    } else {
        $options_page = add_submenu_page( 'options-general.php',
            'My Google Analytics Configuration',
            'My Google Analytics',
            'manage_options', 'ch2pho-my-google-analytics',
            'ch2pho_config_page' );
    }
    if ( !empty( $options_page ) ) {
        add_action( 'load-' . $options_page, 'ch2pho_help_tabs' );
    }
}
```

6. In the process_ch2pho_options function, replace the call to update_option with a call to update_site_option:

```
update_site_option( 'ch2pho_options', $options );
```

7. Still in the `process_ch2pho_options` function, make the following changes around the `wp_redirect` function call with new elements shown in bold:

```
if ( is_multisite() ) {
    $redirect_page = '/network/settings.php';
} else {
    $redirect_page = 'options-general.php';
}

wp_redirect( add_query_arg(
            array( 'page' => 'ch2pho-my-google-analytics',
                   'message' => '1' ),
            admin_url( $redirect_page ) ) );
```

8. Modify the `ch2pho_config` page function to modify the form action so that it finds `admin-post.php` in the multisite installations with the new code shown in bold:

```
<form method="post"
      action="<?php echo admin_url( 'admin-post.php' ); ?>">
```

9. Save and close the plugin file.

10. In a Network installation of WordPress, visit the **Plugins** section of Network Admin.

11. **Network Activate** the `Chapter 2 - Page Header Output` plugin. You will see that a new item is now available under the Settings menu.

12. Visit any site in the network and look at the page source to see that the Google Analytics code is added to the page header with the user account configured on our administration page.

How it works...

When creating a network-level plugin, the `is_multisite` function becomes very useful to determine whether or not a site is configured as a multisite. In the recipe, we used it to register callbacks to be called when building different menus (the regular single site administration menu and the network management menu). We also used the `is_multisite` function when registering the actual menu item and to determine where users should be redirected after saving options.

The other useful functions in these modifications are `get_site_option` and `update_site_option`. When called in a multisite configuration, these functions will retrieve network-level options from the database. Alternatively, when running on a regular single site, they will default to access site-level options. By using these functions in our updated code, we make all the interactions with site options compatible with single and multisite installations.

The last element of this recipe relates to how we activated this plugin at the network level. This means that it will be active in all sites created in the network. More specifically, in the case of our plugin, this means that all the sites will output Google Analyics code in their header, with the associated account being specified once on the network configuration.

See also

- The *Accessing user settings from action and filter hooks* recipe

4

The Power of Custom Post Types

This chapter covers one of the most powerful features of WordPress, custom post types, through the following topics:

- Creating a custom post type
- Adding a new section to the custom post type editor
- Displaying single custom post type items using custom layout
- Displaying custom post type data in shortcodes
- Adding custom categories for custom post types
- Adding custom fields to categories
- Hiding the category editor from the custom post type editor
- Displaying additional columns in the custom post list page
- Adding filters for custom categories to the custom post list page
- Adding Quick Edit fields for custom categories
- Updating a page title to include custom post data using plugin filters

Introduction

Building on its history of openness and ease of use, WordPress reached new heights in customization when it introduced custom post types.

Custom post types are new categories of items that are created by using the WordPress API and that appear in the WordPress administration interface as complete new sections, next to the default Posts and Pages sections. These custom items can be used to store any type of information, including events, bug reports, recipes, movie reviews, and many more.

When using custom post types to implement this kind of functionality, developers are able to take advantage of WordPress internal content editing capabilities, including its powerful text editor and user-friendly media uploader. Custom post types also simplify data management for developers, since all of the information related to these new entries is stored in the site database using the existing table structures. Finally, custom post types can leverage the established theme and template system to display the information that site administrators store in these new content types.

If you have ever taken a peek at the MySQL database behind a WordPress site, you know that posts, pages, attachments, revisions, and navigation menu items share the same tables. In essence, all of these data elements are custom post types, with some of them using the standard text editor, while others, such as the navigation menus, have a custom management interface. Each of these types of items also has a different mechanism to be displayed on a site.

Using custom post types opens up endless possibilities to tailor the functionality of a WordPress installation and provide a custom solution to end users without needing to invest a large amount of time re-inventing the wheel. This chapter covers all facets of creating custom post types through the creation of a Book Review system, including the creation of new types of elements, displaying the newly stored information on the website, and customizing the environment to create an editor with unique capabilities.

Creating a custom post type

The initial creation of a custom post type is extremely easy. It only requires a single function to be called from an action hook callback. Once in place, a lot of functionality immediately becomes available to administrators and site visitors. This recipe shows how to create a new custom post type that will be used to store Book Reviews.

Getting ready

You should have access to a WordPress development environment, either on your local computer or a remote server, where you will be able to load your new plugin files.

How to do it...

1. Navigate to the WordPress plugin directory of your development installation.
2. Create a new directory called `ch4-book-reviews`.
3. Navigate to this directory and create a new text file called `ch4-book-reviews.php`.
4. Open the new file in a code editor and add an appropriate header at the top of the plugin file, naming the plugin `Chapter 4 - Book Reviews`.
5. Add the following line of code to register a function that will be executed during the initialization phase every time WordPress generates a page:

```
add_action( 'init', 'ch4_br_create_book_post_type' );
```

6. Add the following code block to provide an implementation for the `ch4_br_create_book_post_type` function:

```
function ch4_br_create_book_post_type() {
    register_post_type( 'book_reviews',
        array(
            'labels' => array(
                'name' => 'Book Reviews',
                'singular_name' => 'Book Review',
                'add_new' => 'Add New',
                'add_new_item' => 'Add New Book Review',
                'edit' => 'Edit',
                'edit_item' => 'Edit Book Review',
                'new_item' => 'New Book Review',
                'view' => 'View',
                'view_item' => 'View Book Review',
                'search_items' => 'Search Book Reviews',
                'not_found' => 'No Book Reviews found',
                'not_found_in_trash' =>
                    'No Book Reviews found in Trash',
                'parent' => 'Parent Book Review'
            ),
            'public' => true,
            'menu_position' => 20,
            'supports' =>
```

```
                    array( 'title', 'editor', 'comments',
                        'thumbnail', 'custom-fields' ),
                'taxonomies' => array( '' ),
                'menu_icon' =>
                    plugins_url( 'book-reviews.png', __FILE__ ),
                'has_archive' => true,
                'exclude_from_search' => true
            )
        );
    }
```

7. Save and close the plugin file.

8. Find and download a PNG format book icon measuring 24 x 24 pixels from a site, such as IconArchive (`http://www.iconarchive.com`), resize it to 20 x 20 pixels, and save it as `book-reviews.png` in the plugin directory.

9. Navigate to the Plugins management page and **Activate** the `Chapter 4 – Book Reviews` plugin.

10. Click on the newly available **Book Reviews** menu item, located under the **Pages** section, to see the Book Review creation and management interface.

11. Click on the **Add New** button, next to the section title, to display the Book Review editor featuring the complete WordPress text editor, the custom fields editor, comments control, publishing controls, and the featured image section.

12. Fill in the new entry by specifying the Book Review title (for example, `WordPress Plugin Development Cookbook`) and a short description.

13. Scroll to the **Custom Fields** section and type `book_author` as the **Name** of the field and `Yannick Lefebvre` as the **Value**. Click **Add Custom Field** to create a second field.

If some custom fields already exist in your WordPress installation (from other plugin data entry), you will need to click on **Enter new** before being able to set the Name to book_author.

14. Set the **Name** of the second field to book_rating and its **Value** to 5.
15. Find and download a book cover image from a website such as Google Images (https://images.google.com) or Packt (https://www.packtpub.com).
16. Click on the **Set featured image** link located in the right-hand sidebar of the editing interface.
17. Click on **Select Files** to pick the image that you downloaded to your computer and have WordPress upload it to the wp-content/uploads folder of your site.
18. Once the file is uploaded and WordPress displays information about it, look at the bottom of the media upload dialog and click on the **Set featured image** link to associate it with the **Book Review** that you are creating.

19. Click on the **Publish** button to save this first **Book Review**.
20. Visit the **Permalinks** section of the **Settings** menu and click on the **Save Changes** button (without changing your **Permalinks** settings).
21. Go back to the Book Review you created and click on the **View Book Review** button to see the newly created content in your web browser.

How it works...

By making a call to the `register_post_type` function, the entire WordPress environment becomes aware of the existence of this new post type. This awareness includes the creation of a dedicated section to create and edit posts of this type and the ability to process web page requests for Book Reviews.

As mentioned at the beginning of this recipe, the function is quite simple to use and only requires two arguments:

```
register_post_type( $post_type, $args );
```

The first argument is a text string that indicates the name of the post type. Please note when choosing this name that it will be used as the default value for the permalinks of all items that use the new type, and that it should be unique enough to avoid potential conflicts with other plugins.

The second argument is an array of properties that specify the characteristics of the new post type and determine how this type will be edited.

In this specific example, the first element of the properties array is actually another array, which contains a number of labels. These labels indicate the text strings that should be displayed when managing items created under the new post type. For example, if we look at the screenshot before step 11, the message **No Book Reviews found** came directly from the definition of the `not_found` label in this array.

The second argument, named `public`, determines whether the post type's administration interface should be shown to manage it and if visitors should be able to view single items. Next is the `menu_position` member of the configuration array, indicating the desired position of the new element in the administration menu. In this example, a value of 20 indicates that it should be displayed following to the **Pages** menu item. Visit the WordPress Codex (`https://codex.wordpress.org/Function_Reference/register_post_type`) for a full list of potential values for this parameter and their associated positions.

The `supports` parameter is another array that indicates which parts of the content editor should be displayed for items that use the custom post type. In this case, we left out some sections, such as `author`, `excerpt`, `trackbacks`, `revisions`, `page-attributes`, and `post-formats`, as they were not desirable for Book Reviews.

The next few parameters in the configuration array indicate that we do not want to define custom taxonomies at this time, and specify the path and name of the image file that should be displayed next to the post type's name in the administration menu. Finally, the last two arguments determines whether WordPress should present an archive listing page for the new type when users visit the `/book_reviews` page on the site and whether or not book reviews should be excluded from search results.

There are actually many other parameters that can be included in the configuration array to get more precise control over some aspects of the new custom post type. Please visit the WordPress Codex (`https://codex.wordpress.org/Function_Reference/register_post_type`) to learn more about them.

There's more...

While the internal post type name is used by default to generate post permalinks, it can actually be overridden to create better-looking URLs.

Changing the custom post type permalinks slug

An optional member of the custom post type configuration is the `rewrite` parameter. It can be defined as follows:

```
'rewrite' => array( 'slug' => 'awesome-book-reviews' )
```

Although this may seem very simple, the permalinks will only change over after you go to the **Permalinks** section and **Save Changes**, as we did in the recipe. Alternatively, it is possible to make calls from the WordPress rewrite module to programmatically request for the permalinks configuration to be rebuilt. As this is not something that should be done every time WordPress displays a page, but would be too early to do when a plugin gets initialized or upgraded, a good place to call these functions would be within the plugin options storage function. You might even decide to give administrators the ability to specify their own slug in a plugin configuration page. The code to reset the permalinks rules is as follows:

```
global $wp_rewrite;
$wp_rewrite->flush_rules();
```

Adding a new section to the custom post type editor

While the custom post editor that has been put in place so far is functional, it is not the friendliest of user interfaces, especially with the custom fields section, where users need to type or select the names of each field as they create new items. A cleaner approach is to create a custom interface using the meta box mechanism that we saw in the previous chapter to display all the data associated with Book Reviews.

This recipe shows how to create a meta box that will be associated with a custom post type and how to save the information that is entered in that new interface.

Getting ready

You should have already followed the *Creating a custom post type* recipe to have a starting point for this recipe, and the resulting plugin should still be active in your development site. Alternatively, you can get the resulting code (`Chapter 4/ch4-book-reviews/ch4-book-reviews-v1.php`) from the code bundle downloaded from the Packt website (`https://www.packtpub.com/support`) and rename the file `ch4-book-reviews.php`.

How to do it...

1. Navigate to the `ch4-book-reviews` folder of the WordPress plugin directory of your development installation.
2. Open the `ch4-book-reviews.php` file in a code editor.
3. Add the following line of code after the existing functions to register a function to be called when the administration interface is visited:

```
add_action( 'admin_init', 'ch4_br_admin_init' );
```

4. Add the following code section to provide an implementation for the
   `ch4_br_admin_init` function and register a meta box to be associated with the
   `book_reviews` post type:

```
function ch4_br_admin_init() {
    add_meta_box( 'ch4_br_review_details_meta_box',
                  'Book Review Details',
                  'ch4_br_display_review_details_meta_box',
                  'book_reviews', 'normal', 'high' );
}
```

5. Insert this function to implement the
   `ch4_br_display_review_details_meta_box` function and render the meta
   box contents:

```
function ch4_br_display_review_details_meta_box( $book_review ) {
    // Retrieve current author and rating based on review ID
    $book_author =
        esc_html( get_post_meta( $book_review->ID,
                                 'book_author', true ) );
    $book_rating =
        intval( get_post_meta( $book_review->ID,
                               'book_rating', true ) );
    ?>
    <table>
        <tr>
            <td style="width: 100%">Book Author</td>
            <td><input type="text" size="80"
                    name="book_review_author_name"
                    value="<?php echo $book_author; ?>" /></td>
        </tr>
        <tr>
            <td style="width: 150px">Book Rating</td>
            <td>
                <select style="width: 100px"
                        name="book_review_rating">
                <!-- Loop to generate items in dropdown list -->
                <?php
                for ( $rating = 5; $rating >= 1; $rating -- ) { ?>
                <option value="<?php echo $rating; ?>"
                <?php echo selected( $rating, $book_rating ); ?>>
                <?php echo $rating; ?> stars
                <?php } ?>
                </select>
            </td>
        </tr>
    </table>
```

```
<?php }
```

6. Add the following code segment to register a function that will be called when posts are saved to the database:

```
add_action( 'save_post', 'ch4_br_add_book_review_fields', 10, 2 );
```

7. Add an implementation for the `ch4_br_add_book_review_fields` function defined in the previous `add_action` call:

```
function ch4_br_add_book_review_fields( $book_review_id,
                                        $book_review ) {
    // Check post type for book reviews
    if ( 'book_reviews' == $book_review->post_type ) {
        // Store data in post meta table if present in post data
        if ( isset( $_POST['book_review_author_name'] ) ) {
            update_post_meta( $book_review_id, 'book_author',
                sanitize_text_field(
                    $_POST['book_review_author_name'] ) );
        }
        if ( isset( $_POST['book_review_rating'] ) &&
            !empty( $_POST['book_review_rating'] ) ) {
            update_post_meta( $book_review_id, 'book_rating',
                intval( $_POST['book_review_rating'] ) );
        }
    }
}
```

8. Find the `ch4_br_create_book_post_type` function, where the new book type was originally created, and remove the `custom-fields` element from the `supports` array:

```
'supports' => array( 'title', 'editor', 'comments', 'thumbnail' ),
```

9. Save and close the plugin file.
10. Open the previously created Book Review to see the new **Book Review Details** meta box, containing a text field to specify the author and a drop-down list for the rating:

Book Review Details   ▲

Book Author   Yannick Lefebvre

Book Rating   5 stars   ▼

How it works...

This recipe uses the WordPress built-in meta box system to create a clean interface that will allow users to manage fields specific to custom post types without having to use the cumbersome default **Custom Fields** editor. As we saw in Chapter 3, *User Settings and Administration Pages*, custom meta boxes can be created using the add_meta_box function. In addition to declaring the meta box and associating it with the custom post type, add_meta_box defines a callback that is responsible for rendering the contents of the box.

The next section of the recipe implements the function that renders the meta box content. As we can see, this box receives an object variable that contains information about the Book Review that is being displayed in the post editor. Using this object, our code retrieves the post ID and uses it to query the site database for a book author and rating associated with the entry. Once the custom field data has been retrieved from the database, it can be used to render the author and rating fields onscreen. When new Book Reviews are created, both calls to get_post_meta will return an empty string, resulting in the display of an empty text field and the last entry in the drop-down list.

The get_post_meta function is used to retrieve data that was stored in the custom fields section of the post editor and has three parameters:

```
get_post_meta( $post_id, $field_name, $single );
```

The first parameter is the post ID, which can easily be retrieved using the get_the_ID() template function. This ID is used to identify the post to which the custom information is associated. The second argument is the custom field name, which should match the name specified when it is created in the post editor. The third and final argument indicates whether the return value should be a single value or an array of values. If set to false, it will produce an array containing a single element even if the custom field only contains a single value. In most cases, it should be set to true to receive a single value that can be accessed directly.

The last steps of this recipe take care of registering a function that will be called when posts of all types are saved or deleted by the site administrator. Since it will deal with all types of data, the saving callback must first check the type of the received post data. If it's a Book Review, the code proceeds to check if the received data is valid and stores the information in the post meta data table. In this recipe, the parameters for the `update_post_meta` function are similar to the `get_post_meta` function, except for the third argument, which is used to specify the data to be stored.

One last detail that should be mentioned about this recipe is the use of the fourth parameter of the `add_action` function when associating a callback to the `save_post` action hook. This argument indicates that two arguments will be received by the registered callback. If this argument is not set, the callback function will never receive that second piece of data.

See also

- The *Creating a custom post type* recipe
- The *Formatting admin pages using meta boxes* recipe in `Chapter 3`, *User Settings and Administration Pages*

Displaying single custom post type items using a custom layout

When displaying an entry created in our new custom post type, the default layout offered by our current site theme may not always be able to pleasantly display the information it contains. In most cases, you will be able to see the main post content, but not any of the custom fields data that is associated with the post.

This recipe shows how to create a custom layout to display all the elements that we stored in the Book Review created in the previous recipe.

Getting ready

You should have already followed the *Adding a new section to the custom post type editor* recipe to have a starting point for this recipe and the resulting plugin should still be active in your development site. Alternatively, you can get the resulting code (Chapter 4/ch4-book-reviews/ch4-book-reviews-v2.php) from the downloaded code bundle and rename the file ch4-book-reviews.php.

How to do it...

1. Navigate to the ch4-book-reviews folder of the WordPress plugin directory of your development installation.

2. Open the ch4-book-reviews.php file in a code editor.

3. Add the following line of code after the existing functions to register a function to be called when WordPress is deciding which theme template to use to render content:

```
add_filter( 'template_include', 'ch4_br_template_include', 1 );
```

4. Add the following code section to provide an implementation for the ch4_br_template_include function:

```
function ch4_br_template_include( $template_path ) {
    if ( 'book_reviews' == get_post_type() ) {
        if ( is_single() ) {
            // checks if the file exists in the theme first,
            // otherwise install content filter
            if ( $theme_file = locate_template( array
                ( 'single-book_reviews.php' ) ) ) {
                $template_path = $theme_file;
            } else {
                add_filter( 'the_content',
                            'ch4_br_display_single_book_review',
                            20 );
            }
        }
    }
    return $template_path;
}
```

5. Add the following code section to implement the
`ch4_br_display_single_book_review` function to display Book Reviews,
including their custom fields:

```php
function ch4_br_display_single_book_review( $content ) {
    if ( !empty( get_the_ID() ) ) {
        // Display featured image in right-aligned floating div
        $content = '<div style="float: right; margin: 10px">';
        $content .= get_the_post_thumbnail( get_the_ID(),
                                            'medium' );
        $content .= '</div>';

        $content .= '<div class="entry-content">';

        // Display Author Name
        $content .= '<strong>Author: </strong>';
        $content .= esc_html( get_post_meta( get_the_ID(),
                                             'book_author',
                                             true ) );
        $content .= '<br />';

        // Display yellow stars based on rating -->
        $content .= '<strong>Rating: </strong>';

        $nb_stars = intval( get_post_meta( get_the_ID(),
                                           'book_rating',
                                           true ) );

        for ( $star_counter = 1; $star_counter <= 5;
                $star_counter++ ) {
            if ( $star_counter <= $nb_stars ) {
                $content .= '<img src="' .
                            plugins_url( 'star-icon.png',
                                         __FILE__ ) . '"
                            />';
            } else {
                $content .= '<img src="' .
                            plugins_url( 'star-icon-grey.png',
                                         __FILE__ )
                            . '" />';
            }
        }

        // Display book review contents
        $content .= '<br /><br />';
        $content .= get_the_content( get_the_ID() );
        $content .= '</div>';
```

```
            return $content;
        }
    }
```

6. Save and close the plugin file.

7. Find and download a PNG format pixel star icon measuring 32 x 32 pixels from a site such as IconArchive (`http://www.iconarchive.com`), and save it as `star-icon.png` in the plugin directory.

8. Create a grayscale version of the star icon using any graphic processing tool (for example, the free multi-platform XnViewMP tool, found at `http://www.xnview.com/en/`) and save it as `star-icon-grey.png`.

9. Go to the **Book Reviews** management page and click on the **View** link under the existing entry created in the previous recipe to see the content rendered using the new template.

How it works...

When rendering any web page, the default WordPress functionality is to search the current theme directory for an applicable template suitable for the content at hand. In the case of a single custom post type item, such as a Book Review, it first looks for a single item template named `single-<post-type-name>.php`, where the latter part is the actual post type name. If it does not find this file, it defaults to the general single item template. In the first recipe of this chapter, the template that was used to show the Book Review was the default single item template, simply named `single.php`.

To add better support for our new post type, this recipe associates a function with the `template_include` filter hook to change that behavior. More specifically, we use the `locate_template` function to check whether the user provided a template for the `book_reviews` post type in the theme directory. If no template is found, we register a filter to overwrite the page contents with our own layout. This gives users the flexibility to use our predefined layout or to provide their own.

The rest of the recipe implements our fallback filter function for Book Review content. This code makes use of many WordPress template functions, such as `get_the_ID()` and `get_the_content()`, as well as the `get_post_meta` function, to display various elements of the current item, including the book author and its rating, as well as the main post content and the featured image.

To help users build their own theme template for your custom post type, you should provide code snippets in your plugin documentation, showing how to retrieve your custom post type's custom fields.

See also

- The *Creating a custom post type* recipe

Displaying custom post type data in shortcodes

To help visitors navigate through the items added using our new custom post type, we will need to display a list of all the book reviews on the site, along with navigation elements to be able to handle large numbers of items. While WordPress offers a built-in mechanism to list post items in the form of the archive page, it is not easy for a plugin to be able to modify the layout of the resulting page in a consistent way across all possible user themes. A better solution to display a list of custom post type items is to create a shortcode that will display one or more posts in any place selected by the user, including a page, a post, or even on the site's front page.

This recipe shows how to create a shortcode that will retrieve and display five book reviews at a time with accompanying navigation links.

Getting ready

You should have already followed the *Displaying single custom post type items using a custom layout* recipe to have a starting point for this recipe, and the resulting plugin should still be active in your development site. Alternatively, you can get the resulting code (Chapter 4/ch4-book-reviews/ch4-book-reviews-v3.php) from the downloaded code bundle and rename the file ch4-book-reviews.php.

How to do it...

1. Navigate to the ch4-book-reviews folder of the WordPress plugin directory of your development installation.
2. Open the ch4-book-reviews.php file in a code editor.
3. Add the following line of code after the existing functions to register a function that declares the new shortcode:

```
add_shortcode( 'book-review-list', 'ch4_br_book_review_list' );
```

4. Add the following code section to provide an implementation for the ch4_br_book_review_list function:

```
function ch4_br_book_review_list() {
    // Preparation of query array to retrieve 5 book reviews
    $query_params = array( 'post_type' => 'book_reviews',
                           'post_status' => 'publish',
                           'posts_per_page' => 5 );

    // Execution of post query
    $book_review_query = new WP_Query;
    $book_review_query->query( $query_params );

    // Check if any posts were returned by the query
    if ( $book_review_query->have_posts() ) {
        // Display posts in table layout
        $output = '<table>';

        $output .= '<tr><th style="width: 350px"><strong>';
        $output .= 'Title</strong></th>';
        $output .= '<th><strong>Author</strong></th></tr>';

        // Cycle through all items retrieved
        while ( $book_review_query->have_posts() ) {
            $book_review_query->the_post();
```

```
                        $output .= '<tr><td><a href="' . get_permalink();
                        $output .= '">';
                        $output .= get_the_title( get_the_ID() ) . '</a></td>';
                        $output .= '<td>';
                        $output .= esc_html( get_post_meta( get_the_ID(),
                                                            'book_author',
                                                            true ) );
                        $output .= '</td></tr>';
                    }

                    $output .= '</table>';
                    // Display page navigation links
                    if ( $book_review_query->max_num_pages > 1 ) {
                        $output .= '<nav id="nav-below">';
                        $output .= '<div class="nav-previous">';
                        $output .= get_next_posts_link (
                            '<span class="meta-nav">&larr;</span>' .
                            ' Older reviews',
                            $book_review_query->max_num_pages );
                        $output .= '</div>';
                        $output .= '<div class="nav-next">';
                        $output .= get_previous_posts_link(
                                'Newer reviews ' .
                                '<span class="meta-nav">&rarr;</span>',
                                $book_review_query->max_num_pages );
                        $output .= '</div>';
                        $output .= '</nav>';
                    }

                    // Reset post data query
                    wp_reset_postdata();
                }

            return $output;
        }
```

5. Save the plugin file.
6. Create a new page and insert the shortcode [book-review-list].
7. **Publish** and **View** the page to see that a list of Book Reviews will be displayed in place of the shortcode.

BOOK REVIEWS	Title	Author
Edit	Hybrid Mobile Development with Ionic	Gaurav Saini
	Game Development Patterns and Best Practices	John P. Doran, Matt Casanova
	The Node Craftsman Book	Manuel Kiessling
	Learning Windows Server Containers	Srikanth Machiraju
	Python Programming with Raspberry Pi	Sai Yamanoor, Srihari Yamanoor
	← Older reviews	

8. If more than five Book Reviews exist in the system, click on the navigation links that are displayed. You will see that the URL in the browser address bar changes, but the list of entries shows the same first five items as before.

9. Back in the ch4-book-reviews.php file, add the following highlighted code near the top of ch4_br_book_review_list, right after the line initializing the value of the $query_params variable:

```
// Preparation of query string to retrieve 5 book reviews
$query_params = array( 'post_type' => 'book_reviews',
                       'post_status' => 'publish',
                       'posts_per_page' => 5 );

// Retrieve page query variable, if present
$page_num = ( get_query_var( 'paged' ) ?
             get_query_var( 'paged' ) : 1 );

// If page number is higher than 1, add to query array
if ( $page_num != 1 ) {
    $query_params['paged'] = $page_num;
}
```

10. Save and close the plugin file. Refresh the page that includes our new shortcode and use the navigation links to see that the list of items now changes properly.

How it works...

As we saw in `Chapter 3`, *User Settings and Administration Pages*, shortcodes are text elements that can be inserted in any page and post, that will be replaced with the content generated by the plugin when they are found. The registered callback function must prepare the output and send it back as a return value at the end of its execution.

The first part of the `ch4_br_book_review_list` function takes care of preparing a query array to be passed to a new instance of the `WP_Query` class. This class allows developers to easily extract information from the site database's post table. In this example, the parameters that are being set in the query are the internal post type name (`post_type`), the status of the items that we want to display (`post_status`), and the number of items that should be retrieved at a time (`posts_per_page`).

Once the query string is in place, we create a global variable called `book_review_query` and assign to it a new instance of a `WP_Query` object. Once created, we initialize it using the query string that was just assembled. If posts are found by the object, we output HTML code to create a table and use a `while` loop to cycle through all the items found and display their title and author using a code similar to the previous two recipes.

As part of this recipe, we have seen that if more entries exist for the custom post type than the value specified with the `posts_per_page` query argument, navigation controls are added under the table of entries but will not work correctly, since we manually created the query string. To rectify the situation, we use the `get_query_var` function to see if a page number was requested. If that is the case, and the page number is not 1, we add that number to our query parameters.

There's more...

As mentioned in the beginning of this recipe, there may be instances where a list of custom post type items needs to be displayed as part of a theme template. The following section shows how to get shortcode content to be displayed as part of a template file.

do_shortcode function

The `do_shortcode` function can be called from any theme template file, for the front page or any other section of the site, to render content associated with a shortcode. It takes a single argument, the shortcode string including any parameters. To display the content created in this recipe, we would simply need to call the following:

```
<?php echo do_shortcode( '[book-review-list]' ); ?>
```

Adding custom categories for custom post types

To keep items organized on a site, administrators often use the built-in WordPress categories and terms to identify similar items. Looking back at the **Book Reviews** system that we have been putting in place so far in this chapter, a type of categorization that would be helpful is a book type (for example, Science Fiction, Documentary, Fiction, Poetry, and so on).

This recipe shows how to create a new category (known as a **taxonomy** in the WordPress backend) and associate it with the Book Review custom post type.

Getting ready

You should have already followed the *Displaying custom post type data in shortcodes* recipe, to have a starting point for this recipe, and the resulting plugin should still be active in your development site. Alternatively, you can get the resulting code (`Chapter 4/ch4-book-reviews/ch4-book-reviews-v4.php`) from the downloaded code bundle and rename the file `ch4-book-reviews.php`.

How to do it...

1. Navigate to the `ch4-book-reviews` folder of the WordPress plugin directory of your development installation.
2. Open the `ch4-book-reviews.php` file in a code editor.
3. Find the `ch4_br_create_book_post_type` function and add the following code after the existing call to `register_post_type` to create the new taxonomy:

```
register_taxonomy(
    'book_reviews_book_type',
    'book_reviews',
    array(
        'labels' => array(
            'name' => 'Book Type',
            'add_new_item' => 'Add New Book Type',
            'new_item_name' => 'New Book Type Name'
        ),
        'show_ui' => true,
        'show_tagcloud' => false,
        'hierarchical' => true
    )
);
```

4. Save and close the plugin file.
5. Open the previously created Book Reviews to see the newly added **Book Type** meta box on the right-hand side of the post editor.
6. Click on the **+ Add New Book Type** link to create a new item and assign it as the current item's type. Click on the **Update** button in the top-right section of the post editor to save the review:

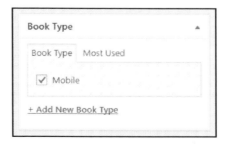

7. Look at the left-hand administration menu to see that a new menu item was added to manage book types, leading to an editor similar to the post and page category editor:

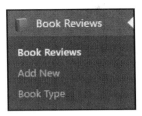

8. Back in the plugin file, add the following code to the `ch4_br_display_single_book_review` function after the section displaying the rating to display the book type:

```
$book_types = wp_get_post_terms( get_the_ID(),
                                 'book_reviews_book_type' );

$content .= '<br /><strong>Type: </strong>';

if ( $book_types ) {
    $first_entry = true;
    for ( $i = 0; $i < count( $book_types ); $i++ ) {
        if ( !$first_entry ) {
            $content .= ', ';
        }
        $content .= $book_types[$i]->name;
        $first_entry = false;
    }
} else {
    $content .= 'None Assigned';
}
```

9. Save and close the template file.
10. Visit a Book Review page to see the book type displayed under the rating.

How it works...

The `register_taxonomy` function is used to create a new type of category in WordPress and associate it to a post type. It has three parameters:

```
register_taxonomy( $taxonomy_name, $post_type, $options );
```

The first argument is a unique identifier for the taxonomy. The second parameter is the post type that it should be associated with, which should match the type declared with the `register_post_type` function. The third argument is an array of parameters that determine how the new taxonomy will behave.

In this example, we have set a few taxonomy options, including a first item called **labels** that contains an array of text strings that will be used in the interface when referring to the new taxonomy. We also specified a second element, called `show_ui`, which controls the display of the taxonomy meta box in the post editor and the presence of a link to access the taxonomy editor in the administration menu. Next is an option called `show_tagcloud`, which we set to `false` to avoid displaying a tag cloud of all taxonomy values. Finally, the last item in the options array is called `hierarchical`. When set to `true`, taxonomy items will be able to have parent/child relationships and will be accessible as a list of checkboxes in the post editor. If set to `false`, all taxonomies are organized as a flat list and can be selected using an interface similar to the tag window in the post and page editor.

There are many more options available for the `register_taxonomy` function, as can be seen if you visit the WordPress Codex website (`https://codex.wordpress.org/Function_Reference/register_taxonomy`), but the ones found here are the essential ones to define a basic taxonomy.

See also

- The *Creating a custom post type* recipe

Adding custom fields to categories

In addition to specifying names for categories, it may be useful to attach additional information to custom taxonomies created in a WordPress plugin. For example, we may want to assign custom colors to categories that will be used when they are displayed, or we might want to identify the categories of content that are only accessible to paying members on a website.

This recipe shows how to display additional fields in the taxonomy editor and how to store the additional data in the site's database.

Getting ready

You should have already followed the *Adding custom categories for custom post types* recipe to have a starting point for this recipe, and the resulting plugin should still be active in your development site. Alternatively, you can get the resulting code (`Chapter 4/ch4-book-reviews/ch4-book-reviews-v5.php`) from the downloaded code bundle and rename the file `ch4-book-reviews.php`.

How to do it...

1. Navigate to the `ch4-book-reviews` folder of the WordPress plugin directory of your development installation.
2. Open the `ch4-book-reviews.php` file in a code editor.
3. Add the following lines of code after the existing functions to assign a function to two action hooks that will be called when users create or edit taxonomy items:

```
add_action( 'book_reviews_book_type_edit_form_fields',
            'ch4_br_book_type_new_fields', 10, 2 );
add_action( 'book_reviews_book_type_add_form_fields',
            'ch4_br_book_type_new_fields', 10, 2 );
```

4. Add the following code section to provide an implementation for the `ch4_br_book_type_new_fields` function:

```
function ch4_br_book_type_new_fields( $tag ) {
    $mode = 'new';

    if ( is_object( $tag ) ) {
        $mode = 'edit';
        $book_cat_color = get_term_meta( $tag->term_id,
                                         'book_type_color',
                                         true );
    }
    $book_cat_color = empty( $book_cat_color ) ?
                             '#' : $book_cat_color;

    if ( 'edit' == $mode ) {
        echo '<tr class="form-field">';
```

```
            echo '<th scope="row" valign="top">';
        } elseif ( 'new' == $mode ) {
            echo '<div class="form-field">';
        } ?>

        <label for="tag-category-url">Color</label>
        <?php if ( 'edit' == $mode ) {
            echo '</th><td>';
        } ?>

        <input type="text" id="book_type_color"
                name="book_type_color"
                value="<?php echo $book_cat_color; ?>" />
        <p class="description">Color associated with book type
                        (e.g. #199C27 or #CCC)</p>

        <?php if ( 'edit' == $mode ) {
            echo '</td></tr>';
        } elseif ( 'new' == $mode ) {
            echo '</div>';
        }
    }
```

5. Add the following lines of code at the end of the file to assign a function that will be called when users create or update taxonomy items:

```
add_action( 'edited_book_reviews_book_type',
            'ch4_br_save_book_type_new_fields', 10, 2 );
add_action( 'created_book_reviews_book_type',
            'ch4_br_save_book_type_new_fields', 10, 2 );
```

6. Add the following code section to provide an implementation for the `ch4_br_save_book_type_new_fields` function:

```
function ch4_br_save_book_type_new_fields( $term_id, $tt_id ) {
    if ( !$term_id ) {
        return;
    }

    if ( isset( $_POST['book_type_color'] )
            && ( '#' == $_POST['book_type_color']
        || preg_match( '/#([a-f0-9]{3}){1,2}\b/i',
                        $_POST['book_type_color'] ) ) ) {
        $returnvalue = update_term_meta( $term_id,
                        'book_type_color',
                        $_POST['book_type_color'] );
    }
}
```

7. Save and close the plugin file.
8. Edit one of the **Book Type** entries created in the previous recipe to see the newly added Color field. Enter a color code and **Update** the entry to see the data saved:

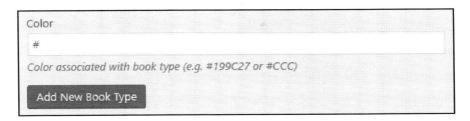

How it works...

This recipe uses many variable name action hooks to register functions to be called when users create or modify book types in the taxonomy editor. The first two calls to `add_action` refer to the `<taxonomy>_edit_forms_fields` and `<taxonomy>_add_form_fields` hooks. While you might expect to see two different functions associated with each of these action hooks, we actually register the same function in both cases, since rendering an additional field is similar in both cases. That being said, part of the function we register checks to see whether it receives a valid object as a parameter to know how it should render the new field so that it fits on the page if the user is creating a new category or editing an existing one.

We use a similar technique with the `edited_<taxonomy>` and `created_<taxonomy>` action hooks, which are respectively called when you first save a new taxonomy and update an existing one. In this case, the code does not have any significant differences depending on the action, since we only need to validate and save the incoming value for the new field.

See also

- The *Adding custom categories for custom post types* recipe

Hiding the category editor from the custom post type editor

As we saw in the previous recipe, when we associate a new taxonomy with the Book Review custom post type, the `show_ui` option controls the visibility of the taxonomy assignment meta box and the admin menu link to the taxonomy editor. In some cases, it is desirable to give users access to the full taxonomy editor, but only let editors choose from a controlled drop-down list when they create new entries in the custom post type editor.

This recipe shows how to hide the taxonomy interface from the post editor and how to update the custom post type meta box created in the previous recipe to assign a type to new Book Reviews and save this information in the site's database.

Getting ready

You should have already followed the *Adding custom fields to categories* recipe to have a starting point for this recipe, and the resulting plugin should still be active in your development site. Alternatively, you can get the resulting code (`Chapter 4/ch4-book-reviews/ch4-book-reviews-v6.php`) from the downloaded code bundle and rename the file `ch4-book-reviews.php`.

How to do it...

1. Navigate to the `ch4-book-reviews` folder of the WordPress plugin directory of your development installation.
2. Open the `ch4-book-reviews.php` file in a code editor.
3. Find the call to the `register_taxonomy` function within the `ch4_br_create_book_post_type` function and add a new member to the configuration array named `meta_box_cb` with a value set to `false` highlighted in bold:

```
'show_tagcloud' => false,
'meta_box_cb' => false,
'hierarchical' => true
```

4. Save the plugin and edit a Book Review to see that the **Book Type** taxonomy box is no longer displayed.

5. Locate the `ch4_br_display_review_details_meta_box` function in the code and add the following code within the existing table rendering code to add a new row containing a drop-down selection box for the book type:

```php
<tr>
    <td>Book Type</td>
    <td>
    <?php
        // Retrieve array of types assigned to post
        $assigned_types = wp_get_post_terms( $book_review->ID,
                            'book_reviews_book_type' );
        // Retrieve array of all book types in system
        $book_types = get_terms( 'book_reviews_book_type',
                            array( 'orderby' => 'name',
                                   'hide_empty' => 0) );

        if ( $book_types ) {
            echo '<select name="book_review_book_type"';
            echo ' style="width: 400px">';

            foreach ( $book_types as $book_type ) {
                echo '<option value="' . $book_type->term_id;
                echo '" ';
                if ( !empty( $assigned_types ) ) {
                    selected( $assigned_types[0]->term_id,
                            $book_type->term_id );
                }
                echo '>' . esc_html( $book_type->name );
                echo '</option>';
            }

            echo '</select>';
        } ?>
    </td>
</tr>
```

6. Find the `ch4_br_add_book_review_fields` function and add the following code segment within the if statement, checking to see whether the post type is a Book Review, to save the selected book type in the site's database upon the submission of the post:

```php
if ( isset( $_POST['book_review_book_type'] )
    && !empty( $_POST['book_review_book_type'] ) ) {
    wp_set_post_terms( $book_review->ID,
```

```
                                 intval( $_POST['book_review_book_type'] ),
                                 'book_reviews_book_type' );
        }
```

7. Save and close the plugin file.
8. Open a previously created Book Review to see the updated **Book Review Details** meta box containing a new drop-down list to specify **Book Type**:

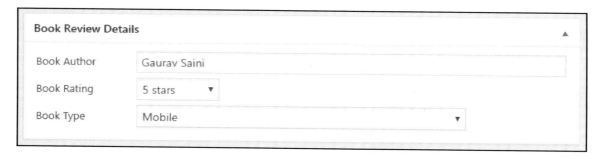

How it works...

This recipe uses one of the many parameters of the `register_taxonomy` function to remove the ability for book review creators and editors to create new book types and creates a drop-down list to be able to assign a single book type to reviews.

In this process, the recipe makes use of three functions related to storing and retrieving taxonomy entries related to posts. The first, `wp_get_post_terms`, retrieves an array of terms associated with a post based on its ID and the name of the taxonomy. The second, `wp_set_post_terms`, assigns a term to a post based on its ID and the taxonomy name. Finally, `get_terms` retrieves an array of all the terms in the taxonomy, ordered based on the query string found in the second argument.

See also

- The *Adding custom categories for custom post types* recipe

Displaying additional columns in the custom post list page

After customizing the post editor to give content creators a tailored environment to create and edit custom post type entries, this recipe turns its efforts toward the Book Reviews management page, where all the entries for this type are listed. By default, custom post type listings are quite simple and only show the title, publication date, and the number of comments for each item. To make it easier to identify, sort, and find data in this management page, WordPress offers a number of customization capabilities, starting with the ability to change the columns that are displayed.

This recipe shows how to add and remove columns in the post management page, as well as make sorting in new columns possible.

Getting ready

You should have already followed the *Hiding the category editor from the custom post type editor* recipe to have a starting point for this recipe, and the resulting plugin should still be active in your development site. Alternatively, you can get the resulting code (Chapter 4/ch4-book-reviews/ch4-book-reviews-v7.php) from the downloaded code bundle and rename the file to ch4-book-reviews.php.

How to do it...

1. Navigate to the ch4-book-reviews folder of the WordPress plugin directory of your development installation.
2. Open the ch4-book-reviews.php file in a code editor.
3. Add the following line of code after the existing functions to register a function to be called when the **Book Reviews** listings page is being prepared:

```
add_filter( 'manage_edit-book_reviews_columns',
            'ch4_br_add_columns' );
```

4. Add the following code section to provide an implementation for the ch4_br_add_columns function:

```
function ch4_br_add_columns( $columns ) {
    $columns['book_reviews_author'] = 'Author';
    $columns['book_reviews_rating'] = 'Rating';
```

```
        $columns['book_reviews_type'] = 'Type';

        unset( $columns['comments'] );

        return $columns;
    }
```

5. Add the following line of code to assign a function to be called when the columns data is being retrieved for each row in the post listing:

```
add_action( 'manage_posts_custom_column',
            'ch4_br_populate_columns' );
```

6. Insert the following code segment to provide an implementation for the ch4_br_populate_columns function:

```
function ch4_br_populate_columns( $column ) {
    if ( 'book_reviews_author' == $column ) {
        $book_author = esc_html( get_post_meta( get_the_ID(),
                                                'book_author',
                                                true ) );
        echo $book_author;
    } elseif ( 'book_reviews_rating' == $column ) {
        $book_rating = get_post_meta( get_the_ID(), 'book_rating',
                                      true );
        echo $book_rating . ' stars';
    } elseif ( 'book_reviews_type' == $column ) {
        $book_types = wp_get_post_terms( get_the_ID(),
                          'book_reviews_book_type' );
        if ( $book_types ) {
            $book_cat_color = get_term_meta(
                                  $book_types[0]->term_id,
                                  'book_type_color', true );

            if ( '#' != $book_cat_color ) {
                echo '<span style="background-color: ';
                echo $book_cat_color . '; ';
                echo 'color: #fff; padding: 6px;">';
                echo $book_types[0]->name . '</span>';
            } else {
                echo $book_types[0]->name;
            }
        } else {
            echo 'None Assigned';
        }
    }
}
```

7. Save the plugin file and navigate to the **Book Reviews** listing page to see that the list of columns has been altered and that data stored in the post custom fields is now displayed for each item in the list.

8. Back in the code editor, add the following code at the end of the plugin file to register a function to be called when WordPress identifies columns that will be sortable for the Book Reviews custom post type:

```
add_filter( 'manage_edit-book_reviews_sortable_columns',
            'ch4_br_author_column_sortable' );
```

9. Append the following code to provide an implementation for the ch4_br_author_column_sortable function:

```
function ch4_br_author_column_sortable( $columns ) {
    $columns['book_reviews_author'] = 'book_reviews_author';
    $columns['book_reviews_rating'] = 'book_reviews_rating';

    return $columns;
}
```

10. Add the following block of code to register a function that will be called when data is requested to display post lists:

```
add_filter( 'request', 'ch4_br_column_ordering' );
```

11. Insert the following code segment to implement the ch4_br_column_ordering function:

```
function ch4_br_column_ordering( $vars ) {
    if ( !is_admin() ) {
        return $vars;
    }

    if ( isset( $vars['orderby'] ) &&
         'book_reviews_author' == $vars['orderby'] ) {
        $vars = array_merge( $vars, array(
            'meta_key' => 'book_author',
            'orderby' => 'meta_value' ) );
    } elseif ( isset( $vars['orderby'] ) &&
               'book_reviews_rating' == $vars['orderby'] ) {
        $vars = array_merge( $vars, array(
                              'meta_key' => 'book_rating',
                              'orderby' => 'meta_value_num' ) );
    }
    return $vars;
}
```

12. Save and close the plugin file.
13. Refresh the **Book Reviews** listing to see that the **Author** and **Rating** column headers are links that can be clicked to sort these columns:

Title	Date	Author	Rating ▼	Type
Vulkan Cookbook	Published 2017/05/01	Pawel Lapinski	5 stars	None Assigned
Python Programming with Raspberry Pi	Published 2017/05/01	Sai Yamanoor, Srihari Yamanoor	5 stars	None Assigned

How it works...

Customizing the post listings page requires an intricate mix of action and filter hooks to achieve the final goal. The first function we registered is associated with the variable filter name `manage_edit-<post_type>_columns`, where `<post_type>` is replaced with the internal post type name. When the registered function is called, it receives the default column list that will be shown while listing Book Reviews entries as an argument. Using this data, it proceeds to add three columns for `author`, `rating`, and `type` and removes the `comments` column from the array. Once finished, it returns the modified array.

The second part of the recipe registers the function that will be responsible for populating the new columns. Since this function gets called when any custom post type column is rendered, the code checks which column is currently requested before echoing the requested data to the browser. The function makes calls to `get_the_ID()` to get the index of the currently displayed row and to be able to find its associated data using `get_post_meta` and `wp_get_post_terms`.

At this point in the recipe, the new columns are visible in the **Book Reviews** management page and data is displayed for each of them. The purpose of the rest of the recipe is to make the `author` and `rating` columns sortable. This is done by first registering a function with the variable filter name `manage_edit-<post_type>_sortable_columns`, where `<post_type>` is replaced with the post type name. When the function is executed, it adds two items to the array of columns that will be sorted. This takes care of making the column header links that can be clicked for sorting, associated with the appropriate URLs.

The last function that is registered is associated with the request filter and takes care of adding elements to the query array based on the variables that came through in the query URL.

The final result allows administrators to easily reorder **Book Reviews** based on these two columns which can be sorted, as well as to see information about each entry's type.

See also

- The *Adding custom categories for custom post types* recipe

Adding filters for custom categories to the custom post list page

A second customization method for the custom post listings is to create a drop-down box that will allow administrators to only display items that belong to a single category at a time. This can help significantly reduce the number of entries that are shown to quickly find the desired entry.

This recipe shows how to add a filter mechanism based on the Book Review type to the listings page.

Getting ready

You should have already followed the *Displaying additional columns in the custom post list page* recipe to have a starting point for this recipe and the resulting plugin should still be active in your development site. Alternatively, you can get the resulting code (Chapter 4/ch4-book-reviews/ch4-book-reviews-v8.php) from the downloaded code bundle and rename the file ch4-book-reviews.php.

How to do it...

1. Navigate to the `ch4-book-reviews` folder of the WordPress plugin directory of your development installation.
2. Open the `ch4-book-reviews.php` file in a code editor.
3. Add the following line of code after the existing functions to register a function to be called when WordPress is preparing the filter drop-down boxes for the post listings:

```
add_action( 'restrict_manage_posts',
            'ch4_br_book_type_filter_list' );
```

4. Add the following code section to provide an implementation for the `ch4_br_book_type_filter_list` function:

```
function ch4_br_book_type_filter_list() {
    $screen = get_current_screen();
    global $wp_query;
    if ( 'book_reviews' == $screen->post_type ) {
        wp_dropdown_categories( array(
            'show_option_all' =>  'Show All Book Types',
            'taxonomy'        =>  'book_reviews_book_type',
            'name'            =>  'book_reviews_book_type',
            'orderby'         =>  'name',
            'selected'        =>
            ( isset( $wp_query->query['book_reviews_book_type'] )
              ? $wp_query->query['book_reviews_book_type'] : '' ),
            'hierarchical'    =>  false,
            'depth'           =>  3,
            'show_count'      =>  false,
            'hide_empty'      =>  true,
        ) );
    }
}
```

5. Insert the following line of code to register a function that will be called when the post display query is being prepared:

```
add_filter( 'parse_query', 'ch4_br_perform_book_type_filtering' );
```

6. Implement the `ch4_br_perform_book_type_filtering` function with the following code segment:

```
function ch4_br_perform_book_type_filtering( $query ) {
    $qv = &$query->query_vars;

    if ( isset( $qv['book_reviews_book_type'] ) &&
         !empty( $qv['book_reviews_book_type'] ) &&
         is_numeric( $qv['book_reviews_book_type'] ) ) {
        $term = get_term_by( 'id',
                             $qv['book_reviews_book_type'],
                             'book_reviews_book_type' );
        $qv['book_reviews_book_type'] = $term->slug;
    }
}
```

7. Save and close the plugin file.

8. Visit the **Book Reviews** listings to see the new dropdown to restrict what book types are displayed:

How it works...

This recipe starts by registering an action callback that will be executed when WordPress renders the various filter controls that are available for each post type listing. When the function is called, it retrieves a global variable to know the post type that is currently being displayed and determine if it should show the book type filter list. It also accesses the global post query variable to see if a book type filter is already in place and sets the correct drop-down list entry to be selected, if there is one.

The callback then proceeds to use the `wp_dropdown_categories` function to display a list of all of the taxonomy items registered for book types. This utility function expects to receive an array of parameters that determine which taxonomy list to display, the name of the drop-down list field name, and the label to be displayed for the option to show all the types. This array should also contain a few parameters to determine the order in which the items should be displayed, specify the item to set as selected, indicate the maximum depth to show for hierarchical taxonomies, and determine whether or not items count and empty items be shown.

Once the new book type selection list is in place, selecting an entry and clicking on the **Filter** button triggers a refresh of the web page and leads to the second registered callback that was put in place after being executed. The filter function receives the current WordPress post query object and starts by first getting a pointer to the query variables that are stored inside of the query object. With this in hand, it moves on to verify that a book type is part of the query variables and that it is numeric. If the result is positive, it replaces the numeric value with the textual name for the selected book type so that the query can take place.

Once all of this code is executed, users are able to quickly filter which book types should be displayed in the **Book Reviews** management page. They are also still able to use the column sorting mechanism implemented in the previous recipe.

See also

- The *Adding custom categories for custom post types* recipe

Adding Quick Edit fields for custom categories

A great feature of WordPress is the ability for site editors to quickly make changes to any post in the admin section by clicking on the Quick Edit link associated with any of the items shown. While our custom post type taxonomy appears in the Quick Edit section, it is not a drop-down list of choices as we had in the book review editor. Also, the author and rating fields do not appear in any way in the Quick Edit section.

This recipe shows how to add custom fields while quickly editing book reviews. As you perform the following steps, you will see that some of the code that we put in place is not as cleanly written as code from previous recipes, since the WordPress Quick Edit customization infrastructure is not as well-formed as other areas of the platform.

Getting ready

You should have already followed the *Adding filters for custom categories to the custom post list page* recipe to have a starting point for this recipe, and the resulting plugin should still be active in your development site. Alternatively, you can get the resulting code (Chapter 4/ch4-book-reviews/ch4-book-reviews-v9.php) from the downloaded code bundle and rename the file ch4-book-reviews.php.

How to do it...

1. Navigate to the ch4-book-reviews folder of the WordPress plugin directory of your development installation.

2. Open the ch4-book-reviews.php file in a code editor.

3. Find the call to the register_taxonomy function within the ch4_br_create_book_post_type function and add a new member to the configuration array named show_in_quick_edit with a value set to false highlighted in bold:

```
'show_tagcloud' => false,
'meta_box_cb' => false,
'show_in_quick_edit' => false,
'hierarchical' => true,
```

4. Add the following line of code after the existing functions to register a function to be called when WordPress is preparing to render the contents of the **Quick Edit** section:

```
add_action( 'quick_edit_custom_box',
            'ch4_br_display_custom_quickedit_link', 10, 2 );
```

5. Add the following code section to provide an implementation for the ch4_br_display_custom_quickedit_link function:

```
function ch4_br_display_custom_quickedit_link( $column_name,
                                               $post_type ) {
```

```php
if ( 'book_reviews' == $post_type ) {
    switch ( $column_name ) {
        case 'book_reviews_author': ?>
            <fieldset class="inline-edit-col-right">
            <div class="inline-edit-col">
                <label><span class="title">Author</span></label>
                <input type="text"
                        name='book_reviews_author_input'
                        id='book_reviews_author_input' value="">
            </div>
            <?php break;
        case 'book_reviews_rating': ?>
            <div class="inline-edit-col">
                <label>
                    <span class="title">Rating</span>
                </label>
                <select name='book_reviews_rating_input'
                        id='book_reviews_rating_input'>
                <?php // Generate all items of drop-down list
                for ( $rating = 5; $rating >= 1; $rating -- ) {
                ?>  <option value="<?php echo $rating; ?>">
                    <?php echo $rating; ?> stars
                <?php } ?>
                </select>
            </div>
            <?php break;
        case 'book_reviews_type': ?>
            <div class="inline-edit-col">
                <label><span class="title">Type</span></label>
                <?php
                $terms = get_terms( array( 'taxonomy' =>
                                    'book_reviews_book_type',
                                    'hide_empty' => false ) );
                ?>
                <select name='book_reviews_type_input'
                        id='book_reviews_type_input'>
                <?php foreach ($terms as $index => $term) {
                    echo '<option ';
                    echo 'class="book_reviews_type-option"';
                    echo 'value="' . $term->term_id . '"';
                    selected( 0, $index );
                    echo '>' . $term->name. '</option>';
                } ?>
                </select>
            </div>
        <?php break;
    }
}
```

```
    }
```

6. Add the following line of code to register a function to be called when WordPress is rendering the footer of the administration pages:

```
add_action( 'admin_footer', 'ch4_br_quick_edit_js' );
```

7. Implement the ch4_br_quick_edit_js function with the following code snippet:

```
function ch4_br_quick_edit_js() {
    global $current_screen;
    if ( ( 'edit-book_reviews' !== $current_screen->id ) ||
        ( 'book_reviews' !== $current_screen->post_type ) ) {
      return;
    } ?>

    <script type="text/javascript">
    function set_inline_book_reviews( reviewArray ) {
        // revert Quick Edit menu so that it refreshes properly
        inlineEditPost.revert();
        var inputBookAuthor =
            document.getElementById('book_reviews_author_input');
        inputBookAuthor.value = reviewArray[0];

        var inputRating =
            document.getElementById('book_reviews_rating_input');
        for (i = 0; i < inputRating.options.length; i++) {
            if ( inputRating.options[i].value == reviewArray[1] ) {
                inputRating.options[i].setAttribute( 'selected',
                                                      'selected' );
            } else {
                inputRating.options[i].removeAttribute(
                    'selected' );
            }
        }

        var inputBookType =
            document.getElementById('book_reviews_type_input');
        for (i = 0; i < inputBookType.options.length; i++) {
            if ( inputBookType.options[i].value ==
                    reviewArray[2] ) {
                inputBookType.options[i].setAttribute( 'selected',
                    'selected' );
            } else {
                inputBookType.options[i].removeAttribute(
                    'selected' );
            }
```

```
            }
        }
    </script>
    <?php }
```

8. Add the following code to register a function to replace the original Quick Edit code that is generated for each post in the book reviews page:

```
add_filter( 'post_row_actions', 'ch4_br_quick_edit_link', 10, 2 );
```

9. Add the following block of code to provide an implementation for the `ch4_br_quick_edit_link` function:

```php
function ch4_br_quick_edit_link( $act, $post ) {
    global $current_screen;
    $post_id = '';

    if ( ( isset( $current_screen ) &&
            $current_screen->id != 'edit-book_reviews' &&
            $current_screen->post_type != 'book_reviews' )
        || ( isset( $_POST['screen'] ) &&
            $_POST['screen'] != 'edit-book_reviews' ) ) {
        return $act;
    }

    if ( !empty( $post->ID ) ) {
        $post_id = $post->ID;
    } elseif ( isset( $_POST['post_ID'] ) ) {
        $post_id = intval( $_POST['post_ID'] );
    }

    if ( !empty( $post_id ) ) {
        $book_author = esc_html( get_post_meta( $post_id,
                                'book_author', true ) );
        $book_rating = esc_html( get_post_meta( $post_id,
                                'book_rating', true ) );
        $book_reviews_types = wp_get_post_terms( $post_id,
                                'book_reviews_book_type',
                                array( 'fields' => 'all' ) );
        if ( empty( $book_reviews_types ) ) {
            $book_reviews_types[0] =
                (object) array( 'term_id' => 0 );
        }

        $idx = 'inline hide-if-no-js';
        $act[$idx] = '<a href="#" class="editinline" ';
        $act[$idx] .= " onclick=\"var reviewArray = new Array('";
        $act[$idx] .= "{$book_author}', '{$book_rating}', ";
```

```
        $act[$idx] .= "'{$book_reviews_types[0]->term_id}');";
        $act[$idx] .= "set_inline_book_reviews( reviewArray )\">";
        $act[$idx] .= __( 'Quick Edit' );
        $act[$idx] .= '</a>';
    }
    return $act;
}
```

10. Add the following function call to register a function that will be executed when post data is updated from the **Quick Edit** section:

```
add_action( 'save_post', 'ch4_br_save_quick_edit_data', 10, 2 );
```

11. Provide an implementation for the `ch4_br_save_quick_edit_data` function with the following block of code:

```
function ch4_br_save_quick_edit_data( $ID = false,
                                      $post = false ) {
    // Do not save if auto-saving, not book reviews, no permissions
    if ( ( defined( 'DOING_AUTOSAVE' ) && DOING_AUTOSAVE ) ||
        ( isset( $_POST['post_type'] )
          && 'book_reviews' != $_POST['post_type'] ) ||
        !current_user_can( 'edit_page', $ID ) ) {
        return $ID;
    }

    $post = get_post( $ID );
    if ( !empty( $post ) && 'revision' != $post->post_type ) {
        if ( isset( $_POST['book_reviews_author_input'] ) ) {
            update_post_meta( $ID, 'book_author',
                sanitize_text_field(
                    $_POST['book_reviews_author_input'] ) );
        }

        if ( isset( $_POST['book_reviews_rating_input'] ) ) {
            update_post_meta( $ID, 'book_rating',
                intval( $_POST['book_reviews_rating_input'] ) );
        }

        if ( isset( $_POST['book_reviews_type_input'] ) ) {
            $term = term_exists(
                intval( $_POST['book_reviews_type_input'] ),
                    'book_reviews_book_type' );
            if ( !empty( $term ) ) {
                wp_set_object_terms( $ID,
                    intval( $_POST['book_reviews_type_input'] ),
                        'book_reviews_book_type' );
            }
```

```
                    }
                }
            }
```

12. Save and close the plugin file.

13. Visit the **Book Reviews** listings page and click on **Quick Edit** to see the newly added **Author**, **Rating**, and **Type** fields.

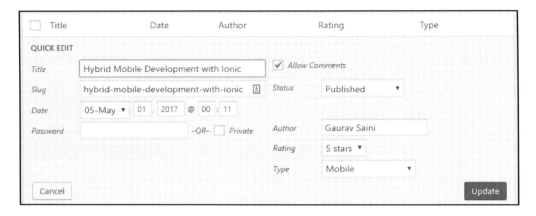

14. Change the values in these fields and save them using the **Update** button. You will see that the values get updated in the Book Reviews list, accordingly.

How it works...

While the Quick Edit box is a great tool that WordPress users appreciate, customizing it is a bit tricky in current versions of WordPress. While we could easily add data to each individual item in sections, such as the post editor, for our new custom post type, the Quick Edit section requires more work to add custom fields. The root of the issue stems from the fact that there is really only a single instance of the Quick Edit section that gets rendered as part of the edit page. That section is hidden at first, then appears, and moves to the correct position when a user clicks on the Quick Edit link. With this in mind, we cannot assign proper values to custom fields in the Quick Edit box and, therefore, need to store hidden information as each item gets listed to be able to update each field appropriately based on which item is being edited.

The first section of our recipe code starts off by rendering a text input field and two drop-down lists within the Quick Edit section. You will notice that we do not set the value of the text field or set options to be selected in the select lists. Another interesting point with this callback is that it sends us the same list of columns that we used in the *Displaying additional columns in the custom post list page* recipe. This means that if we wanted to add fields other than the ones we have added to the post table, we would still have to place these field names in the list of columns and then use some tricks to hide them from the table.

Once these extra fields are in place, we will add the code to the admin page footer of the book review editor to create a Javascript function that we will call when it is time to update our new custom fields in the Quick Edit section. The function receives an array of data, then locates the custom fields in the page using the `document.getElementById` function, and updates their values based on the incoming data array.

The next block of code we added creates a new Quick Edit link to replace the original one for each book review item. The new link not only enables users to display the Quick Edit section, but also embeds values for each item within the `onclick` Javascript code along with a call to the function that we added to the footer so that a new set of values is assigned to each field when the user decides to quickly edit a book review.

Finally, we store data from our custom fields when the user clicks on the **Update** button. Interestingly, we do this by registering a second callback for the `save_post` action. This means that both of our functions will be called when posts are saved. However, this second saving function checks for a number of conditions to be true before actually saving values, and the names of the fields that it saves are different than the save function we put in place for the post editor.

Updating page title to include custom post data using plugin filters

A last customization touch that can be put in place to support our Book Reviews custom post type is to add custom information about the posts in the title bar when displaying them. For example, we could add the author's name next to the book title.

This recipe shows how to use the `document_title_parts` filter to alter the post title for Book Reviews.

Getting ready

You should have already followed the *Adding Quick Edit fields for custom categories* recipe to have a starting point for this recipe, and the resulting plugin should still be active in your development site. Alternatively, you can get the resulting code (Chapter 4/ch4-book-reviews/ch4-book-reviews-v10.php) from the downloaded code bundle and rename the file ch4-book-reviews.php.

How to do it...

1. Navigate to the ch4-book-reviews folder of the WordPress plugin directory of your development installation.
2. Open the ch4-book-reviews.php file in a code editor.
3. Add the following line of code after the existing functions to register a function to be called when WordPress prepares the text to be displayed in the browser's title bar:

```
add_filter( 'document_title_parts',
            'ch4_br_format_book_review_title' );
```

4. Add the following code section to provide an implementation for the ch4_br_format_book_review_title function:

```
function ch4_br_format_book_review_title( $the_title ) {
    if ( 'book_reviews' == get_post_type() && is_single() ) {
        $book_author = esc_html( get_post_meta( get_the_ID(),
                                 'book_author', true ) );
        if ( !empty( $book_author ) ) {
            $the_title['title'] .= ' by ' . $book_author;
        }
    }

    return $the_title;
}
```

5. Save and close the plugin file.

6. Visit a Book Review page. You will see that the book's author is now displayed after the name in the title:

How it works...

The `document_title_parts` filter allows plugins to modify or completely replace the page title contents. In this case, the code of the function that we associated with the filter hook receives the title that WordPress intends to display as an array. It then proceeds to check whether the item that is being prepared for display is a Book Review and whether or not it is a single item. While the first condition is something obvious to check for, the `is_single` verification is done to make sure that the code does not try to add a book author to the Book Reviews archive listing page.

5
Customizing Post and Page Editors

In this chapter, you will learn how to customize the core post and page editors through the following recipes:

- Capturing and displaying information using custom meta boxes
- Displaying custom post data via filter functions
- Hiding the Custom Field section in the post editor
- Extending the post editor to allow users to upload files directly

Introduction

In the last few chapters, you learned how to create custom plugin configuration panels and how to set up custom post types. With this knowledge in hand, we will now see how to customize the post and page editors using meta boxes.

Meta boxes are a very useful tool in the creation of WordPress plugins. They were first used to organize large administration panels into manageable sections in Chapter 3, *User Settings and Administration Pages*, and then continued to be a key element in the creation of tailored interfaces to edit custom post types in Chapter 4, *The Power of Custom Post Types*.

This chapter explores how meta boxes can be used to augment the default post and page editors' capabilities. While WordPress posts and pages already offer a lot of functionalities in a default installation, custom data entry fields go a long way in crafting a user experience that is much smoother than using the custom fields editor. These extra fields can be used to store anything. For example, they could be used to specify alternative language links for blog entries or to assign a pop-up dialog to specific articles on a site.

Capturing and displaying information using custom meta boxes

The WordPress post and page editors are organized in a series of collapsible sections with headers called meta boxes. While WordPress is mainly responsible for populating these containers with all of the appropriate elements, plugin developers can insert their own sections by registering user meta boxes.

To demonstrate this capability, this recipe shows how to add a custom meta box that will be used to display and capture information about the name and web address of the source materials used when writing a new post or page entry.

Getting ready

You should have access to a WordPress development environment, either on your local computer or a remote server, where you will be able to load your new plugin files.

How to do it...

1. Navigate to the WordPress plugin directory of your development installation.
2. Create a new directory called `ch5-post-source-link`.
3. Navigate to the directory and create a text file called `ch5-post-source-link.php`.
4. Open the new file in a code editor and add an appropriate header at the top of the plugin file, naming the plugin `Chapter 5 - Post Source Link`.
5. Add the following line of code to register a function that will be executed when WordPress is preparing a list of meta boxes for all the administration areas:

```
add_action( 'add_meta_boxes', 'ch5_psl_register_meta_box' );
```

6. Add the following code segment to provide an implementation for the `ch5_psl_register_meta_box` function:

```php
function ch5_psl_register_meta_box() {
    add_meta_box( 'ch5_psl_source_meta_box', 'Post/Page Source',
                  'ch5_psl_source_meta_box', 'post', 'normal');
    add_meta_box( 'ch5_psl_source_meta_box', 'Post/Page Source',
                  'ch5_psl_source_meta_box', 'page', 'normal');
}
```

7. Insert this code to provide an implementation for the `ch5_psl_source_meta_box` function, responsible for rendering the meta box contents:

```php
function ch5_psl_source_meta_box( $post ) {
    // Retrieve current source name and address for post
    $post_source_name =
        esc_html( get_post_meta( $post->ID, 'post_source_name',
                                 true ) );
    $post_source_address =
        esc_html( get_post_meta( $post->ID,
                                 'post_source_address',
                                 true ) );
    ?>
    <!-- Display fields to enter source name and address -->
    <table>
        <tr>
            <td style="width: 100px">Source Name</td>
            <td>
                <input type="text" size="40"
                       name="post_source_name"
                       value="<?php echo $post_source_name; ?>" />
            </td>
        </tr>
        <tr>
            <td>Source Address</td>
            <td>
                <input type="text" size="40"
                       name="post_source_address"
                       value="<?php echo $post_source_address; ?>"
                />
            </td>
        </tr>
    </table>
    <?php }
```

8. Insert the following block of code to register a function that will be called when any type of post is saved:

```
add_action( 'save_post', 'ch5_psl_save_source_data', 10, 2 );
```

9. Append the following code section to provide an implementation for the ch5_psl_save_source_data function:

```
function ch5_psl_save_source_data( $post_id = false,
                                   $post = false ) {
    // Check post type for posts or pages
    if ( 'post' == $post->post_type ||
         'page' == $post->post_type ) {
        // Store data in post meta table if present in post data
        if ( isset( $_POST['post_source_name'] ) ) {
            update_post_meta( $post_id, 'post_source_name',
                sanitize_text_field(
                    $_POST['post_source_name'] ) );
        }

        if ( isset( $_POST['post_source_address'] ) ) {
            update_post_meta( $post_id, 'post_source_address',
                esc_url( $_POST['post_source_address'] ) );
        }
    }
}
```

10. Save and close the plugin file.
11. Navigate to the **Plugins** management page and **Activate** the Chapter 5 - Post Source Link plugin.
12. Go to the **Posts** section of the administration, click on one of the entries to open the post editor, and see the new **Post/Page Source** meta box:

How it works...

Every time an administrator or content manager visits the platform's backend, WordPress creates a number of meta boxes for all of its internal editors (posts, pages, links, and so on) using the add_meta_box function that we have seen in the previous two chapters.

In this recipe, we will use the same add_meta_box function twice to associate a new box to the page and post editors, with both calls registering the same callback function, since we want the same functionality in both places. As WordPress stores posts and pages in the same database table, it will automatically make sure that all the entries have unique IDs between both types of entries.

The other function that we have seen before is get_post_meta, which is used to retrieve custom metadata associated with post entries.

The content of the meta box itself is displayed using standard HTML. As this box will be part of a larger editor, there is no need to worry about declaring a form in this box.

Once the new dialog section is created, the next task is to put code in place to store data from the additional fields upon submission through the use of the save_post action. Functions associated with this hook are called when posts of any type are saved. When executed, the associated function receives two parameters from WordPress that contain the ID of the post being saved and a copy of all the data that has been processed to be saved so far. The callback also has access to all the server post data received from the user, and uses the sanitize_text_field and esc_url functions to make sure that no malicious content was received.

As indicated in the previous chapter, it is important to set the fourth parameter of the add_action call--that is, accepted_args--for actions and filters that receive more than one argument. If it is not specified, these additional arguments will not be available to the receiving hook function.

Working with the assumption that the meta box was only added to the post and page editors, the code contained in the ch5_psl_save_source_data function first checks to see whether the post type is set as a post or page. If it is one of these two types, it moves on to check for the presence of post data for the source name and address fields. If found, update_post_meta is called once for each field to store the new information in the site's database associated with the posts that it belongs to. Making a call to the update_post_meta function actually updates the post custom field data if it exists or creates it in the case of new post or page entries.

There's more...

While this recipe specifically adds a new section to the post and page editors, it may be desirable to make the new fields available to all post types, including custom ones.

Adding a new meta box to all post types (including custom ones)

This recipe made two function calls to register meta boxes with the post and page editors. This concept does not expand well to register a custom section with all the post types, since custom types created by other plugins are not known. Thankfully, there is an easy way to get an array of all the post types that can be used to associate the new meta box with all the post editors, using a quick `foreach` loop.

The following code shows how the `ch5_psl_register_meta_box` function can be re-written to associate the new box with all the post types:

```
function ch5_psl_register_meta_box() {
    $post_types = get_post_types( array(), 'objects' );
    foreach ( $post_types as $post_type ) {
        add_meta_box( 'ch5_psl_post_source_meta_box',
                    'Post/Page Source',
                    'ch5_psl_source_meta_box',
                    $post_type->name, 'normal' );
    }
}
```

Displaying custom post data using filter functions

Once we have captured additional data in the post editor, the next logical step will be to add code to display it when visitors view posts and pages. In the case of our source link data, the most logical place to show this link is after each post's content, which can easily be accomplished by assigning a function to the filter `the_content`.

This recipe explains how to create a filter function to display the source data associated with a post or page item as a clean link.

Getting ready

You should have already followed the *Capturing and displaying information using custom meta boxes* recipe to have a starting point for this recipe and the resulting plugin should still be active in your development site. Alternatively, you can get the resulting code (`Chapter 5/ch5-post-source-link/ch5-post-source-link-v1.php`) from the code bundle you downloaded from the Packt Publishing website (`https://www.packtpub.com/support`) and rename the file as `ch5-post-source-link.php`.

How to do it...

1. Navigate to the `ch5-post-source-link` folder of the WordPress plugin directory of your development installation.
2. Open the `ch5-post-source-link.php` file in a code editor.
3. Add the following line of code to register a filter function to be called when the post and page content is prepared for display:

   ```
   add_filter( 'the_content', 'ch5_psl_display_source_link' );
   ```

4. Add the following code section to provide an implementation for the `ch5_psl_display_source_link` function:

   ```php
   function ch5_psl_display_source_link ( $content ) {
       $post_id = get_the_ID();

       if ( !empty( $post_id ) ) {
           if ( 'post' == get_post_type( $post_id ) ||
                'page' == get_post_type( $post_id ) ) {

               // Retrieve current source name and address for post
               $post_source_name =
                   get_post_meta( $post_id, 'post_source_name',
                               true );
               $post_source_address =
                   get_post_meta( $post_id, 'post_source_address',
                               true );

               // Output information to browser
               if ( !empty( $post_source_name ) &&
                    !empty( $post_source_address ) ) {
                   $content .= '<div class="source_link">Source: ';
                   $content .= '<a href="';
                   $content .= esc_url( $post_source_address );
   ```

```
                              $content .= '">' . esc_html( $post_source_name );
                              $content .= '</a></div>';
                    }
               }
          }
          return $content;
     }
```

5. Save and close the plugin file.

6. Add source data to one of your site's posts and view it to see the new **Source** link displayed on the page.

APRIL 9, 2017 BY YLEFEBVRE

Hello world!

Welcome to WordPress. This is your first post. Edit or delete it, then start writing!

Source: Packt Publishing

How it works...

Similarly to what was done in `Chapter 2`, *Plugin Framework Basics*, in the *Adding text after each item's content using plugin filters* recipe, this recipe registers a callback with the `the_content` filter hook, which allows us to add an additional link after each post or page where the source name and source address fields have been filled in. We use the `get_post_type` function in our callback to first check whether the item being displayed is in one of these two categories. Then, we use `get_post_meta` to retrieve the information and display the source link if both fields contain information.

We also use the `esc_url` and `esc_html` functions as a precaution to be sure that the data stored in these two post meta fields is clean.

See also

- The *Capturing and displaying information using custom meta boxes* recipe

Hiding the Custom Field section in the post editor

After having full control over which meta boxes are shown when creating custom post type editor controls and putting together plugin configuration pages, things are a little different when it comes to altering the basic post and page editors. More specifically, instead of choosing which meta boxes to display, the editor sections created by WordPress need to be removed to tailor the user experience.

This recipe shows how to remove the **Custom Fields** meta boxes from the post and page editors:

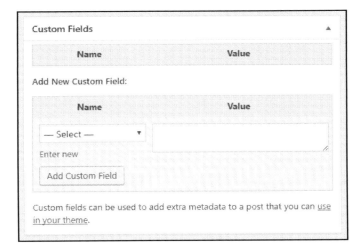

Getting ready

You should have access to a WordPress development environment, either on your local computer or a remote server, where you will be able to load your new plugin files.

How to do it...

1. Navigate to the WordPress plugin directory of your development installation.
2. Create a new directory called `ch5-hide-custom-fields`.

3. Navigate to this directory and create a new text file called `ch5-hide-custom-fields.php`.

4. Open the new file in a code editor and add an appropriate header at the top of the plugin file, naming the plugin `Chapter 5 - Hide Custom Fields`.

5. Add the following line of code to register a function that will be executed when WordPress is preparing a list of meta boxes for all the administration areas:

```
add_action( 'add_meta_boxes',
            'ch5_hcf_remove_custom_fields_metabox' );
```

6. Add the following code section to provide an implementation for the `ch5_hcf_remove_custom_fields_metabox` function:

```
function ch5_hcf_remove_custom_fields_metabox() {
    remove_meta_box( 'postcustom', 'post', 'normal' );
    remove_meta_box( 'postcustom', 'page', 'normal' );
}
```

7. Save and close the plugin file.

8. Navigate to the **Plugins** management page and **Activate** the `Chapter 5 - Hide Custom Fields` plugin.

9. Go to the **Posts** section of the administration and click on one of the entries to open the post editor. You will see that the **Custom Fields** section is no longer visible in the editor and does not show up in the **Screen Options** configuration tab either:

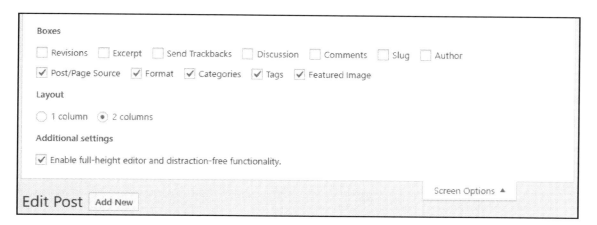

How it works...

This short recipe contains only a few lines of code which register a function to be called when WordPress is preparing meta boxes for all the administration sections, followed by the implementation of this function. The function itself makes two calls to the `remove_meta_box` function to remove the custom fields section from the post and page editors. This function requires three parameters:

```
remove_meta_box( $id, $page, $context );
```

The first argument is the meta box identifier that was used when it was first created. While you may not know where the creation code for a given meta box is located within the WordPress source code, a quick look at the box's `div id` in the page source from a browser reveals its name. In this case, the `id` is `postcustom`. The other two arguments indicate the name of the editor from which the meta box is to be removed and the context of the meta box (`normal`, `advanced`, or `side`).

Once the plugin is activated, the designated box disappears from the interface immediately.

Extending the post editor to allow users to upload files directly

WordPress offers a very complete media upload dialog. However, some projects might require users to be able to attach files right from the post editor. This recipe shows how to modify the post editor form to be able to attach files to articles and how to store these files once they have been uploaded. While any type of file could be attached using this technique, the code will be written to accept only items with a PDF file extension.

Getting ready

You should have access to a WordPress development environment, either on your local computer or a remote server, where you will be able to load your new plugin files.

How to do it...

1. Navigate to the WordPress plugin directory of your development installation.
2. Create a new directory called `ch5-custom-file-uploader`.
3. Navigate to this directory and create a new text file called `ch5-custom-file-uploader.php`.
4. Open the new file in a code editor and add an appropriate header at the top of the plugin file, naming the plugin `Chapter 5 - Custom File Uploader`.
5. Add the following line of code to register a function that will be executed when WordPress is rendering the HTML code at the beginning of the post editor form:

```
add_action( 'post_edit_form_tag', 'ch5_cfu_form_add_enctype' );
```

6. Add the following code section to provide an implementation for the `ch5_cfu_form_add_enctype` function:

```
function ch5_cfu_form_add_enctype() {
    echo ' enctype="multipart/form-data"';
}
```

7. Insert the following line of code to register a function to be called when WordPress is preparing the meta boxes for all the administration sections:

```
add_action( 'add_meta_boxes', 'ch5_cfu_register_meta_box' );
```

8. Add the following block of code to implement the `ch5_cfu_register_meta_box` function:

```
function ch5_cfu_register_meta_box() {
    add_meta_box( 'ch5_cfu_upload_file', 'Upload File',
                'ch5_cfu_upload_meta_box', 'post', 'normal' );
    add_meta_box( 'ch5_cfu_upload_file', 'Upload File',
                'ch5_cfu_upload_meta_box', 'page', 'normal' );
}
```

9. Implement the function responsible for rendering the meta box contents, `ch5_cfu_upload_meta_box`, with the following code:

```
function ch5_cfu_upload_meta_box( $post ) { ?>
    <table>
        <tr>
            <td style="width: 150px">PDF Attachment</td>
            <td>
            <?php
            // Retrieve attachment data for post
            $attachment_data = get_post_meta( $post->ID,
                                               'attach_data',
                                               true );
            // Display post link if data is present
            if ( empty ( $attachment_data ) ) {
                echo 'No Attachment Present';
            } else {
                echo '<a target="_blank" href="';
                echo esc_url( $attachment_data['url'] );
                echo '">' . 'Download Attachment</a>';
            }
            ?>
            </td>
        </tr>
        <tr>
            <td>Upload File</td>
            <td><input name="upload_pdf" type="file" /></td>
        </tr>
        <tr>
            <td>Delete File</td>
            <td><input type="submit" name="delete_attachment"
                        class="button-primary"
                        id="delete_attachment"
                        value="Delete Attachment" /></td>
        </tr>
    </table>
<?php }
```

10. Add the following line of code, which calls the `add_action` function to register a callback that will be executed when post data is processed to be saved:

```
add_action( 'save_post', 'ch5_cfu_save_uploaded_file', 10, 2 );
```

11. Implement `ch5_cfu_save_uploaded_file` with the following code:

```
function ch5_cfu_save_uploaded_file( $post_id = false,
                                      $post = false ) {
```

```
if ( isset($_POST['delete_attachment'] ) ) {
    $attach_data = get_post_meta( $post_id, 'attach_data',
                                    true );

    if ( !empty( $attach_data ) ) {
        unlink( $attach_data['file'] );
        delete_post_meta( $post_id, 'attach_data' );
    }
} elseif ( 'post' == $post->post_type ||
            'page' == $post->post_type ) {

    // Look to see if file has been uploaded by user
    if( array_key_exists( 'upload_pdf', $_FILES ) &&
        !$_FILES['upload_pdf']['error'] ) {

        // Retrieve file type and store lower-case version
        $file_type_array = wp_check_filetype( basename(
            $_FILES['upload_pdf']['name'] ) );
        $file_ext = strtolower( $file_type_array['ext'] );

        // Display error message if file is not a PDF
        if ( 'pdf' != $file_ext ) {
            wp_die( 'Only files of PDF type are allowed.' );
            exit;
        } else {
            // Send uploaded file data to upload directory
            $upload_return = wp_upload_bits(
                $_FILES['upload_pdf']['name'], null,
                file_get_contents(
                $_FILES['upload_pdf']['tmp_name'] ) );

            // Replace backslashes with slashes for Windows
            // web servers
            $upload_return['file'] =
                str_replace( '\\', '/',
                            $upload_return['file'] );

            // Set upload path data if successful.
            if ( isset( $upload_return['error'] ) &&
                        $upload_return['error'] != 0 ) {
                $errormsg = 'There was an error uploading';
                $errormsg .= 'your file. The error is: ';
                $errormsg .= $upload_return['error'];
                wp_die( $errormsg );
                exit;
            } else {
                $attach_data = get_post_meta( $post_id,
                                                'attach_data',
```

```
                                                 true );

                    if ( !empty( $attach_data ) ) {
                        unlink( $attach_data['file'] );
                    }
                    update_post_meta( $post_id, 'attach_data',
                                      $upload_return );
                }
            }
        }
    }
}
```

12. Add the following line of code to register a filter function to be called when the post and page content is prepared for display:

```
add_filter( 'the_content', 'ch5_cfu_display_pdf_link' );
```

13. Insert the following code to provide an implementation for the `ch5_cfu_display_pdf_link` function:

```php
function ch5_cfu_display_pdf_link ( $content ) {
    $post_id = get_the_ID();

    if ( !empty( $post_id ) ) {
        if ( 'post' == get_post_type( $post_id ) ||
             'page' == get_post_type( $post_id ) ) {

            $attachment_data =
                get_post_meta( $post_id, 'attach_data', true );

            if ( !empty( $attachment_data ) ) {
                $content .= '<div class="file_attachment">';
                $content .= '<a target="_blank" href="';
                $content .= esc_url( $attachment_data['url'] );
                $content .= '">' . 'Download additional ';
                $content .= 'information</a></div>';
            }
        }
    }
    return $content;
}
```

14. Save and close the plugin file.

15. Navigate to the **Plugins** management page and **Activate** the **Chapter 5 - Custom File Uploader** plugin.

16. Edit any post on your site to see the new **Upload File** meta box and click on **Update** to save the post and upload the selected PDF file to be associated with the item:

17. View the post to see the link to download the attached file:

How it works...

The default WordPress post editor declares a simple form that does not have an encoding type defined and, therefore, can only accept regular text input. Fortunately, we have access to an action hook to register a callback function that will output additional code when the form gets created, allowing us to upload files. This callback is implemented in the first part of this recipe.

The next code section registers a meta box, as we have seen in many recipes so far, to display a new editor section that will display a link to an attached file if present, a file selection box to upload a new file, and a button to request for the attachment to be deleted.

Moving on to the function responsible for processing the post data, the recipe's code first checks whether the user requested to delete a file associated with a post. If that is the case, it will proceed with the deletion of the file and remove the associated post metadata. In other circumstances, if the item's post type is a post or page, the plugin will proceed to search for a file uploaded by the user within the PHP global `$_FILES` array. This array contains information on any uploads that have been processed as part of a form's post data. If an entry is found, we will use the `wp_check_filetype` function to retrieve information about the file type and proceed to convert the resulting extension to a lowercase string to make comparisons easier.

As this example only expects to receive PDF files, the code then checks to see whether the file extension is correct to decide whether it will display an error message using the `wp_die` function or move the file from the web server's temp directory to the `wp-content/uploads` directory in WordPress, using the `wp_upload_bits` function. In the latter case, it also stores the resulting file's path and URL in the post custom field table.

Once this is done, this recipe implements a filter function for `the_content` to display a link to associated PDF attachments under posts and pages.

See also

- The *Adding extra fields to the post editor using custom meta boxes* recipe

6
Accepting User Content Submissions

In this chapter, we will be focusing on giving visitors the ability to make submissions to a website. We will cover the following recipes:

- Creating a client-side content submission form
- Saving user-submitted content in custom post types
- Sending email notifications upon new submissions
- Implementing a CAPTCHA on user forms using an online service
- Using a local library to implement a CAPTCHA on user forms

Introduction

Giving users the ability to contribute content to a website is always a good way to engage the community and keep content fresh on a website. Going back to the book review system that was put in place in `Chapter 4`, *The Power of Custom Post Types*, this chapter explains how to allow visitors to add their own book reviews to a website.

Creating a client-side content submission form

The first step toward giving visitors the ability to contribute to a website is to present a form that they will be able to use to submit new content. This recipe shows how to create a shortcode that can easily be inserted on any WordPress page to render a simple form.

Getting ready

You should be running the final version of the Book Reviews plugin created in `Chapter 4`, *The Power of Custom Post Types*, or using the final resulting code (`Chapter 4/ch4-book-reviews/ch4-book-reviews-v11.php`) from the downloaded code bundle.

How to do it...

1. Navigate to the WordPress plugin directory of your development installation.
2. Create a new directory called `ch6-book-review-user-submission` and open it.
3. Create a text file called `ch6-book-review-user-submission.php`.
4. Open the new file in a code editor and add an appropriate header at the top of the plugin file, naming the plugin `Chapter 6 - Book Review User Submission`.
5. Add the following line of code to declare a new shortcode and its associated function:

   ```
   add_shortcode( 'submit-book-review', 'ch6_brus_book_review_form' );
   ```

6. Add the following code segment to provide an implementation for the `ch6_brus_book_review_form` function:

   ```
   function ch6_brus_book_review_form() {
       // make sure user is logged in
       if ( !is_user_logged_in() ) {
           echo '<p>You need to be a website member to be able to ';
           echo 'submit book reviews. Sign up to gain access!</p>';
           return;
       }
   ?>
   ```

```
<form method="post" id="add_book_review" action="">

<!-- Nonce fields to verify visitor provenance -->
<?php wp_nonce_field( 'add_review_form', 'br_user_form' ); ?>

<table>
    <tr>
        <td>Book Title</td>
        <td><input type="text" name="book_title" /></td>
    </tr>
    <tr>
        <td>Book Author</td>
        <td><input type="text" name="book_author" /></td>
    </tr>
    <tr>
        <td>Review</td>
        <td><textarea name="book_review_text"></textarea></td>
    </tr>
    <tr>
      <td>Rating</td>
        <td><select name="book_review_rating">
        <?php
        // Generate all rating items in drop-down list
        for ( $rating = 5; $rating >= 1; $rating-- ) { ?>
            <option value="<?php echo $rating; ?>">
                        <?php echo $rating; ?> stars
        <?php } ?>
        </select>
        </td>
    </tr>
    <tr>
        <td>Book Type</td>
        <td>
        <?php
        // Retrieve array of all book types in system
        $book_types = get_terms( 'book_reviews_book_type',
                        array( 'orderby' => 'name',
                                'hide_empty' => 0 ) );

        // Check if book types were found
        if ( !is_wp_error( $book_types ) &&
            !empty( $book_types ) ) {

            echo '<select name="book_review_book_type">';

            // Display all book types
            foreach ( $book_types as $book_type ) {
                echo '<option value="' . $book_type->term_id;
```

```
                        echo '">' . $book_type->name . '</option>';
                    }

                    echo '</select>';
                } ?>
                </td>
            </tr>
        </table>

        <input type="submit" name="submit" value="Submit Review" />
        </form>
    <?php }
```

7. Save and close the plugin file.
8. **Activate** the Chapter 6 - Book Review User Submission plugin.
9. Create a new page and insert the newly created [submit-book-review] shortcode in the item's content.
10. Publish and view the page to see the form. If you submit the form, nothing will happen at the moment, since we have not implemented a processing function to parse and save the submitted data:

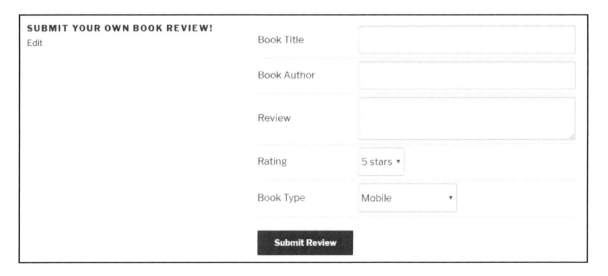

How it works...

As seen in the previous chapters, shortcodes are special blocks of text that can be easily added in any post or page to be replaced by content when they are found in pages visited by users. This recipe uses the `add_shortcode` function to declare a new shortcode that gets replaced with a review submission form.

The form itself is created using standard HTML and displays a number of text fields. It also uses a bit of PHP code to dynamically build the list of ratings and book types defined in the system. The form also includes a PHP call to the `wp_nonce_field` function, which was previously seen when creating plugin configuration panels, to add hidden fields that will be used as a security measure in the associated data processing function. Finally, the code checks to see whether the user visiting the page is logged in to the website and displays a short message instead of the submission form when the check is negative.

When submitted, the form action will send visitor content to the page where the book review form is displayed. This new content will be intercepted and processed in the code that will be added in the next recipe.

See also

- The *Creating a new simple shortcode* recipe in `Chapter 2`, *Plugin Framework Basics*

Saving user-submitted content in custom post types

When visitors click on the **Submit** button on the form created in the previous recipe, the target of the form is set to be the same page that is hosting the submission form. Since this page is not capable of handling form data, we must implement an action hook that intercepts this post data and sends it to a processing function that we will define. This recipe shows how to implement a function responsible for processing user input.

Getting ready

You should be running the final version of the Book Reviews plugin created in Chapter 4, *The Power of Custom Post Types,* and should have already followed the *Creating a client-side content submission form* recipe. Alternatively, you can get the files from the code bundle (Chapter 4/ch4-book-reviews/ch4-book-reviews-v11.php and Chapter 6/ch6-book-review-user-submission/ch6-book-review-user-submission-v1.php), and rename ch6-book-review-user-submission-v1.php to ch6-book-review-user-submission.php.

How to do it...

1. Navigate to the ch6-book-review-user-submission directory of the WordPress plugin folder of your development installation.

2. Open the file ch6-book-review-user-submission.php in a text editor.

3. Add the following line of code to register a function that will intercept user-submitted book reviews:

```
add_action( 'template_redirect',
           'ch6_brus_match_new_book_reviews' );
```

4. Add the following block of code to implement the ch6_brus_match_new_book_reviews function:

```
function ch6_brus_match_new_book_reviews( $template ) {
    if ( !empty( $_POST['ch6_brus_user_book_review'] ) ) {
        ch6_brus_process_user_book_reviews();
    } else {
        return $template;
    }
}
```

5. Insert the following code to provide an implementation for the ch6_brus_process_user_book_reviews:

```
function ch6_brus_process_user_book_reviews() {
    // Check that all required fields are present and non-empty
    if ( wp_verify_nonce( $_POST['br_user_form'],
                          'add_review_form' ) &&
        !empty( $_POST['book_title'] ) &&
        !empty( $_POST['book_author'] ) &&
        !empty( $_POST['book_review_text'] ) &&
```

```
            !empty( $_POST['book_review_book_type'] ) &&
            !empty( $_POST['book_review_rating'] ) ) ) {
        // Create array with received data
        $new_book_review_data = array(
            'post_status' => 'publish',
            'post_title' => $_POST['book_title'],
            'post_type' => 'book_reviews',
            'post_content' => $_POST['book_review_text'] );

        // Insert new post in website database
        // Store new post ID from return value in variable
        $new_book_review_id =
                        wp_insert_post( $new_book_review_data );

        // Store book author and rating
        add_post_meta( $new_book_review_id, 'book_author',
                    wp_kses( $_POST['book_author'], array() ) );
        add_post_meta( $new_book_review_id, 'book_rating',
                    (int) $_POST['book_review_rating'] );

        // Set book type on post
        if ( term_exists( $_POST['book_review_book_type'],
                        'book_reviews_book_type' ) ) {
            wp_set_post_terms( $new_book_review_id,
                            $_POST['book_review_book_type'],
                            'book_reviews_book_type' );
        }
        // Redirect browser to book review submission page
        $redirect_address =
            ( empty( $_POST['_wp_http_referer'] ) ? site_url() :
                            $_POST['_wp_http_referer'] );
        wp_redirect( add_query_arg( 'add_review_message', '1',
                    $redirect_address ) );
        exit;
    } else {
        // Display message if any required fields are missing
        $abort_message = 'Some fields were left empty. Please ';
        $abort_message .= 'go back and complete the form.';
        wp_die( $abort_message );
        exit;
    }
}
```

6. In the original `ch6_brus_book_review_form` function, add the following code after the `wp_nonce_field` function call:

```php
<?php if ( isset( $_GET['add_review_message'] )
        && $_GET['add_review_message'] == 1 ) { ?>

    <div style="margin: 8px;border: 1px solid #ddd;
        background-color: #ff0;">
    Thank for your submission!
    </div>

<?php } ?>

<!-- Post variable to indicate user-submitted items -->
<input type="hidden" name="ch6_brus_user_book_review" value="1" />
```

7. Save and close the plugin file.
8. Go back to the book review submission form and submit a review to send all the fields to the newly created processing function. After processing the new content, the script will return to the form, which will display a confirmation message.

How it works...

After submitting the book review form data to the page containing the book review submission form in the previous recipe, the first few steps of this recipe will be to assign a function to the `template_redirect` action hook to allow us to capture new book review content. This hook function is executed early in the WordPress processing sequence. If found, we will call the processing function that is defined in the rest of the recipe.

The first thing that is done in our processing function is to check whether the proper hidden data field is found as part of the post data, using the `wp_verify_nonce` function. If it is not present, indicating that someone may be trying to post data to the website without having visited the frontend form, it will display an error message.

When we are sure that our data storage script is being called legitimately, we will continue processing the actual data by first checking to see whether all the fields are present and are not empty. If that is not the case, we will display an error message, asking the user to go back and complete the form using the `wp_die` function.

If all the fields have been received correctly, the recipe continues to process the incoming data by preparing an array of information that includes the newly submitted title and review text, along with a post status and the `book_reviews` post type name. The resulting array is sent to the `wp_insert_post` function to store the information. As we can see, `wp_insert_post` only requires a single parameter that is fulfilled using the array that we just created. While we only define four elements of that array, many more are available, which can be seen by consulting the WordPress Codex (`https://developer.wordpress.org/reference/functions/wp_insert_post/`).

Now, calling `wp_insert_post` only takes care of storing some key data elements that belong in the post data. We must follow up this code with calls to `update_post_meta` and `wp_set_post_terms` to store the remaining user information to the website database.

Once all the information is stored, we use a combination of the `wp_redirect` and `add_query_arg` functions to send the user back to the page where he submitted a book review, while making sure that only one instance of the `add_review_message` variable is in the target address.

Last but not least, this recipe makes a small modification to the code that rendered the book review form to add a confirmation message that is shown to visitors when information is accepted by the plugin.

There's more...

In a world of spam bots and real people, who are set on creating bogus content on any website, setting new book reviews to be immediately visible on the website might not be wise.

Moderating user-submitted content

Instead of setting a status of publish for new post entries, we can use a value of draft to make the new entry visible only in the backend administration area. To give plugin users more flexibility, you could also give them a way to decide what method they prefer in a configuration panel.

See also

- The *Creating a client-side content submission form* recipe
- The *Processing and storing plugin configuration data* recipe in Chapter 3, *User Settings and Administration Pages*
- The *Adding a new section to the custom post type editor* recipe in Chapter 4, *The Power of Custom Post Types*

Sending email notifications upon new submissions

Just like WordPress sends out email notifications to the administrator when new comments are posted, sending out emails when visitors post new book reviews allows website managers to review new content as it comes in and decide if they approve it to be published online.

This recipe shows how to prepare email data and send it using the wp_mail function.

Getting ready

You should be running the final version of the Book Reviews plugin created in Chapter 4, *The Power of Custom Post Types,* and should have already followed the *Saving user-submitted data in custom post types* recipe (including changing the post status to draft as indicated in the *There's more...* section). Alternatively, you can get the resulting files from the code bundle (Chapter 4/ch4-book-reviews/ch4-book-reviews-v11.php and Chapter 6/ch6-book-review-user-submission/ch6-book-review-user-submission-v2.php) and rename ch6-book-review-user-submission-v2.php to ch6-book-review-user-submission.php. Finally, you should have access to a WordPress installation on a hosted web server, as emails are usually not sent when running it on a local installation. Be sure to have access to the email account associated with the website administrator to see the resulting email.

How to do it...

1. Navigate to the `ch6-book-review-user-submission` directory of the WordPress plugin folder of your development installation.
2. Open the file `ch6-book-review-user-submission.php` in a text editor.
3. Insert the following line of code to register a function to be called back when new posts are submitted:

```
add_action( 'wp_insert_post', 'ch6_brus_send_email', 10, 2 );
```

4. Insert the following block of code to implement the `ch6_brus_send_email` function:

```
function ch6_brus_send_email( $post_id, $post ) {

    // Only send emails for user-submitted book reviews
    if ( isset( $_POST['ch6_brus_user_book_review'] ) &&
        'book_reviews' == $post->post_type ) {

        $admin_mail = get_option( 'admin_email' );
        $headers = 'Content-type: text/html';
        $message = 'A user submitted a new book review to your ';
        $message .= 'WordPress website database.<br /><br />';
        $message .= 'Book Title: ' . $post->post_title ;
        $message .= '<br /><a href="';
        $message .= add_query_arg( array(
                                    'post_status' => 'draft',
                                    'post_type' => 'book_reviews' ),
                                    admin_url( 'edit.php' ) );
        $message .= '">Moderate new book reviews</a>';
        $email_title = htmlspecialchars_decode( get_bloginfo(),
            ENT_QUOTES ) . " - New Book Review Added: " .
            htmlspecialchars( $_POST['book_title'] );
        // Send email
        wp_mail( $admin_mail, $email_title, $message, $headers );
    }
}
```

5. Save and close the plugin file.

6. Go back to the book review submission form and submit a book review. An email will be sent to the address associated with the website administrator, containing some information from the new review:

How it works...

The `wp_mail` function can be used by any plugin to send out email messages. It takes five arguments to define all the elements of the outgoing message:

```
wp_mail( $destination, $subject, $message, [$headers],
         [$attachments] );
```

The first three arguments are required and respectively define the email address of the intended recipient, the title of the message, and its content. As we have seen in this recipe, the content is mainly specified using standard HTML syntax, while the target email address is retrieved from the options table using the `get_option` function. As for the title, it is built from a number of textual elements, such as the blog title and book review title, to create the final result.

The next parameter is optional and provides header information for the email, with the most important piece of information in that section being the character set. The last parameter can optionally be used to specify the path of one or more files to be sent as email attachments.

To make it easier for website administrators to manage new entries, part of the message body contains a link to the custom post management page of the WordPress website administration area to quickly display all the unapproved entries (set as draft items).

See also

- The *Creating a client-side content submission form* recipe

Implementing a CAPTCHA on user forms using an online service

A common security measure on website forms is to use CAPTCHA codes, where distorted letters or some other form of test is displayed to check that the person submitting data is not a spam robot. The form that we have been building to accept visitor-submitted book reviews could benefit from this type of technology to avoid weeding through unwanted entries.

This recipe shows how to integrate Google's reCAPTCHA service in our book review submission form. If you prefer using a local CAPTCHA script to avoid being dependent on an online service or to be sure that your form can be used in all countries, jump to the next recipe, titled *Using a local library to implement a CAPTCHA on user forms*.

Getting ready

You should be running the final version of the Book Reviews plugin created in Chapter 4, *The Power of Custom Post Types*, and should have already followed the *Sending email notifications upon new submissions* recipe. Alternatively, you can get the resulting files from the code bundle (Chapter 4/ch4-book-reviews/ch4-book-reviews-v11.php and Chapter 6/ch6-book-review-user-submission/ch6-book-review-user-submission-v3.php) and rename ch6-book-review-user-submission-v3.php to ch6-book-review-user-submission.php before starting the recipe.

This recipe requires having a Google account to be able to register for the reCAPTCHA service.

How to do it...

1. Visit the Google reCAPTCHA administrator website (`https://www.google.com/recaptcha/admin`) and log in if you are not already connected to Google services.

2. **Register a new website** by specifying a **Label** (for example, `Development website`) and setting the type of reCAPTCHA to **reCAPTCHA V2** using the radio selector.

3. Enter the domain name of the web server you will be using to test your code in the **Domains** field. If you are running a local development server, it is likely to be `localhost`.

4. Check the box to accept the terms of service, then click on **Register** to complete the new website creation process.

5. In the resulting page, take note of the website and secret keys that the service assigned to your test website.

6. Navigate to the `ch6-book-review-user-submission` directory of your plugin folder and open the file named `ch6-book-review-user-submission.php` in a code editor.

7. Insert the following line of code at the end of the file to register a function that will be called when WordPress prepares the list of scripts to be loaded on the website:

```
add_action( 'wp_enqueue_scripts', 'ch6_brus_recaptcha_script' );
```

8. Add the following block of code to provide an implementation for the `ch6_brus_recaptcha_script` function:

```
function ch6_brus_recaptcha_script() {
    wp_enqueue_script( 'google_recaptcha',
                        'https://www.google.com/recaptcha/api.js',
                        array(), false, true );
}
```

9. Locate the `ch6_brus_book_review_form` function in your code and add an extra row to the form table to display the CAPTCHA, replacing **[my-website-key]** with the website key obtained earlier from the reCAPTCHA service:

```
<tr>
    <td colspan="2">
        <div class="g-recaptcha"
             data-sitekey="[my-website-key]"></div>
    </td>
</tr>
```

10. Save your plugin and visit your book review submission page. You should now see the Google reCAPTCHA box appear in the form.

11. Visit the Google reCAPTCHA GitHub page (`https://github.com/google/reca ptcha`) and download the latest version of the repository to your computer.

12. Extract the repository contents and copy the resulting `src` folder to the `ch6-book-review-user-submission` directory.

13. Rename the `src` folder to `recaptcha`.

14. Locate the `ch6_brus_process_user_book_reviews` function in your code and add the following lines of code at the top of the function implementation, replacing `[my-secret-key]` with the secret key obtained earlier from the reCAPTCHA service:

```
require_once plugin_dir_path( __FILE__ ) .
             '/recaptcha/autoload.php';

$recaptcha = new \ReCaptcha\ReCaptcha( '[my-secret-key]' );
$resp = $recaptcha->verify( $_POST['g-recaptcha-response'],
                            $_SERVER['REMOTE_ADDR'] );

if ( ! $resp->isSuccess() ) {
```

```
                        // Display message if any required fields are missing
                        $abort_message = 'Missing or incorrect captcha.<br />';
                        $abort_message .= 'Please go back and try again.';
                        wp_die( $abort_message );
                        exit;
                } else {
```

15. Add an extra closing bracket (}) just before the end of the `ch6_brus_process_user_book_reviews` function to close out the `else` section of the code inserted in the previous step.

16. Save and close the code file.

17. Submit a new book review without checking the reCAPTCHA checkbox to see that it will not be accepted by the processing function.

How it works...

Google's reCAPTCHA service is a free service that can generate and display a CAPTCHA box in your form. It has evolved over time from asking users to decipher a scrambled message in an image to displaying addresses and other street signs and asking users to enter what they saw. In its latest incarnation, reCAPTCHA simply asks the user to check a box to indicate that they are not a robot and only asks more advanced questions if it suspects the visitor from being an automated system. When visitors check the box, a hidden field is populated with a validation code that gets sent to our data processing function along with the rest of the form data.

Adding a reCAPTCHA to our form is actually quite easy, only requiring us to load a Javascript script and add a line of code to our form that gets transformed into the service's trademark checkbox. Once the form data is posted, validating it is a bit more complex than the nonces we have used before since our plugin needs to communicate with Google's servers to check the validation code. Thankfully, Google offers an easy-to-use library to hide away much of this operation's complexity. If the reCAPTCHA code received is valid, the previously created data processing and storage code is executed as before. Otherwise, an error message is displayed to users. In addition to being easy to integrate, a benefit of using a third-party service is that most code updates are done by the service provider. You would still need to check for occasional updates to the PHP validation library, but that is only a small part of this service's functionality.

If you are planning to distribute a plugin that makes use of the reCAPTCHA service for more than one person or customer, it would not make sense to leave your own website and secret keys in the final plugin code, as we have done here. Instead, you should create an administration panel, as you learned to do in `Chapter 3`, *User Settings and Administration Pages*, so that users can enter their own keys and have them be used on the website.

It should be noted that while Google reCAPTCHA is one of the most popular CAPTCHA-generation services, it does not work for Chinese visitors at the time of writing and has not worked there for some time. If you are developing a plugin for a wide audience, you might want to consider supporting more than one CAPTCHA service or library to make sure that users have options, no matter where they or their audience resides. Read the next recipe for an example of using a local library to generate a CAPTCHA.

See also

- The *Sending email notifications upon new submissions* recipe
- The *Creating an administration page menu item in the Settings menu* recipe
- The *Rendering the admin page contents using HTML* recipe
- The *Processing and storing plugin configuration data* recipe
- The *Displaying a confirmation message when options are saved* recipe

Using a local library to implement a CAPTCHA on user forms

As discussed in the previous recipe, *Implementing a CAPTCHA on user forms using an online service*, adding a CAPTCHA to visitor-facing forms helps reduce unwanted submissions to a website. After seeing how to integrate an online third-party service, this recipe shows how to download and integrate a local PHP script to generate and validate CAPTCHA images locally.

Getting ready

You should be running the final version of the Book Reviews plugin created in `Chapter 4`, *The Power of Custom Post Types*, and should have already followed the *Sending email notifications upon new submissions* recipe. Alternatively, you can get the resulting files from the code bundle (`Chapter 4/ch4-book-reviews/ch4-book-reviews-v11.php` and `Chapter 6/ch6-book-review-user-submission/ch6-book-review-user-submission-v3.php`) and rename `ch6-book-review-user-submission-v3.php` to `ch6-book-review-user-submission.php` before starting the recipe.

The GD and FreeType libraries need to be installed and activated in your development web server's PHP installation to be able to generate a CAPTCHA image. Most of the pre-packaged local web servers listed in the *Installing a web server on your computer* recipe from `Chapter 1`, *Preparing a Local Development Environment*, come with these libraries activated. They are also commonly enabled on most hosted web servers, but you should still mention that they are required when distributing a plugin containing the following code to a larger audience.

How to do it...

1. Visit the Securimage website (`https://www.phpcaptcha.org/download/`) to download the latest version of their CAPTCHA library.
2. Open the resulting archive and extract the entire `securimage` directory to the `ch6-book-review-user-submission` folder of your plugin directory.
3. In the plugin directory, open the file named `ch6-book-review-user-submission.php` in a code editor.
4. Locate the `ch6_brus_book_review_form` function in your code and add an extra row to the form table to display the CAPTCHA:

```
<tr>
    <td>Enter text from image</td>
    <td>
        <img id="captcha"
            src="<?php echo plugins_url(
                        'securimage/securimage_show.php',
                        __FILE__ ); ?>"
            alt="CAPTCHA Image" />
        <input type="text" name="captcha_code"
            size="10" maxlength="6" />
        <a href="#"
            onclick="document.getElementById( 'captcha' ).src =
```

```
'<?php echo plugins_url(
            '/securimage/securimage_show.php',
            __FILE__ ); ?>?'
+ Math.random(); return false">[ Different Image ]</a>
    </td>
</tr>
```

5. Save your plugin and visit your book review submission page. You should now see the CAPTCHA image appear in the form:

6. Locate the `ch6_brus_process_user_book_reviews` function in your code and add the following lines of code at the top of the function implementation:

```
if ( PHP_SESSION_NONE == session_status() ) {
    session_start();
}

include_once plugin_dir_path( __FILE__ ) .
            '/securimage/securimage.php';
$securimage = new Securimage();

if ( false == $securimage->check( $_POST['captcha_code'] ) ) {
    // Display message if any required fields are missing
    $abort_message = 'Missing or incorrect captcha.<br />';
    $abort_message .= 'Please go back and try again.';
    wp_die( $abort_message );
    exit;
} else {
```

7. Add an extra closing bracket (}) just before the end of the `ch6_brus_process_user_book_reviews` function to close out the `else` section of the code inserted in the previous step.

8. Save and close the code file.

9. Submit a new book review without entering the CAPTCHA code to see that it will not be accepted by the processing function.

How it works...

The `Securimage` script is a simple tool that can generate and display a CAPTCHA image, as well as store the string that it generated using session data.

The recipe's code displays the CAPTCHA image by using a standard HTML `img` tag that uses one of the scripts in the `securimage` directory as the image path. On the data processing side, our code first starts by calling `session_start` to reconnect to the session that was initiated by the image generator to store the CAPTCHA code. It then proceeds to check whether the user CAPTCHA text matches the image that was displayed using the `check` method of the `securimage` class. Based on this result, we display an error message or continue verifying that the rest of the required data fields have been submitted correctly.

While there are many PHP scripts available to generate CAPTCHA images, this particular one was selected for this recipe since it is an open source script that uses the BSD license, which is compatible with WordPress licensing. This means that you would be able to distribute this script with your plugin on the official WordPress plugin repository.

 When using a third-party library in your plugin, you should regularly check whether that library has been updated by its author and incorporate new versions in your work as soon as possible to make sure that you don't expose your plugin to security vulnerabilities.

For more advanced content filtering methods, look up the Akismet API (`https://akismet.com/development/api/`).

See also

- The *Implementing a CAPTCHA on user forms using an online service* recipe

7
Customizing User Data

This chapter will show us how to augment the WordPress user editor and use the additional data associated with users through the following topics:

- Adding custom fields to the user editor
- Processing and storing user custom data
- Displaying new user data in the user list page
- Using custom user data in containing shortcode

Introduction

After learning how to customize the post editor and taxonomies with custom data fields, the next area that we will be making additions to is the user creation and edition tool. This type of addition can be used for many different purposes, including tracking when users have last visited a site or storing additional data on the types of services they are interested in. This chapter expands on the private content plugin that we started in Chapter 2, *Plugin Framework Basics* and Chapter 3, *User Settings and Administration Pages* in the recipes entitled *Creating a new enclosing shortcode* and *Storing stylesheet data in user settings*, by adding a second level of content protection that will restrict some posts or pages so that they are only available to paid users.

Adding custom fields to the user editor

Similar to the taxonomy editor, the user editor allows developers to add extra fields through action hooks and facilitates this task by using the same HTML structure, whether a new user is being created or an existing one is modified. This recipe shows how to assign a callback function to add a new section to the user editor.

Getting ready

To create a complete plugin with a stylesheet and administration panel, you should have already followed the *Storing stylesheet data in user settings* recipe in Chapter 3, *User Settings and Administration Pages*, to have a starting point for this recipe. Alternatively, you can get the resulting code (Chapter 3/ch2-private-item-text-edit-stylesheet/ch2-private-item-text.php) from the downloaded code bundle and rename ch2-private-item-text-edit-stylesheet to ch2-private-item-text.

It is also possible to just create a new empty plugin file and follow this chapter's recipes by making a folder called ch2-private-item-text in your plugin directory with a text file called ch2-private-item-text.php, and only adding a standard plugin header at the top.

How to do it...

1. Navigate to the ch2-private-item-text folder of the WordPress plugin directory of your development installation.
2. Open the ch2-private-item-text.php file in a text editor.
3. Add the following code snippet at the end of the file to declare a global variable and initialize the variable's content:

```
global $user_levels;
$user_levels = array( 'regular' => 'Regular', 'paid' => 'Paid' );
```

4. Add the following lines of code to register a function to be called when new users are added to the site through the administration interface or when users are edited:

```
add_action( 'user_new_form', 'ch2pit_show_user_profile' );
add_action( 'edit_user_profile', 'ch2pit_show_user_profile' );
```

5. Add the following block of code to provide an implementation for the ch2pit_show_user_profile function:

```
function ch2pit_show_user_profile( $user ) {
    global $user_levels;
    if ( 'add-new-user' == $user ) {
        $current_user_level = '';
    } elseif ( !empty( $user ) && isset( $user->data->ID ) ) {
        $user_id = $user->data->ID;
        $current_user_level =
```

```
                get_user_meta( $user_id, 'user_level', true );
    } ?>

    <h3>Site membership level</h3>
    <table class="form-table">
        <tr>
            <th>Level</th>
            <td><select name="user_level" id="user_level">
            <?php foreach( $user_levels as
                         $user_level_index => $user_level ) { ?>
            <option value="<?php echo $user_level_index; ?>"
            <?php selected( $current_user_level,
                          $user_level_index ); ?>>
            <?php echo $user_level; ?></option>
            <?php } ?>
            </select></td>
        </tr>
    </table>
<?php }
```

6. Save and close the plugin file.
7. Go to the **Plugins** section of the administration interface and make sure that the `Chapter 2 - Private Item Text` plugin is activated.
8. Select the **Add New User** menu item under the **Users** section to view the user creation page and see the new **Site membership level** section at the bottom of the form:

9. Edit one of the existing users on the site to see that the additional section is also displayed. If you try to save the user in either situation, the newly added field will not be saved until you perform the steps in the next recipe.

How it works...

The `user_new_form` and `edit_user_profile` action hooks allow developers to add content to the user editor when a new user is added to the site and when users are edited, respectively.

WordPress offers a third action hook called `show_user_profile`. Functions associated with that hook get called when users view their own profile. You should carefully consider whether or not it makes sense to register a function with this action hook, depending on the nature of your plugin and the additional information to be stored. That being said, if you do not register any function with this hook, as we are doing in this recipe, you will not see the additional fields created when viewing your own user profile on the site, even if you are the administrator. You will still be able to see paid content, since we will display it to users with administrator privileges.

Our callback function first checks to see whether it received a valid user through the `$user` parameter or whether a new user is being created. Based on the result, it retrieves the associated user level data by calling the `get_user_meta` function or initializes a blank variable. The syntax of `get_user_meta` follows the same structure as the `get_post_meta` and `get_term_meta` functions, with the first parameter being used to specify the user ID and the remaining fields indicating the field name to be retrieved and whether data should be returned as a single variable or an array:

```
get_user_meta( $user_id, $field_name, $single );
```

The rest of our callback functions are responsible for rendering a basic HTML select list and selecting one of the items in the list based on the current user membership level.

The only additional element that we put in place in this recipe is the declaration of an array of user membership levels as a `global` variable that we will be referencing in multiple functions in this chapter.

See also

- The *Storing stylesheet data in user settings* recipe

Processing and storing user custom data

As user profiles are created or updated, WordPress offers an easy way to register a callback to save custom user data in the site's database. This recipe shows how to use this action hook.

Getting ready

You should have already followed the *Adding custom fields to the user editor* recipe to have a starting point for this recipe and the resulting plugin should still be active in your development site. Alternatively, you can get the resulting code (`Chapter 7/ch2-private-item-text/ch2-private-item-text-v3.php`) from the downloaded code bundle, renaming it as `ch2-private-item-text.php`.

How to do it...

1. Navigate to the `ch2-private-item-text` folder of the WordPress plugin directory of your development installation.

2. Open the `ch2-private-item-text.php` file in a text editor.

3. Add the following lines of code at the end of the file to register functions to be called when user data is stored upon initial creation or when a user is updated:

```
add_action( 'user_register', 'ch2pit_save_user_data' );
add_action( 'profile_update', 'ch2pit_save_user_data' );
```

4. Add the following block of code to provide an implementation for the `ch2pit_save_user_data` function:

```
function ch2pit_save_user_data( $user_id ) {
    global $user_levels;
    if ( isset( $_POST['user_level'] ) &&
        !empty( $_POST['user_level'] ) &&
        array_key_exists( $_POST['user_level'],
                          $user_levels ) ) {
        update_user_meta( $user_id, 'user_level',
                          $_POST['user_level'] );
    } else {
        update_user_meta( $user_id, 'user_level', 'regular' );
    }
}
```

5. Save and close the plugin file.

6. Edit one of the existing users on the site or create a new one to see that the user level value is saved.

How it works...

Similarly to adding fields to the user editor, WordPress offers two different action hooks to register functions that will be called when a user is initially registered (`user_register`) and when a user profile is updated (`profile_update`). As you can see, we are registering the same callback function in both cases, where we check to see whether we received a value indicating the desired user level and use the `update_user_meta` function to save it. Similar to the post and term meta update functions, this function has three parameters to indicate the user ID that the information should be associated with, the name of the custom data field, and the value to be stored:

```
update_user_meta( $user_id, $field_name, $single );
```

As an additional precaution, we check to see whether the value we received is present in our global array of user levels using the PHP `array_key_exists` function.

The `else` branch of the `if` statement is put in place to set a default user level if the field is absent, which can happen if the site allows visitors to register for accounts by themselves.

Of course, this current process of classifying users as regular users or paid users is very manual, requiring site administrators to log in to the site's dashboard and update their status individually. A more elaborate solution could be to set the value of this field based on receiving a payment to the site using an online payment service.

See also

- The *Adding custom fields to the user editor* recipe

Displaying new user data in user list page

As new fields are added to user profiles, it can be very useful for site administrators to see this data in the site user list and be able to filter users to see only the ones that were assigned certain values. This recipe shows how to add extra columns to the user listing of the WordPress administration area and how to add a filter function to reduce the number of records shown.

Getting ready

You should have already followed the *Processing and storing user custom data* recipe to have a starting point for this recipe and the resulting plugin should still be active in your development site. Alternatively, you can get the resulting code (Chapter 7/ch2-private-item-text/ch2-private-item-text-v4.php) from the downloaded code bundle, renaming it ch2-private-item-text.php.

How to do it...

1. Navigate to the ch2-private-item-text folder of the WordPress plugin directory of your development installation.

2. Open the ch2-private-item-text.php file in a text editor.

3. Add the following line of code to register a function to be called when WordPress is preparing the list of columns to be displayed in the user listing page:

```
add_filter( 'manage_users_columns', 'ch2pit_add_user_columns' );
```

4. Add an implementation for the ch2pit_add_user_columns function with the following block of code:

```
function ch2pit_add_user_columns( $columns ) {
    $new_columns = array_slice( $columns, 0, 2, true ) +
                   array( 'level' => 'User Level' ) +
                   array_slice( $columns, 2, NULL, true );
    return $new_columns;
}
```

5. Add the following line of code to assign a function to be called when WordPress prepares the content of each column as it displays a list of all the users:

```
add_filter( 'manage_users_custom_column',
            'ch2pit_display_user_columns_data', 10, 3 );
```

6. Provide an implementation for the `ch2pit_display_user_columns_data` function by inserting the following code section:

```
function ch2pit_display_user_columns_data( $val, $column_name,
                                           $user_id ) {
    global $user_levels;
    if ( 'level' == $column_name ) {
        $current_user_level = get_user_meta( $user_id,
                                    'user_level', true );
        if ( !empty( $current_user_level ) ) {
            $val = $user_levels[$current_user_level];
        }
    }
    return $val;
}
```

7. Add the following code snippet to register a function to be called when WordPress prepares the list of quick actions that can be performed by administrators on the user listing page:

```
add_action( 'restrict_manage_users', 'ch2pit_add_user_filter' );
```

8. Add this code section to provide a body for the `ch2pit_add_user_filter` function:

```
function ch2pit_add_user_filter() {
    global $user_levels;
    $filter_value = '';
    if ( isset( $_GET['user_level'] ) ) {
        $filter_value = $_GET['user_level'];
    } ?>

    <select name="user_level" class="user_level"
            style="float:none;">
    <option value="">No filter</option>
    <?php foreach( $user_levels as
                    $user_level_index => $user_level ) { ?>
        <option value="<?php echo $user_level_index; ?>"
        <?php selected( $filter_value, $user_level_index ); ?>>
        <?php echo $user_level; ?></option>
    <?php } ?>
```

```
            <input type="submit" class="button" value="Filter">
    <?php }
```

9. Add the following line of code to register a function to be called when WordPress is rendering the footer of the administration pages:

```
add_action( 'admin_footer', 'ch2pit_user_filter_js' );
```

10. Provide an implementation for the `ch2pit_user_filter_js` function by adding the following code section:

```
function ch2pit_user_filter_js() {
    global $current_screen;
    if ( 'users' != $current_screen->id ) {
        return;
    } ?>

    <script type="text/javascript">
        jQuery( document ).ready( function() {
            jQuery( '.user_level' ).first().change( function() {
                jQuery( '.user_level' ).
                    last().val( jQuery( this ).val() );
            });

            jQuery( '.user_level' ).last().change( function() {
                jQuery( '.user_level' ).
                    first().val( jQuery( this ).val() );
            });
        });
    </script>
    <?php }
```

11. Add this line of code to register a function that will be executed when WordPress is preparing the query to retrieve the list of users from the database:

```
add_filter( 'pre_get_users', 'ch2pit_filter_users' );
```

12. Insert the following block of code to define the `ch2pit_filter_users` function:

```
function ch2pit_filter_users( $query ) {
    global $pagenow;
    global $user_levels;

    if ( is_admin() && 'users.php' == $pagenow &&
        isset( $_GET['user_level'] ) ) {
        $filter_value = $_GET['user_level'];
        if ( !empty( $filter_value ) &&
            array_key_exists( $_GET['user_level'],
                              $user_levels ) ) {
            $query->set( 'meta_key', 'user_level' );
            $query->set( 'meta_query', array(
                         array( 'key' => 'user_level',
                                'value' => $filter_value ) ) );
        }
    }
}
```

13. Save and close the plugin file.

14. Visit the **Users** section of the administration interface to see the new **User Level** column.

15. Use the filter drop-down list and click on **Filter** to limit the number of records displayed.

How it works...

The first code section in this recipe is a filter function that gets a list of all columns that the system intends on displaying in the users section of the administration interface. While we could have just added our new entry at the end of the array, similar to what we did in the *Displaying additional columns in the custom post list page* recipe in `Chapter 4`, *The Power of Custom Post Types*, we take a more advanced approach in this recipe; we use the PHP `array_slice` function to split the columns array into two sections and insert our new column name between the existing items.

We continue this recipe by providing a function that displays the user level assigned to each user. This is done by simply retrieving the information based on the current user ID and returning the data to be displayed. It should be noted that the user management page takes an approach that is slightly different from the post and pages custom column content, since it uses a filter function where we return data instead of using an action hook that directly sends content to the browser.

The next code section is responsible for rendering a drop-down list of user levels that can be used to filter the user list; this is done by using standard HTML and code to loop through the list of user levels and display them. Unfortunately, WordPress complicates things by calling our function twice, before and after listing users, resulting in two drop-down lists on the same page with no way to differentiate them. To avoid having issues with the two drop-down lists being set to different values and sending these conflicting values to our filtering code, the next function places Javascript code in the page footer of all the user listing pages. This allows us to synchronize either drop-down list with the other's value when the user interacts with them.

Our last step consists of modifying the user query if we find a filtering argument in the page URL when displaying the user listing. If an argument is found and the page is the correct one, we will check whether the value is part of our user levels array and then add it to the system's current query variables.

See also

- The *Processing and storing user custom data* recipe

Using custom user data in containing shortcode

Now that we have additional data stored in user profiles and have facilitated the viewing of this information in the administration pages, the only missing component to achieve our goal of restricting some site content to paid users is to introduce a new enclosing shortcode that will check a user's level before displaying content. The recipe will show how to create this new shortcode.

Getting ready

You should have already followed the *Display new user data in user list page* recipe to have a starting point for this recipe and the resulting plugin should still be active in your development site. Alternatively, you can get the resulting code (`Chapter 7/ch2-private-item-text/ch2-private-item-text-v5.php`) from the `Chapter 7, *Customizing User Data* section of the downloaded code bundle, renaming it as `ch2-private-item-text.php`.

How to do it...

1. Navigate to the `ch2-private-item-text` folder of the WordPress plugin directory of your development installation.
2. Open the `ch2-private-item-text.php` file in a text editor.
3. Add the following line of code to define a new shortcode and define the function to be called when it is used:

```
add_shortcode( 'paid', 'ch2pit_paid_shortcode' );
```

4. Provide an implementation for `ch2pit_paid_shortcode` with the following code section:

```
function ch2pit_paid_shortcode( $atts, $content = null ) {
    if ( is_user_logged_in() ) {
        $current_user = wp_get_current_user();
        $current_user_level = get_user_meta( $current_user->ID,
                                        'user_level', true );
        if ( 'paid' == $current_user_level ||
            current_user_can( 'activate_plugins' ) ) {
            return '<div class="paid">' . $content . '</div>';
```

```
            }
        }
        $output = '<div class="register">';
        $output .= 'You need to be a paid member to access ';
        $output .= 'this content.</div>';
        return $output;
    }
```

5. Save and close the plugin file.
6. Create a new post and wrap some or all of the content with the `[paid]` and `[/paid]` tags. View the page as an administrator, a visitor who is not logged in, a registered regular user, and a registered paid user to validate that the content is only displayed in the first and last cases.

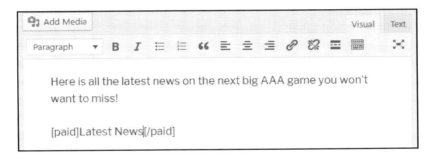

How it works...

Similar to the `[private]` shortcode that we created back in the *Creating a new enclosing shortcode* recipe in Chapter 2, *Plugin Framework Basics*, the new `[paid]` shortcode that this recipe puts in place can be used by content creators to identify one or more sections of a post or page that can only be viewed by users whose user level is set as a paid member.

To do this, our shortcode implementation first checks whether the visitor is logged in. If that is the case, it further validates the user by asking WordPress to provide data on the current user, then uses the user ID to retrieve the `user_level` metadata that we stored in the previous recipes in this chapter. Alternatively, it checks if the user is a site administrator by using the `current_user_can` WordPress function and specifying `'activate_plugins'` as the argument, since only administrators can perform this action. If all of these conditions are met, the enclosed post content will be displayed. Otherwise, a message will be shown to indicate that users must be paid members to see this content.

See also

- The *Display new user data in user list page* recipe

8
Creating Custom MySQL Database Tables

In this chapter, we will cover the following topics around the creation of custom database tables:

- Creating new database tables
- Deleting custom tables on plugin removal
- Updating custom table structure on plugin upgrade
- Displaying custom table data on an admin page
- Inserting and updating records in custom tables
- Deleting records from custom tables
- Displaying custom database table data in shortcodes
- Implementing a search function to retrieve custom table data
- Importing data from a user file into custom tables

Introduction

As seen in Chapter 4, *The Power of Custom Post Types*, custom post types provide a very powerful and easy way to create and manage custom content in a WordPress installation. That being said, if the new items that you wish to create do not benefit from having access to the built-in text editor and have a large amount of data fields that need to be stored in the system, storing them using custom post types can actually become cumbersome. More specifically, each custom field requires a separate function call to be associated with a custom post. Also, custom fields have limited functionality, since they store all their information in simple text fields, making it difficult to perform ordered queries based on special data types, such as dates.

An alternative solution to manage custom content is to create new tables in the website's database and offer a custom interface to manage these new items.

While working directly with the website database might sound like a tall order, and should really only be done if custom post types don't work as desired, WordPress actually offers a utility class that makes it very easy to create new database tables, store information in these new structures, and perform data retrieval queries. While having a basic level of **Structured Query Language** (**SQL**) knowledge will help understand all of the recipes in this chapter while we create a bug tracking system, each recipe thoroughly explains how each command works to produce the end result.

Creating new database tables

The first step in the creation of custom data elements to be stored in a custom database table is to create the table itself. This is done by preparing a standard SQL command that specifies the name of the table and its desired structure and then getting WordPress to execute it on the website's database.

This recipe shows how to prepare and execute a query that creates a table to hold bug reports.

Getting ready

You should have access to a WordPress development environment, either on your local computer or on a remote server, where you will be able to load your new plugin files.

How to do it...

1. Navigate to the WordPress plugin directory of your development installation.
2. Create a new directory called `ch8-bug-tracker`.
3. Navigate to the directory and create a text file called `ch8-bug-tracker.php`.
4. Open the new file in a code editor and add an appropriate header at the top of the plugin file, naming the plugin `Chapter 8 - Bug Tracker`.
5. Add the following line of code to register a function to be called on plugin activation:

```
register_activation_hook( __FILE__, 'ch8bt_activation' );
```

6. Add the following code segment to provide an implementation for the `ch8bt_activation` function:

```
function ch8bt_activation() {
    // Get access to global database access class
    global $wpdb;
    // Create table on main blog in network mode or single blog
    ch8bt_create_table( $wpdb->get_blog_prefix() );
}
```

7. Insert the following code to provide an implementation for the `ch8bt_create_table` function responsible for the actual table creation:

```
function ch8bt_create_table( $prefix ) {
    // Prepare SQL query to create database table
    // using function parameter

    $creation_query = 'CREATE TABLE IF NOT EXISTS ' .
                      $prefix . 'ch8_bug_data (
                      `bug_id` int(20) NOT NULL AUTO_INCREMENT,
                      `bug_description` text,
                      `bug_version` varchar(10) DEFAULT NULL,
                      `bug_report_date` date DEFAULT NULL,
                      `bug_status` int(3) NOT NULL DEFAULT 0,
                      PRIMARY KEY (`bug_id`)
                      );';
    global $wpdb;
    $wpdb->query( $creation_query );
}
```

8. Save and close the plugin file.

9. Navigate to the **Plugins** management page and **Activate** the `Chapter 8 - Bug Tracker` plugin.

10. Using `phpMyAdmin`, connect to your MySQL database to see that a new table was created when the plugin was activated:

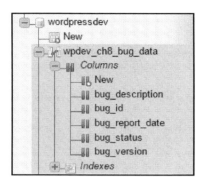

How it works...

Similar to the creation of configuration options that we covered back in the *Creating default user settings on plugin initialization* recipe from `Chapter 3`, *User Settings and Administration Pages*, custom database tables are typically created when a plugin is activated in a WordPress installation. By using the activation hook, we register code to be executed when the plugin is first activated and when upgrades are performed. When the callback is executed, we will have our first encounter with the global `wpdb` class. This utility class is instantiated by WordPress and gives us access to a number of methods that can be used to interact with the underlying MySQL website database, as well as to help prevent data-related security risks. These methods vary in complexity, ranging from simple calls that will quickly insert or update records to more complex member functions that require knowledge of SQL commands to produce the expected results.

Before making the call to create the actual table, the activation function makes a call to the `get_blog_prefix` method of the `wpdb` class to retrieve the table prefix associated with the website (set to `wp_` in a default installation). On retrieval, this prefix is immediately sent to the `ch8bt_create_table` function to build an SQL command designed to create a new table.

While the SQL command has multiple lines, we can see that it is actually quite simple if we break it down into small sections. The first line of the command specifies that a new table named `<prefix>ch8_bug_data` should be created if it does not exist already on the server. If the creation takes place, the following five lines specify the name and data type for each field, along with information indicating whether the field can contain a NULL value and what the default value should be in some cases. There is also a special command associated with the `bug_id` field, called the AUTO_INCREMENT command, which tells the system to automatically populate this field with auto-incrementing values when new records are added to the table. Last, but not least, the last line of the code indicates that the primary key for the table is the `bug_id` field.

Once the query is ready, it is stored in a variable and executed by calling the `query` method of the `wpdb` object. This method executes any SQL command on the website database and returns a numeric value indicating how many rows were affected by the query.

There's more...

While the previous code is relatively manageable, things might get a bit more complicated when dealing with a larger number of fields or with network WordPress installation.

Using phpMyAdmin to simplify code creation

Instead of writing the table creation code from scratch, the `phpMyAdmin` database management tool can come in handy to prepare this code:

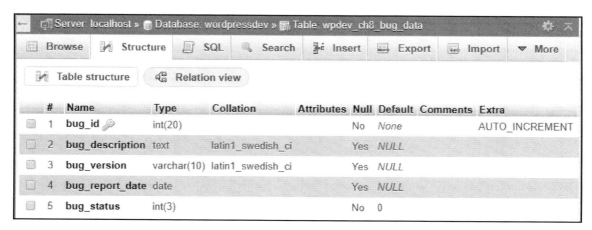

For example, to create the table that was used in this recipe, follow these steps:

1. Select the `wordpressdev` database in `phpMyAdmin`.
2. Under the Create table section, enter `wpdev_ch8_bug_data` in the **Name** field and the number 5 as Number of fields.
3. Click on the **Go** button.
4. In the table creation grid that is displayed, set the name of each **Field** based on the Column names listed in the previous screenshot.
5. Set the **Type** of each Field based on the Type column in the previous screenshot.
6. For items that have a value in parentheses next to their Type, use the numeric value to indicate the **Length/Values** of these items.
7. Set the **Default** value for each field based on the previous screenshot. You can select **NULL** from the drop-down list for the items that have a **NULL** default. For items that have a specific value, select **As defined:** in the drop-down and indicate the value in the adjacent field.
8. For items that are allowed to have a **NULL** value (shown with a Yes in the previous screenshot), make sure that the **Null** box is checked.

9. Select **PRIMARY** under the Index drop-down list for the `bug_id` field to indicate that it will be the primary key for the table. Then, click on **Go** in the index creation pop-up dialog that appears.
10. Check the **A_I** box for the **bug_id** field to indicate that it should auto-increment when new values are inserted in the table.
11. Click on the **Save** button to complete the table creation process.

At this time, phpMyAdmin will create the table on the server. To access the SQL command used to create the table, click on the **Export** tab and click on **Go** to download a text file containing the SQL code. While the export file will contain some extra information, the important section is the actual CREATE TABLE segment that, as you will see, looks very similar to the code written in this recipe.

Create tables in network installation

One of WordPress's many strengths is the ability to create and manage multiple websites from a single installation. In these situations, each site has its own set of tables in the MySQL database. Therefore, when preparing a plugin that creates custom tables and may be used in network installations, extra code must be put in place to create the new tables under each site's structure.

The first changes are done in the `ch8bt_activation` function, where we check whether we are dealing with a multisite installation. If that is the case, we will cycle through each existing site and make a call to create the new table, as we saw in the main recipe code:

```
function ch8bt_activation() {
    // Get access to global database access class
    global $wpdb;

    // Check to see if WordPress installation is a network
    if ( is_multisite() ) {
        // If it is, cycle through all blogs, switch to them
        // and call function to create plugin table
        if ( !empty( $_GET['networkwide'] ) ) {
            $start_blog = $wpdb->blogid;
            $blog_list =
                $wpdb->get_col( 'SELECT blog_id FROM ' . $wpdb->blogs );
            foreach ( $blog_list as $blog ) {
                switch_to_blog( $blog );
                // Send blog table prefix to creation function
                ch8bt_create_table( $wpdb->get_blog_prefix() );
            }
            switch_to_blog( $start_blog );
```

```
            return;
        }
    }

    // Create table on main blog in network mode or single blog
    ch8bt_create_table( $wpdb->get_blog_prefix() );
}
```

While this will handle creating custom tables in all the existing network sites when the plugin is activated, additional code needs to be put in place to create the additional table when new sites are created:

```
// Register function to be called when new blogs are added
// to a network site
add_action( 'wpmu_new_blog', 'ch8bt_new_network_site' );

function ch8bt_new_network_site( $blog_id ) {
    global $wpdb;

    // Check if this plugin is active when new blog is created
    // Include plugin functions if it is
    if ( !function_exists( 'is_plugin_active_for_network' ) ) {
        require_once( ABSPATH . '/wp-admin/includes/plugin.php' );
    }

    // Select current blog, create new table and switch back
    if ( is_plugin_active_for_network( plugin_basename( __FILE__ ) ) ) {
        $start_blog = $wpdb->blogid;
        switch_to_blog( $blog_id );

        // Send blog table prefix to table creation function
        ch8bt_create_table( $wpdb->get_blog_prefix() );
        switch_to_blog( $start_blog );
    }
}
```

The `ch8bt_create_table` function itself does not require any modifications, since it was already designed to receive a table prefix from other functions and use it to build a query.

Deleting custom tables on plugin removal

It is always a good practice for plugins to provide an uninstallation procedure to remove content that they added to a website's database or filesystem. When dealing with custom database tables, all records should be dropped along with the table itself when a website administrator decides to delete a plugin.

This recipe shows how to implement a data removal script to delete the bug storage table that was created in the previous recipe.

Getting ready

You should have already followed the *Creating new database tables* recipe to have an existing table to remove. Alternatively, you can get the resulting code (`Chapter 8/ch8-bug-tracker/ch8-bug-tracker-v1-1.php`) from the code bundle and rename the file as `ch8-bug-tracker.php`.

How to do it...

1. Navigate to the WordPress plugin directory of your development installation.
2. Create a text file called `uninstall.php` in the `ch8-bug-tracker` directory and open it in a code editor.
3. Start the new script with the standard `<?php` opening tags.
4. Implement a new function called `ch8bt_drop_table` by adding this code to the file:

```
function ch8bt_drop_table( $prefix ) {
    global $wpdb;
    $wpdb->query( 'DROP TABLE ' . $prefix . 'ch8_bug_data' );
}
```

5. Add the following code to perform the deletion of tables created to store bugs from a single or network WordPress installation:

```
// Check that file was called from WordPress admin
if( !defined( 'WP_UNINSTALL_PLUGIN' ) ) {
    exit();
}

global $wpdb;

// Check if site is configured for network installation
if ( is_multisite() ) {
    if ( !empty( $_GET['networkwide'] ) ) {
        // Get blog list and cycle through all blogs
        $start_blog = $wpdb->blogid;
        $blog_list = $wpdb->get_col( 'SELECT blog_id FROM ' .
                                          $wpdb->blogs );
        foreach ( $blog_list as $blog ) {
            switch_to_blog( $blog );
            // Call function to delete bug table with prefix
            ch8bt_drop_table( $wpdb->get_blog_prefix() );
        }
        switch_to_blog( $start_blog );
        return;
    }
}

ch8bt_drop_table( $wpdb->prefix );
```

6. Save and close the code file.
7. Navigate to the **Plugins** management page and **Deactivate** the **Chapter 8 - Bug Tracker** plugin.
8. Make a copy of the entire plugin directory before performing the next step, to avoid deleting all of your work.
9. Click on the plugin's **Delete** link and then click **OK** in the dialog that asks for confirmation before deleting the plugin and its data.
10. Using `phpMyAdmin`, connect to your MySQL database to verify that the bug data table has been deleted.

How it works...

As we saw in `Chapter 2`, *Plugin Framework Basics*, all of the code contained in a file called `uninstall.php` gets executed when a plugin is deleted. In this case, our code's main purpose is to run a query against the website database to remove the bug table.

Before doing so, the first few lines of the file check for the presence of a variable (`WP_UNINSTALL_PLUGIN`) to confirm that the code has been called as part of the plugin deletion process and not by an external user.

Once the legitimacy of the execution has been confirmed, the code that runs is similar to the table creation code, where we first get access to the WordPress database management class, followed by a check to see whether the WordPress installation is a single site or a network installation. In the first case, we make a single call to the `ch8bt_drop_table` function to drop the bug table, while we make multiple calls to that function for every existing site under a network environment.

The query to remove the table is actually quite simple, making a call to the `query` method of the `wpdb` class to execute a `DROP TABLE` SQL command.

See also

- The *Creating new database tables* recipe

Updating custom table structure on plugin upgrade

Over the lifetime of a plugin, as it gets expanded to provide additional functionality, there may be a need to store more data than was originally intended in custom database tables. As you may know, WordPress itself makes regular changes to its own database structure during the upgrade process to store new information. To do this, it uses a simple function called `dbDelta`, which we can also access from our plugin's code.

This recipe shows how to alter the previous table creation code to load the WordPress upgrade API and use the database upgrade function to add an extra field to the existing bug storage table.

Getting ready

You should have already followed the *Creating new database tables* recipe to have the creation code to modify. Alternatively, you can get the resulting code (Chapter 8/ch8-bug-tracker/ch8-bug-tracker-v1-1.php) from the code bundle and rename the file ch8-bug-tracker.php.

How to do it...

1. Navigate to the WordPress plugin directory of your development installation.
2. Navigate to the ch8-bug-tracker directory and edit ch8-bug-tracker.php.
3. Locate the ch8bt_create_table function.
4. Remove the IF NOT EXISTS text on the first line of the table creation query.
5. Add an extra line to the table creation code to add a field to hold the bug title, shown as follows in bold:

```
$creation_query = 'CREATE TABLE ' . $prefix .
                  'ch8_bug_data (
                  `bug_id` int(20) NOT NULL AUTO_INCREMENT,
                  `bug_description` text,
                  `bug_version` varchar(10) DEFAULT NULL,
                  `bug_report_date` date DEFAULT NULL,
                  `bug_status` int(3) NOT NULL DEFAULT 0,
                  `bug_title` VARCHAR( 128 ) NULL,
                  PRIMARY KEY (`bug_id`)
                  );';
```

6. Locate the following lines of code:

```
global $wpdb;
wpdb->query( $creation_query );
```

They should be replaced with the following lines of code:

```
require_once( ABSPATH . 'wp-admin/includes/upgrade.php' );
dbDelta( $creation_query );
```

7. Save and close the plugin file.
8. Navigate to the **Plugins** management page.
9. **Deactivate** and re-**Activate** the **Chapter 8 - Bug Tracker** plugin.

10. Using phpMyAdmin, connect to your MySQL database to see that the new `bug_title` field has been added to the bug storage table:

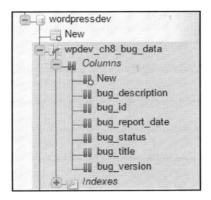

How it works...

The `dbDelta` function is part of the utility functions that WordPress calls when performing version upgrades. When called, it parses the table creation SQL command that it receives and figures out the difference between the table structure that it describes and the current table, if the table exists. Once that difference has been established, it performs the necessary changes to align the two structures.

If both the structures are identical, it leaves the table as it is. With this approach in place, any changes to the structure can simply be implemented by altering the table creation query. As such, the `dbDelta` function can actually be used from the first version of a plugin to ensure an easy upgrade path.

See also

- The *Creating new database tables* recipe

Displaying custom table data on an admin page

After creating one or more custom database tables to store data, the next step in the creation of a custom item management system is to build an interface to populate them. While custom post types have a very organized structure to edit entries, creating an interface for custom tables is much more similar to creating plugin configuration panels, as we saw in Chapter 3, *User Settings and Administration Pages*.

This recipe shows how to create an interface that will display a list of bugs stored in the system, provide a link to create new entries, and offer a way to edit existing entries.

Getting ready

You should have already followed the *Updating custom table structure on plugin upgrade* recipe to have a custom table in place with the required structure. Alternatively, you can get the resulting code (Chapter 8/ch8-bug-tracker/ch8-bug-tracker-v2.php) from the code bundle and rename the file ch8-bug-tracker.php.

How to do it...

1. Navigate to the WordPress plugin directory of your development installation.
2. Navigate to the ch8-bug-tracker directory and edit ch8-bug-tracker.php.
3. Insert the following line of code to register a function to be called when the administration menu is being built:

```
add_action( 'admin_menu', 'ch8bt_settings_menu' );
```

4. Add the following code to provide an implementation for the ch8bt_settings_menu function:

```
function ch8bt_settings_menu() {
    add_options_page( 'Bug Tracker Data Management',
                      'Bug Tracker',
                      'manage_options', 'ch8bt-bug-tracker',
                      'ch8bt_config_page' );
}
```

5. Append the following block of code to provide an implementation for the ch8bt_config_page function responsible to render the configuration page:

```php
function ch8bt_config_page() {
    global $wpdb;
    ?>

    <!-- Top-level menu -->
    <div id="ch8bt-general" class="wrap">
    <h2>Bug Tracker <a class="add-new-h2" href="<?php echo
        add_query_arg( array( 'page' => 'ch8bt-bug-tracker',
                              'id' => 'new' ),
                    admin_url('options-general.php') ); ?>">
    Add New Bug</a></h2>
    <!-- Display bug list if no parameter sent in URL -->
    <?php if ( empty( $_GET['id'] ) ) {
        $bug_query = 'select * from ' . $wpdb->get_blog_prefix();
        $bug_query .= 'ch8_bug_data ORDER by bug_report_date DESC';
        $bug_items = $wpdb->get_results( $bug_query, ARRAY_A );
    ?>

    <h3>Manage Bug Entries</h3>

    <table class="wp-list-table widefat fixed">
    <thead><tr><th style="width: 80px">ID</th>
    <th style="width: 300px">Title</th>
    <th>Version</th></tr></thead>

    <?php
        // Display bugs if query returned results
        if ( $bug_items ) {
            foreach ( $bug_items as $bug_item ) {
                echo '<tr style="background: #FFF">';
                echo '<td>' . $bug_item['bug_id'] . '</td>';
                echo '<td><a href="';
                echo add_query_arg( array(
                    'page' => 'ch8bt-bug-tracker',
                    'id' => $bug_item['bug_id'] ),
                    admin_url( 'options-general.php' ) );
                echo '">' . $bug_item['bug_title'] . '</a></td>';
                echo '<td>' . $bug_item['bug_version'];
                echo '</td></tr>';
            }
        } else {
            echo '<tr style="background: #FFF">';
            echo '<td colspan="3">No Bug Found</td></tr>';
        }
    ?>
```

```
        </table><br />
        <?php } ?>
        </div>
    <?php }
```

6. Save and close the plugin file.
7. Navigate to the new **Bug Tracker** item under the administration page's **Settings** menu to see the newly created page, showing that there are currently no bugs stored in the system:

How it works...

The first few steps of the recipe use functions that were previously covered in Chapter 3, *User Settings and Administration Pages*, to register a callback that will add a menu to the Settings section of the admin menu. When the new menu page is visited, the ch8bt_config_page function is called to render the page contents, using a mix of HTML and PHP code.

After rendering the page title, along with a link that will be used to create new bugs, the page display code checks to see whether the page address contains a variable called id. This ID will be used in subsequent recipes to indicate whether the user wants to create or edit bugs. It will not be set when a visitor clicks on the **Bug Tracker** menu item, resulting in the current recipe code getting called.

The next section uses the get_results method of the wpdb database management class to retrieve information from the database. In this call, the first parameter is an SQL query, whereas the second argument indicates the desired format to be used to return data. While we specified that we want an associative array in this case, other options are to return a numerically indexed array (ARRAY_N), an object (OBJECT), or an array of objects (OBJECT_K).

The SELECT * command in the query indicates that we want all the fields in the table to be returned, while the ORDER command specifies the field that should be used to order results and the order direction (ASC or DESC).

Once the get_results method has been executed, we will check to see whether any data was retrieved from the database, and proceed to perform a foreach loop through all the records to display them in a standard HTML table if data is found. If no records are returned by the query, we will display a short message indicating that no bugs were found.

See also

- The *Creating an administration page menu item in the Settings menu* recipe in Chapter 3, *User Settings and Administration Pages*
- The *Rendering the admin page contents using HTML* recipe in Chapter 3, *User Settings and Administration Pages*

Inserting and updating records in custom tables

Now that we have a basic infrastructure in place to display existing bugs, the next logical step is to create a form that will be used to insert and update records in a custom table.

This recipe shows how to add a form to manage bugs when users select an entry in the bug tracking list or indicate that they want to create a new entry by using the appropriate link.

Getting ready

You should have already followed the *Displaying custom table data in an admin page* recipe to have an existing framework in place. Alternatively, you can get the resulting code (Chapter 8/ch8-bug-tracker/ch8-bug-tracker-v3.php) from the code bundle and rename the file ch8-bug-tracker.php.

How to do it...

1. Navigate to the WordPress plugin directory of your development installation.
2. Navigate to the `ch8-bug-tracker` directory and edit `ch8-bug-tracker.php`.
3. Find the `ch8bt_config_page` function and locate the bracket that closes out the `if` statement (`<?php } ?>`) situated toward the end of its body.
4. Insert the following code block right before the closing bracket from the `if` statement identified in the previous step:

```php
<?php } elseif ( isset( $_GET['id'] ) &&
                ( 'new' == $_GET['id'] ||
                  is_numeric( $_GET['id'] ) ) ) {
    $bug_id = intval( $_GET['id'] );
    $mode = 'new';
    // Query database if numeric id is present
    if ( $bug_id > 0 ) {
        $bug_query = 'select * from ' . $wpdb->get_blog_prefix();
        $bug_query .= 'ch8_bug_data where bug_id = %d';

        $bug_data =
            $wpdb->get_row( $wpdb->prepare( $bug_query, $bug_id ),
                            ARRAY_A );

        // Set variable to indicate page mode
        if ( $bug_data ) {
            $mode = 'edit';
        }
    }

    if ( 'new' == $mode ) {
        $bug_data = array(
            'bug_title' => '', 'bug_description' => '',
            'bug_version' => '', 'bug_status' => ''
        );
    }

    // Display title based on current mode
    if ( 'new' == $mode ) {
        echo '<h3>Add New Bug</h3>';
    } elseif ( 'edit' == $mode ) {
        echo '<h3>Edit Bug #' . $bug_data['bug_id'] . ' - ';
        echo $bug_data['bug_title'] . '</h3>';
    }
    ?>
    <form method="post"
```

```
            action="<?php echo admin_url( 'admin-post.php' ); ?>">
    <input type="hidden" name="action" value="save_ch8bt_bug" />
    <input type="hidden" name="bug_id"
            value="<?php echo $bug_id; ?>" />

    <!-- Adding security through hidden referrer field -->
    <?php wp_nonce_field( 'ch8bt_add_edit' ); ?>

    <!-- Display bug editing form -->
    <table>
        <tr>
            <td style="width: 150px">Title</td>
            <td><input type="text" name="bug_title" size="60"
                        value="<?php echo esc_html(
                        $bug_data['bug_title'] ); ?>"/></td>
        </tr>
        <tr>
            <td>Description</td>
            <td><textarea name="bug_description"
            cols="60"><?php echo
esc_textarea( $bug_data['bug_description'] ); ?></textarea></td>
        </tr>
        <tr>
            <td>Version</td>
            <td><input type="text" name="bug_version"
                        value="<?php echo esc_html(
                        $bug_data['bug_version'] ); ?>" /></td>
        </tr>
        <tr>
            <td>Status</td>
            <td>
                <select name="bug_status">
                <?php
                // Display drop-down list of bug statuses
                $bug_statuses = array( 0 => 'Open', 1 => 'Closed',
                                        2 => 'Not-a-Bug' );
                foreach( $bug_statuses as $status_id => $status ) {
                    // Add selected tag when entry matches
                    echo '<option value="' . $status_id . '" ';
                    selected( $bug_data['bug_status'],
                            $status_id );
                    echo '>' . $status;
                }
                ?>
                </select>
            </td>
        </tr>
    </table>
```

```
        <input type="submit" value="Submit" class="button-primary" />
    </form>
```

5. Add the following line of code to register a function that will be called on the
initialization of the administration page:

```
add_action( 'admin_init', 'ch8bt_admin_init' );
```

6. Add the following block of code at the end of the plugin file to register a function
to be called when bugs are created or updated:

```
function ch8bt_admin_init() {
    add_action( 'admin_post_save_ch8bt_bug', 'process_ch8bt_bug' );
}
```

7. Append the following block of code to process user-submitted data and store it in
the website database:

```
function process_ch8bt_bug() {
    if ( !current_user_can( 'manage_options' ) ) {
        wp_die( 'Not allowed' );
    }

    // Check if nonce field is present for security
    check_admin_referer( 'ch8bt_add_edit' );
    global $wpdb;

    // Place all user submitted values in an array (or empty
    // strings if no value was sent)
    $bug_data = array();
    $bug_data['bug_title'] = ( isset( $_POST['bug_title'] ) ?
        sanitize_text_field( $_POST['bug_title'] ) : '' );

    $bug_data['bug_description'] =
        ( isset( $_POST['bug_description'] ) ?
          sanitize_text_field( $_POST['bug_description'] ) : '' );
    $bug_data['bug_version'] = ( isset( $_POST['bug_version'] ) ?
        sanitize_text_field( $_POST['bug_version'] ) : '' );

    // Set bug report date as current date
    $bug_data['bug_report_date'] = date( 'Y-m-d' );

    // Set status of all new bugs to 0 (Open)
    $bug_data['bug_status'] = ( isset( $_POST['bug_status'] ) ?
        intval( $_POST['bug_status'] ) : 0 );

    // Call the wpdb insert or update method based on value
```

```
    // of hidden bug_id field
    if ( isset( $_POST['bug_id'] ) && 0 == $_POST['bug_id'] ) {
        $wpdb->insert( $wpdb->get_blog_prefix() . 'ch8_bug_data',
                        $bug_data );
    } elseif ( isset( $_POST['bug_id'] ) &&
                $_POST['bug_id'] > 0 ) {
        $wpdb->update( $wpdb->get_blog_prefix() . 'ch8_bug_data',
            $bug_data,
            array( 'bug_id' => intval( $_POST['bug_id'] ) ) );
    }

    // Redirect the page to the user submission form
    wp_redirect( add_query_arg( 'page', 'ch8bt-bug-tracker',
                    admin_url( 'options-general.php' ) ) );
    exit;
}
```

8. Save and close the plugin file.
9. Navigate to the new **Bug Tracker** item under the administration page's **Settings** menu and click on the **Add New Bug** link to create an entry:

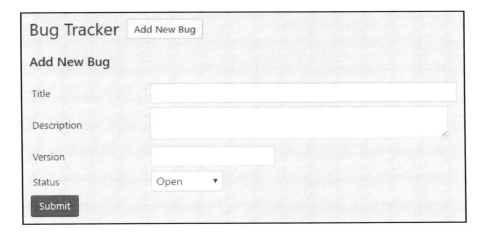

10. Click on **Submit** to store the new bug in the website database. The newly created bug will appear in the bug listing created in the previous recipe.
11. Click on the new entry's name to review its information and update it.

How it works...

If you tried clicking on the **Add New Bug** link created in the previous recipe, you would have been presented with a page that only contained the panel's title. This is due to the fact that we had not implemented the code to display a bug creation and editing form when the id variable is present in the website address.

The first few steps of this recipe aim to rectify this by checking for the presence of a variable called id in the page URL with a value set to the text new or a numeric value.

While both of these situations will result in displaying a bug edition form, the second condition first performs a database query using the wpdb object's get_row method to try to retrieve a bug with the designated ID. The get_row method is similar to the get_results method used in the previous recipe, but will only return a single row, even if more than one result is found by the query. As part of our get_row call, we also use the $wpdb class's prepare method. This method will parse the second argument it receives for security and then use it to replace the placeholder placed in our query. If the query is successful, the values that were retrieved are used to customize the form title and set initial field values.

The form itself is a standard HTML form that includes many of the elements that we have seen in previous recipes, such as a call to wp_nonce_field to provide security from external attacks. We have also added a hidden field containing the bug ID that was found in the page URL to facilitate data processing when a bug is submitted.

Once the form is in place, we make a call to add_action to register a callback that will be executed when the newly created form is submitted.

The callback, named process_ch8bt_bug, starts off by doing a bit of validation. Namely, it checks to see whether the current user has administrative rights and if the nonce field that should be part of the form data is present. If both of these conditions are met, a data array is created from user post data, the current system date, and a hardcoded status value.

The resulting array is stored in the website database using one of two wpdb object methods, insert or update, based on the value found in the hidden bug_id field. Both methods expect to receive the name of the target table, along with an associative array containing the names and values of each table field to be stored. Additionally, the update method requires a third parameter that indicates the field name and value to be used to locate the field to be updated. In both cases, you will notice that the bug_id field is not specified in the array of new values, since it gets automatically set to an incremental value by the database server.

The last step in this function is to build a clean URL to the plugin configuration page and use the resulting address in a call to wp_redirect.

See also

- The *Displaying custom table data in an admin page* recipe

Deleting records from custom tables

After adding data to custom tables, website administrators are likely to delete some of these entries down the road. Since we have been building an interface to view, create, and modify database entries, the task of selecting items to be deleted also falls under our responsibility. Thankfully, we can easily expand the existing bug display list to add checkboxes for selection and a button to trigger the actual deletion.

This recipe shows how to add deletion capabilities to our bug tracking system.

Getting ready

You should have already followed the *Inserting and updating records in custom tables* recipe to have an existing framework to augment. Alternatively, you can get the resulting code (`Chapter 8/ch8-bug-tracker/ch8-bug-tracker-v4.php`) from the code bundle and rename the file `ch8-bug-tracker.php`.

How to do it...

1. Navigate to the WordPress plugin directory of your development installation.
2. Navigate to the `ch8-bug-tracker` directory and edit `ch8-bug-tracker.php`.
3. Find the `ch8bt_config_page` function and locate the `Manage Bug Entries` h3 header in its content.
4. Insert the following highlighted lines of code right after the header to create a form:

```
<h3>Manage Bug Entries</h3>

<form method="post"
      action="<?php echo admin_url( 'admin-post.php' ); ?>">
<input type="hidden" name="action" value="delete_ch8bt_bug" />
<!-- Adding security through hidden referrer field -->
<?php wp_nonce_field( 'ch8bt_deletion' ); ?>
```

5. A few lines down, add an empty column in the table header, before the `ID` field, as highlighted in the following line of code:

```
<thead><tr><th style="width: 50px"></th>
        <th style='width: 80px'>ID</th>
```

6. Within the main bug list display loop, insert the following highlighted code segments to add a checkbox in front of each item:

```
echo '<tr style="background: #FFF">';
echo '<td><input type="checkbox" name="bugs[]" value="';
echo intval( $bug_item['bug_id'] ) . '" /></td>';
echo '<td>' . $bug_item['bug_id'] . '</td>';
```

7. A few lines down, change the value of the `colspan` table row parameter from 3 to 4:

```
echo '<td colspan="4">No Bug Found</td></tr>';
```

8. Append the following highlighted lines of code after the `table` close tag to display a deletion button and terminate the form section:

```
</table><br />

<input type="submit" value="Delete Selected"
        class="button-primary"/>
</form>
```

9. Find the `ch8bt_admin_init` function and add the following function call at the end of its body:

```
add_action( 'admin_post_delete_ch8bt_bug', 'delete_ch8bt_bug' );
```

10. Navigate to the bottom of the file and add the following code block to provide an implementation for the `delete_ch8bt_bug` function responsible for processing deletion requests generated by the new form:

```
function delete_ch8bt_bug() {
    // Check that user has proper security level
    if ( !current_user_can( 'manage_options' ) ) {
        wp_die( 'Not allowed' );
    }

    // Check if nonce field is present
    check_admin_referer( 'ch8bt_deletion' );
```

```
// If bugs are present, cycle through array and call SQL
// command to delete entries one by one
if ( !empty( $_POST['bugs'] ) ) {
    // Retrieve array of bugs IDs to be deleted
    $bugs_to_delete = $_POST['bugs'];
    global $wpdb;

    foreach ( $bugs_to_delete as $bug_to_delete ) {
        $query = 'DELETE from ' . $wpdb->get_blog_prefix();
        $query .= 'ch8_bug_data WHERE bug_id = %d';
        $wpdb->query( $wpdb->prepare( $query,
                        intval( $bug_to_delete ) ) );
    }
}

// Redirect the page to the user submission form
wp_redirect( add_query_arg( 'page', 'ch8bt-bug-tracker',
                admin_url( 'options-general.php' ) ) );
exit;
}
```

11. Save and close the plugin file.
12. Navigate to the new **Bug Tracker** item under the administration page's **Settings** menu to see the new interface elements that were added to the bug listing.

How it works...

While the actual deletion of data from our custom table can be done with a single call to run the DELETE SQL command, we first need the user to indicate which entries need to be removed. This selection interface can be easily added to the existing bug listing created in an earlier recipe.

This recipe starts in familiar territory with the creation of a standard HTML form to surround the original bug listing. In addition to the bug list, the form also includes a hidden field to indicate the name of the action to be called when the user submits the form, along with a nonce field to ensure that access to the deletion process is secure.

With this initial code in place, the next section of the recipe modifies the original table listing to add a checkbox at the front of every row. As can be seen in the code, the `name` property of the checkbox is a bit different than regular HTML syntax, ending with two square parentheses. This syntax, used in conjunction with each item's `bug_id`, results in the creation of an array of checked items and ID numbers that are sent to the form processing function on submission.

The last change that is done in the bug listing display code is to add a deletion button and to close the form.

To associate a callback with the newly created form, the next addition made by the recipe is a call to `add_action` to associate the `admin_post_<actionname>` variable action name with the `delete_ch8bt_bug` function.

When called, the bug deletion function, like most other submission processing code that we have created before, first starts with a few verifications to make sure that the user has appropriate permissions and that the hidden security fields that were placed in the form are present. When both of these formalities are confirmed, the code goes on to check for the presence of a bug array and proceeds to cycle through all the entries if one was found. In that loop, we get access to the global `wpdb` class and we can use it to build and execute SQL queries that delete a single database row at a time using the `bug_id` numbers that were submitted.

As an added security measure, notice the use of the `intval` function in front of the `$bug_to_delete` variable to make sure that no one is trying to get external commands to be processed in an attempt to corrupt or hijack the database.

See also

- The *Inserting and updating records in custom tables* recipe

Displaying custom database table data in shortcodes

The purpose of creating custom tables is often to store information to be shared with website visitors. As such, it is important to give users the ability to easily display their new content stored in custom tables on their website. The most straightforward method to achieve this goal is to create one or more shortcodes that can be inserted on any post or page to render the desired information.

This recipe shows how to implement a new shortcode that will be used to display a bug listing on a page.

Getting ready

You should have already followed the *Deleting records from custom tables* recipe to have an existing framework to augment. Alternatively, you can get the resulting code (Chapter 8/ch8-bug-tracker/ch8-bug-tracker-v5.php) from the code bundle and rename the file ch8-bug-tracker.php.

How to do it...

1. Navigate to the WordPress plugin directory of your development installation.
2. Navigate to the ch8-bug-tracker directory and edit ch8-bug-tracker.php.
3. Add the following line of code at the bottom of the file to declare a new shortcode and its associated display function:

    ```
    add_shortcode( 'bug-tracker-list', 'ch8bt_shortcode_list' );
    ```

4. Insert the following code block right after the section header to implement the ch8bt_shortcode_list function that is responsible for displaying a bug listing:

    ```
    function ch8bt_shortcode_list() {
        global $wpdb;

        // Prepare query to retrieve bugs from database
        $bug_query = 'select * from ' . $wpdb->get_blog_prefix();
        $bug_query .= 'ch8_bug_data ';
        $bug_query .= 'ORDER by bug_id DESC';
        $bug_items = $wpdb->get_results( $bug_query, ARRAY_A );
    ```

```
        // Prepare output to be returned to replace shortcode
        $output = '';
        $output .= '<div class="bug-tracker-list"><table>';

        // Check if any bugs were found
        if ( !empty( $bug_items ) ) {
            $output .= '<tr><th style="width: 80px">ID</th>';
            $output .= '<th style="width: 300px">Title / Desc</th>';
            $output .= '<th>Version</th></tr>';

            // Create row in table for each bug
            foreach ( $bug_items as $bug_item ) {
                $output .= '<tr style="background: #FFF">';
                $output .= '<td>' . $bug_item['bug_id'] . '</td>';
                $output .= '<td>' . $bug_item['bug_title'] . '</td>';
                $output .= '<td>' . $bug_item['bug_version'] . '</td>';
                $output .= '</tr><tr><td></td><td colspan="2">';
                $output .= $bug_item['bug_description'];
                $output .= '</td></tr>';
            }
        } else {
            // Message displayed if no bugs are found
            $output .= '<tr style="background: #FFF">';
            $output .= '<td colspan="3">No Bugs to Display</td>';
        }
        $output .= '</table></div>';

        // Return data prepared to replace shortcode on page/post
        return $output;
    }
```

5. Save and close the plugin file.
6. Create a new page and insert the newly created shortcode `[bug-tracker-list]` in the page body.

7. View the page to see a list of bugs stored in the system:

ID	Title / Desc	Version
5	Cannot save content	1.0
	It is not possible to save content with the latest version.	
4	Refresh issue	1.0
	When visiting the web site, part of the page does not refresh correctly	

How it works...

Creating a new shortcode to display custom table data is done in a very similar way as in previous recipes. First, we declare the new code, along with the name of the function that will be called to generate text to replace it when found in posts or pages. Then, we create a display function to prepare all the output and return it to WordPress.

The only distinction here is in the way we query the information. The recipe uses the `get_results` method of the `wpdb` class to query all the bugs that exist in the custom database table using the SELECT SQL command. After this call is executed, all the items found are returned in an associative array that can easily be displayed in table form using a `foreach` loop.

If no entries were found, the recipe displays a simple message to inform the visitor.

See also

- The *Deleting records from custom tables* recipe

Implementing a search function to retrieve custom table data

While content created using custom post types can be automatically searched by the built-in WordPress search engine, custom database tables don't benefit from the same treatment. Instead, plugin developers choosing this mechanism to store information must build their own search functionality.

This recipe shows how to add a search box to the bug listing created in the previous section and how to use the resulting query data to narrow down the list of bugs that are displayed by the shortcode.

Getting ready

You should have already followed the recipe titled *Displaying custom database table data in shortcodes* to have an existing framework to augment. Alternatively, you can get the resulting code (Chapter 8/ch8-bug-tracker/ch8-bug-tracker-v6.php) from the code bundle and rename the file ch8-bug-tracker.php.

How to do it...

1. Navigate to the WordPress plugin directory of your development installation.
2. Navigate to the ch8-bug-tracker directory and edit ch8-bug-tracker.php.
3. Find the ch8bt_shortcode_list function and add the following highlighted code after the initial global $wpdb call to check whether a search string was entered by a visitor:

```
global $wpdb;

if ( !empty( $_GET['searchbt'] ) ) {
    $search_string = sanitize_text_field( $_GET['searchbt'] );
    $search_mode = true;
} else {
    $search_string = "Search...";
    $search_mode = false;
}
```

4. Insert the following highlighted lines of code in the middle of the existing query string to add the `where` parameters using the user search text, if present:

```
$bug_query = 'select * from ' . $wpdb->get_blog_prefix();
$bug_query .= 'ch8_bug_data ';

// Add search string in query if present
if ( $search_mode ) {
    $search_term = '%'. $search_string . '%';
    $bug_query .= "where bug_title like '%s' ";
    $bug_query .= "or bug_description like '%s' ";
} else {
    $search_term = '';
}

$bug_query .= 'ORDER by bug_id DESC';
```

5. Locate the following line of code:

```
$bug_items = $wpdb->get_results( $bug_query, ARRAY_A );
```

Replace it to the following code:

```
if ( $search_mode ) {
    $bug_items = $wpdb->get_results( $wpdb->prepare(
                    $bug_query, $search_term, $search_term ),
                    ARRAY_A );
} else {
    $bug_items = $wpdb->get_results( $bug_query, ARRAY_A );
}
```

6. Add the following code block, before the table starts rendering, to display a simple search form:

```
$output = '';

$output .= '<div class="ch8_bt_search">';
$output .= '<form method="get" id="ch8_bt_search">';
$output .= '<div>Search bugs ';
$output .= '<input type="text" onfocus="this.value=\'\'" ';
$output .= 'value="' . esc_html( $search_string ) . '" ';
$output .= 'name="searchbt" />';
$output .= '<input type="submit" value="Search" />';
$output .= '</div>';
$output .= '</form></div>';

$output .= '<div class="bug-tracker-list"><table>';
```

7. Save and close the plugin file.
8. Visit the bug display page that was previously created to see the new search form. Enter a search string and click on the **Search** button to see a list of results:

How it works...

This recipe implements a simple search engine by displaying a short form and capturing a user search string using the standard HTML GET method. If a search string is found in the page address, we will modify the bug retrieval query that was in place by adding a `where` clause that looks for the search string anywhere in the `bug_title` or `bug_description` fields.

While it might seem natural to insert the search string directly in the query and execute it, we use the `wpdb` class' `prepare` method to assemble the query and validate the search string to avoid malicious intent. This method works in a very similar way to the standard PHP `sprintf` function, with placeholders to represent the places where variables should be substituted.

The remainder of the shortcode display function remains identical, displaying a list of varying length depending on the presence of a search string and the number of entries that match the query.

See also

- The *Displaying custom database table data in shortcodes* recipe

Importing data from a user file into custom tables

To avoid long data entry sessions, a nice addition to a system, such as the Bug Tracker that we have been putting in place in this chapter, would be to provide users with the ability to import large amounts of entries from an external file in a single operation. To accomplish this task, the **Comma-Separated Values (CSV)** file format is very convenient, since it can be edited by most spreadsheet editors and can be read using standard PHP function calls.

This recipe implements a CSV-based import function in our bug tracking system.

Getting ready

You should have already followed the *Implementing a search function to retrieve custom table data* recipe to have an existing framework to augment. Alternatively, you can get the resulting code (`Chapter 8/ch8-bug-tracker/ch8-bug-tracker-v7.php`) from the code bundle and rename the file `ch8-bug-tracker.php`.

How to do it...

1. Navigate to the WordPress plugin directory of your development installation.
2. Navigate to the `ch8-bug-tracker` directory and edit `ch8-bug-tracker.php`.
3. Find the `ch8bt_config_page` function and add the following highlighted code block at the end of the bug listings section after the end of the existing deletion form:

```
<input type="submit" value="Delete Selected"
       class="button-primary"/>
</form>

<!-- Form to upload new bugs in csv format -->
<form method="post"
      action="<?php echo admin_url( 'admin-post.php' ); ?>"
      enctype="multipart/form-data">

<input type="hidden" name="action" value="import_ch8bt_bug" />
<!-- Adding security through hidden referrer field -->
<?php wp_nonce_field( 'ch8bt_import' ); ?>

<h3>Import Bugs</h3>
```

```
<div class="import_data">Import Bugs from CSV File
    (<a href="<?php echo plugins_url( 'importtemplate.csv',
                                  __FILE__ ); ?>">Template</a>)
        <input name="import_bugs_file" type="file" /></div>
<input type="submit" value="Import" class="button-primary"/>
</form>
```

4. Locate the `ch8bt_admin_init` function and add the following line of code at the end of its body to register a function to process submissions of the bug import form:

```
add_action( 'admin_post_import_ch8bt_bug', 'import_ch8bt_bug' );
```

5. Insert the following block of code to provide an implementation for the `import_ch8bt_bug` function:

```
function import_ch8bt_bug() {
    // Check that user has proper security level
    if ( !current_user_can( 'manage_options' ) ) {
        wp_die( 'Not allowed' );
    }

    // Check if nonce field is present
    check_admin_referer( 'ch8bt_import' );

    // Check if file has been uploaded
    if( array_key_exists( 'import_bugs_file', $_FILES ) ) {
        // If file exists, open it in read mode
        $handle =
            fopen( $_FILES['import_bugs_file']['tmp_name'], 'r' );

        // If file is successfully open, extract a row of data
        // based on comma separator, and store in $data array
        if ( $handle ) {
            while ( FALSE !==
                    ( $data = fgetcsv( $handle, 5000, ',' ) ) ) {
                $row += 1;

                // If row count is ok and row is not header row
                // Create array and insert in database
                if ( count( $data ) == 4 && $row != 1 ) {
                    $new_bug = array(
                        'bug_title' => $data[0],
                        'bug_description' => $data[1],
                        'bug_version' => $data[2],
                        'bug_status' => $data[3],
                        'bug_report_date' => date( 'Y-m-d' ) );
```

```
                            global $wpdb;
                            $wpdb->insert( $wpdb->get_blog_prefix() .
                                        'ch8_bug_data', $new_bug );
                    }
                }
            }
        }

        // Redirect the page to the user submission form
        wp_redirect( add_query_arg( 'page', 'ch8bt-bug-tracker',
                        admin_url( 'options-general.php' ) ) );
        exit;
    }
```

6. Save and close the plugin file.
7. Create a new text file in the plugin directory called importtemplate.csv and open it in a text editor.
8. Insert the following text in the newly created file to provide an example bug to import:

   ```
   "Title","Description","Version","Status"
   "Test Import Bug","This is a test import bug","1.0","0"
   ```

9. Save and close the CSV text file.
10. Navigate to the new **Bug Tracker** item under the administration page's **Settings** menu to see the new **Import Bugs** section.
11. Use the file import dialog to locate the importtemplate.csv.
12. Import the list of bugs in the system to see its content added to the database:

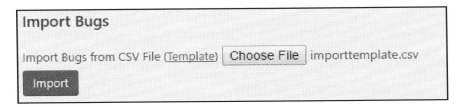

How it works...

This recipe creates a small form on the **Bug Tracker** management page that is solely responsible for uploading one or more bugs to the database. By editing the content of the `importtemplate.csv` file and selecting it in the import dialog, users can quickly populate the system by loading data straight to the custom database table that was created by the plugin when it was first installed.

In addition to the file upload field, the form contains the usual hidden nonce and action name fields. It also features an `enctype` property to allow files to be uploaded.

When the user submits a file to be uploaded, the registered callback function first checks to see whether the user who made the submission has appropriate rights and whether the nonce security fields were present as part of the post data. If both of these conditions are met, the recipe goes on to check whether a file has been correctly uploaded to the web server using the `array_key_exists` function to search through the standard PHP `$_FILES` global variable. As you can see, the text that it searches for is the name of the file upload field from the form.

If a file has been uploaded, the `fopen` function opens it and stores a pointer to it in a local variable. After a quick verification of the pointer's existence, the code moves to a `while` loop to process each line of the incoming file with the `fgetcsv` function. This function reads one line of the file at a time, analyzes its content to find all of the comma-separated fields that are present, and stores the resulting data in a numeric array.

The rest of the `import` function creates an array with the imported data and stores it in the database using the `wpdb` class' `insert` method, as we have seen in a previous recipe.

See also

- The *Inserting and updating records in custom tables* recipe

9

Leveraging JavaScript, jQuery, and AJAX Scripts

This chapter focuses on incorporating JavaScript in plugins by exploring the following topics:

- Safely loading jQuery onto WordPress web pages
- Displaying a pop-up dialog using the built-in ThickBox plugin
- Controlling pop-up dialog display using shortcodes
- Displaying a calendar day selector using the Datepicker plugin
- Adding tooltips to admin page form fields using the TipTip plugin
- Using AJAX to dynamically update partial page contents

Introduction

JavaScript libraries, especially the very popular jQuery library and its numerous plugins, can do wonders in bringing a website to life with slick animations, dynamic data queries, and advanced visual features. Unfortunately, for all of their benefits, these scripts can also be difficult to work with. For example, loading more than one copy of jQuery can destroy all the setup that was done by the other instances and errors in one script usually prevent other scripts from running correctly.

WordPress' answer to this convoluted architecture is twofold. As a first step, it comes pre-packaged with a copy of jQuery and many other popular JavaScript libraries that plugin developers can use without having to load their own versions. Then, to prevent multiple copies from being loaded on a page, it offers easy-to-use functions that queue up scripts and styles to identify duplicates before rendering pages.

This chapter shows how to safely load JavaScript and jQuery files that are provided with WordPress or that come from external sources to add powerful new functionalities to front-facing pages and plugin configuration panels. It also explains how to securely run AJAX queries to refresh partial page sections.

Safely loading jQuery onto WordPress web pages

While it might be tempting to provide your own copy of jQuery as part of a new plugin that uses the popular JavaScript library or to access a copy from the Google API website, WordPress actually provides a copy of jQuery in its installation and makes it very easy to load it.

By using the appropriate utility function to load jQuery, developers make a request to WordPress to load this library instead of doing it themselves. Once all the requests have been received, they are analyzed for duplicates and a single instance of each script is loaded to reduce the chance of conflicts between multiple copies of the same library.

This recipe shows how to load the jQuery script for use on front-facing website pages.

Getting ready

You should have access to a WordPress development environment.

How to do it...

1. Navigate to the WordPress plugin directory of your development installation.
2. Create a new directory called `ch9-load-jquery`.
3. Navigate to the directory and create a text file called `ch9-load-jquery.php`.

4. Open the new file in a code editor and add an appropriate header at the top of the plugin file, naming the plugin `Chapter 9 - Load jQuery`.

5. Add the following line of code to register a function to be called when script loading requests are processed:

```
add_action( 'wp_enqueue_scripts', 'ch9lj_front_facing_pages' );
```

6. Add the following code segment to provide an implementation for the `ch9lj_front_facing_pages` function:

```
function ch9lj_front_facing_pages() {
    wp_enqueue_script( 'jquery' );
}
```

7. Save and close the plugin file.

8. Go to the **Themes** menu section located under **Appearance** in the WordPress administration interface.

9. Click on **Add New** and search for a theme called `Twenty Eleven`.

10. **Install** the theme on your website and **Activate** it.

11. Visit your website and view the page source, searching for instances of the `jquery.js` library. Your search should come up empty unless you have activated other plugins that are asking for jQuery to be loaded.

12. Navigate to the **Plugins** management page and **Activate** the `Chapter 9 - Load jQuery` plugin.

13. Go back to any page on your website and view the page source.

14. Search for the keyword `jquery` to see that a copy of the script is now loaded from the WordPress `wp-includes` folder, along with the `jquery-migrate` script for backward compatibility:

```
<script type='text/javascript' src='http://localhost/
    wp-includes/js/jquery/jquery.js?ver=1.12.4'></script>
<script type='text/javascript' src='http://localhost/
    wp-includes/js/jquery/jquery-
migrate.min.js?ver=1.4.1'></script>
```

How it works...

The key component of this recipe is the `wp_enqueue_script` function, which allows developers to load their own JavaScript files or to ask WordPress to load one of the scripts that it comes packaged with. While the function requires many arguments when loading your own scripts, which we'll cover in a later recipe, it only needs a single argument to load built-in scripts. In this example, that argument is `jquery`. To get a full list of default scripts available with WordPress, check out the code reference page for the function (https://dev eloper.wordpress.org/reference/functions/wp_enqueue_script/).

Once you know which script to load, the call to `wp_enqueue_script` should be made from one of three action hooks, depending on the target page(s) where the script should be loaded. These are `wp_enqueue_scripts` for front-facing pages, `admin_enqueue_scripts` for administration pages, and `login_enqueue_scripts` for the login page, with the first one fulfilling our requirement for this recipe.

We had to go back and install an older theme to be able to see a change after activating our plugin. Many modern themes already make a request for jQuery to be loaded since it is used to animate menus or provide many other common functionalities. That being said, we cannot assume that this will be the case if we plan to distribute our work to a larger audience.

There's more...

Veteran jQuery developers should be aware that the copy delivered with WordPress has a small caveat.

jQuery noconflict mode

To avoid internal conflicts with other JavaScript and jQuery libraries, the version of jQuery that comes bundled with WordPress is configured in the `noconflict` mode. This means that the `$` shortcut that can normally be used to access jQuery will not be available. As such, all the examples found in this chapter spell out the jQuery keyword.

To regain access to this shortcut, you can use the following syntax in your code:

```
jQuery( document ).ready( function($) {
    // $ shortcut is now available for this function
} );
```

Displaying a pop-up dialog using the built-in ThickBox plugin

As annoying as they can be to visitors, pop-up dialogs are a feature that many website administrators are using to help them advertise special offers or get readers to subscribe to their content. Since it uses pop-up dialogs in its own administrative pages, WordPress comes bundled with a jQuery script called ThickBox that can be used to display these types of dialogs.

This recipe shows how to load the ThickBox script and use it to render a pop-up dialog.

Getting ready

You should have access to a WordPress development environment.

How to do it...

1. Navigate to the WordPress plugin directory of your development installation.
2. Create a new directory called ch9-pop-up-dialog.
3. Navigate to the directory and create a text file called ch9-pop-up-dialog.php.
4. Open the new file in a code editor and add an appropriate header at the top of the plugin file, naming the plugin Chapter 9 - Pop-Up Dialog.
5. Add the following line of code to register a function to be called when script loading requests are made:

```
add_action( 'wp_enqueue_scripts', 'ch9pud_load_scripts' );
```

6. Add the following code segment to provide an implementation for the `ch9pud_load_scripts` function:

```
function ch9pud_load_scripts() {
    wp_enqueue_script( 'jquery' );
    add_thickbox();
}
```

7. Insert the following line of code to register a function to display content in the page footer:

```
add_action( 'wp_footer', 'ch9pud_footer_code' );
```

8. Append the following block of code to provide an implementation for the `ch9pud_footer_code` function:

```
function ch9pud_footer_code() { ?>
    <script type="text/javascript">
    jQuery( document ).ready(function() {
        setTimeout( function() {
            tb_show( 'Pop-Up Message', '<?php echo plugins_url(
                    'content.html?width=420&height=220',
                    __FILE__ ); ?>', null );
        }, 2000 );
    } );

</script>
<?php
}
```

9. Save and close the plugin file.
10. Create a new HTML file named `content.html` and open it in a code editor.
11. Insert the following HTML code as the file's content:

```
<!DOCTYPE html>
<html>
    <body>
        <div>This is the pop-up content.</div>
    </body>
</html>
```

12. Save and close the HTML file.

13. Navigate to the **Plugins** management page and **Activate** the `Chapter 9 - Pop-Up Dialog` plugin.

14. Visit any page of the website to see the new pop-up dialog appear two seconds after the whole page is displayed:

How it works...

Similarly to the previous recipe, we start by assigning a function to the `wp_enqueue_scripts` action hook. When executed, the callback makes a call to `wp_enqueue_script` to request for jQuery to be loaded from the local copy of WordPress. The next line calls the `add_thickbox` function, which is a utility function that makes multiple calls to `wp_enqueue_script` and `wp_enqueue_style` to load the appropriate JavaScript and stylesheet in the page header.

Once all the required elements are loaded, the next section of the recipe outputs a block of JavaScript code to the page footer which uses jQuery to register a function that will be called when the entire page is loaded. When this happens, the `setTimeout` JavaScript function is used to register a function that will be called 2000 milliseconds later and will take care of calling `tb_show` to display the pop-up dialog. `tb_show` has three arguments, with the first one indicating the dialog title, the second containing the address of the content to render within the box, and the third expecting a path to a group of images to be displayed. In our case, the last argument is left null. Notice that the width and height (in pixels) of the dialog are indicated as part of the address of the content page to be displayed.

There's more...

While the recipe displays a valid dialog, developers might want a bit more control over how it can be closed and when it gets displayed.

Removing the dialog close button

By default, the ThickBox script offers a close button in the top-right corner of the pop-up dialog that can be used to close it at any time. This may not be desirable if you expect visitors to provide feedback or perform a specific action before dismissing the dialog. By adding the `modal` keyword to the content URL--set to the value of `true`--ThickBox will remove the dialog title bar, including the close button:

```
tb_show( 'Pop-Up Message', '<?php echo plugins_url(
    'content.html?width=420&height=220&modal=true', __FILE__ ); ?>',
    null );
```

Once the close button is gone, we can call the `tb_remove` JavaScript function to close the dialog. The following is an example of a simple link that could be added in `content.html` that will close the dialog:

```
<div><a href="#" onclick="tb_remove();">Close Dialog</a></div>
```

Displaying pop-up dialogs on select pages

While the recipe's original code displays a pop-up dialog on every single page of a website, it may be better to show it only on specific pages, such as the front page, to avoid over-exposure. To accomplish this, we can move the two `add_action` calls inside of an action hook callback and check whether the visitor is making a request to see the front page before loading our scripts:

```
add_action( 'template_redirect', 'ch9pud_template_redirect' );

function ch9pud_template_redirect() {
    if ( is_front_page() ) {
        add_action( 'wp_enqueue_scripts', 'ch9pud_load_scripts' );
        add_action( 'wp_footer', 'ch9pud_footer_code' );
    }
}
```

A similar technique can be used by substituting the `is_front_page` function with the `is_page( 'id_title_or_slug' )` function, which checks whether the current page numeric ID, title, or post slug matches the value that it receives as an argument. In that situation, a plugin configuration page could allow users to easily select one or more pages on which the dialog should appear.

Controlling pop-up dialog display using shortcodes

As you may be aware, loading scripts and styles on a page where they won't be used unnecessarily slows down that page's rendering time, since the browser will still need to download and validate the content of these external files. While the previous recipe's *There's More...* section offered one way to select specific pages where scripts and styles should be loaded, a different approach is to analyze the page contents for the presence of a special code to make that decision.

This recipe shows how to add a filter to the previous recipe to search for a shortcode in posts and pages to decide when to display a pop-up dialog.

Getting ready

You should have already followed the *Displaying a pop-up dialog using the built-in ThickBox plugin* recipe to have a starting point for this recipe. Alternatively, you can get the resulting code (`Chapter 9/ch9-pop-up-dialog/ch9-pop-up-dialog-v1.php`) from the code bundle and rename the file as `ch9-pop-up-dialog.php`.

How to do it...

1. Navigate to the WordPress plugin directory of your development installation.
2. Navigate to the `ch9-pop-up-dialog` directory and then edit `ch9-pop-up-dialog.php`.

3. Find the `ch9pud_load_scripts` function and add the following highlighted lines of code:

```
function ch9pud_load_scripts() {
    // Only load scripts if variable is set to true
    global $load_scripts;

    if ( $load_scripts ) {
        wp_enqueue_script( 'jquery' );
        add_thickbox()
    }
}
```

4. Locate the `ch9pud_footer_code` function and modify the code, adding the following highlighted lines of code to the function body:

```
function ch9pud_footer_code() {
    // Only load scripts if keyword is found on page
    global $load_scripts;
    if ( $load_scripts ) { ?>

    <script type="text/javascript">
        jQuery( document ).ready( function() {
            setTimeout(
                function(){
                    tb_show( 'Pop-Up Message',
                        '<?php echo plugins_url(
                        'content.html?width=420&height=220',
                        __FILE__ ); ?>', null );
                }, 2000 );
        });
    </script>
<?php }
}
```

5. Add the following line of code to register a function that will filter post and page contents before any other parsing and formatting is performed:

```
add_filter( 'the_posts',
            'ch9pud_conditionally_add_scripts_and_styles' );
```

6. Append the following block of code to provide an implementation for the `ch9pud_conditionally_add_scripts_and_styles` function:

```
function ch9pud_conditionally_add_scripts_and_styles( $posts ) {
    // Exit function immediately if no posts are present
    if ( empty( $posts ) ) {
```

```
        return $posts;
    }

    // Global variable to indicate if scripts should be loaded
    global $load_scripts;
    $load_scripts = false;

    // Cycle through posts and set flag true if
    // keyword is found
    foreach ( $posts as $post ) {
        $shortcode_pos = stripos( $post->post_content,
                                  '[popup]', 0 );
        if ( $shortcode_pos !== false ) {
            $load_scripts = true;
            return $posts;
        }
    }

    // Return posts array unchanged
    return $posts;
}
```

7. Insert the following function call to declare a new shortcode along with a function responsible for replacing it with content:

```
add_shortcode( 'popup', 'ch9pud_popup_shortcode' );
```

8. Add the following code block to provide a simple implementation for the ch9pud_popup_shortcode function:

```
function ch9pud_popup_shortcode() {
    return;
}
```

9. Save and close the plugin file.
10. Visit the website's front page and you will notice that the pop-up dialog is no longer displayed.
11. Create a new page and insert the [popup] shortcode in the page contents.
12. View the new page to see that the new pop-up dialog appears, while the [popup] shortcode is not shown.

How it works...

While the existing action hooks were first modified to create and query a global variable to determine whether or not they should load scripts and output code to the page footer, the bulk of the work is actually done by the filter function that gets associated to `the_posts` hook. This function receives an array of all the posts and pages that are destined to be displayed and must determine if a special keyword is present to set the `load_scripts` variable appropriately.

As you can see from the recipe's code, the text that we chose to look for, `[popup]`, is a shortcode. While we could have selected any text as the trigger to display a pop-up dialog, we chose a shortcode, since it would be easy to make it disappear by providing a simple rendering function for it that returns no content.

See also

- The *Displaying a pop-up dialog using the built-in ThickBox plugin* recipe

Displaying a calendar day selector using the Datepicker plugin

For all of its great administrative control panels and user interface elements, WordPress still has a simplistic approach to date selection, making users interact with a drop-down box and text fields to indicate the month, day, year, and time when a post or page is to be published. A much more interesting way to enter this type of information is to use a pop-up calendar that allows users to navigate through visual representations of each month and pick the desired date.

This recipe shows how to use the jQuery Datepicker script that is provided by default with WordPress to display a pop-up calendar to provide an easy way to select dates.

Getting ready

You should have access to a WordPress development environment.

How to do it...

1. Navigate to the WordPress plugin directory of your development installation.
2. Create a new directory called `ch9-calendar-picker` along with a subdirectory called `css`.
3. Visit `https://www.jqueryui.com/download`, toggle all the components to be unchecked, and select only **Datepicker.** Then, select **UI lightness** as the theme to be included and download the latest version of the jQuery UI package.
4. Open the resulting file with an archive management tool and extract the file `jquery-ui.min.css` to the `css` folder of the newly created plugin directory.
5. Extract the entire `images` directory from the archive to the `css` folder.
6. Create a text file called `ch9-calendar-picker.php` in the plugin directory.
7. Open the new file in a code editor and add an appropriate header at the top of the plugin file, naming the plugin `Chapter 9 - Calendar Picker`.
8. Add the following line of code to register a function to be called when script loading requests are made:

```
add_action( 'admin_enqueue_scripts', 'ch9cp_admin_scripts' );
```

9. Add the following code segment to provide an implementation for the `ch9cp_admin_scripts` function:

```
function ch9cp_admin_scripts() {
    $screen = get_current_screen();
    if ( 'post' == $screen->base &&
        'post' == $screen->post_type ) {
        wp_enqueue_script( 'jquery' );
        wp_enqueue_script( 'jquery-ui-core' );
        wp_enqueue_script( 'jquery-ui-datepicker' );
        wp_enqueue_style( 'datepickercss',
            plugins_url( 'css/jquery-ui.min.css',
                __FILE__ ), array(), '1.12.1' );
    }
}
```

10. Insert the following line of code to register a function to be called when meta boxes are created:

```
add_action( 'add_meta_boxes', 'ch9cp_register_meta_box' );
```

11. Append the following block of code to provide an implementation for the `ch9cp_register_meta_box` function:

```
function ch9cp_register_meta_box() {
    add_meta_box( 'ch9cp_datepicker_box', 'Assign Date',
                  'ch9cp_date_meta_box', 'post', 'normal');
}
```

12. Insert the following code block to implement the `ch9cp_date_meta_box` function that was declared in the call to `add_meta_box`:

```
function ch9cp_date_meta_box( $post ) { ?>
    <input type="text" id="ch9cp_date" name="ch9cp_date" />
    <!-- JavaScript function to display calendar button -->
    <!-- and associate date selection with field -->
    <script type='text/javascript'>
        jQuery( document ).ready( function() {
        jQuery( '#ch9cp_date' ).datepicker( { minDate: '+0',
            dateFormat: 'yy-mm-dd', showOn: 'both',
            constrainInput: true} );
        } );
    </script>
<?php }
```

13. Save and close the plugin file.
14. Navigate to the **Plugins** management page and **Activate** the `Chapter 9 - Calendar Picker` plugin.
15. Select any item in the **Posts** management section and edit it to see the new date assignment meta box.
16. Click on the **...** button or click on the **Assign Date** textbox to display the pop-up calendar and select a date:

How it works...

Just like we saw with jQuery and ThickBox in the previous recipes, WordPress comes bundled with many jQuery libraries. Two of these libraries, jQuery UI and jQuery UI Datepicker, can be used to display a pop-up calendar and associate it with a text field on a form. That being said, the distribution of these scripts is missing the associated stylesheet and images that are required to display a fully rendered calendar.

This recipe starts by visiting the jQuery UI website and downloading a copy of the complete library, which includes all the required layout files. Once the download is complete, we are only interested in getting a copy of the style data, since all the other necessary scripts are provided by WordPress. After registering a function with `admin_enqueue_scripts`, we make three function calls to load the required JavaScript files in the admin page header. We also make a call to load the stylesheet that we just downloaded. When copying files from the downloaded archive, we selected the minified versions of the CSS files to have the smallest versions available.

The `wp_enqueue_style` function has many parameters. In this example, we are providing values for the first four of them to indicate the name of the style, the path to the style file, an empty list of dependencies, and a version number. This function also has a fifth parameter, which we are not using here, to indicate if the script should be loaded in the header or footer, where the default is the header.

Once all of the required scripts are in place, the remainder of the code creates a meta box in the post editor, displays a text field in that box, and outputs JavaScript code that will be called when the page is completely rendered to associate the pop-up calendar with the text field. As part of the calendar's options, we specify that the user will only be able to select future dates with the `minDate` parameter along with the desired date format.

Adding tooltips to admin page form fields using the TipTip plugin

Documentation is a very important step of plugin development, as it allows users to understand how to configure the plugins you create. That being said, users will not typically go very far to find the information they need, resulting in many unnecessary questions in discussion forums or in emails.

As discussed in `Chapter 3`, *User Settings and Administration Pages*, one way to provide documentation is to create a help tab that appears in the top-right corner of the plugin's configuration panel. While that approach is much easier for users than to find a Readme file or go back to the official WordPress plugin repository, it still requires them to actively seek and click a link to open that section.

That's where tooltips come into play. Using a jQuery plugin to render clean, good looking tooltips, we can add documentation to a plugin that will be displayed contextually based on the configuration fields that the user is currently interacting with.

This recipe shows how to download and integrate the TipTip jQuery library to display tooltips when configuration fields are used.

Getting ready

You should have already followed the *Displaying a calendar day selector using the Datepicker plugin* recipe to have a starting point for this recipe. Alternatively, you can get the resulting code (`Chapter 9/ch9-calendar-picker/ch9-calendar-picker-v1.php`) from the code bundle and rename the file as `ch9-calendar-picker.php`.

How to do it...

1. Navigate to the WordPress plugin directory of your development installation.
2. Navigate to the `ch9-calendar-picker` directory.
3. Create a new subdirectory called `tiptip`.
4. Visit the TipTip jQuery home page, available at `https://drew.tenderapp.com/kb/tiptip-jquery-plugin/tiptip-downloads`.
5. Download Version 1.3 of the plugin source code to your local computer.
6. Open the resulting file with an archive management tool and extract the `jquery.tipTip.minified.js` and `tipTip.css` files to the `tiptip` directory.
7. Open the main plugin file `ch9-calendar-picker.php` in a code editor.

8. Find the `ch9cp_admin_scripts` function and add the following lines of code at the end of the `if` condition, so that the new scripts are only loaded on the page and post editors, like the others:

```
wp_enqueue_script( 'tiptipjs',
                  plugins_url( 'tiptip/jquery.tipTip.minified.js',
                              __FILE__ ),
                  array(), '1.3' );
wp_enqueue_style( 'tiptip',
                  plugins_url( 'tiptip/tipTip.css', __FILE__ ),
                              array(), '1.3' );
```

9. Locate the `ch9cp_date_meta_box` function and modify the line that renders the textbox, as shown in the following highlighted code:

```
<input type="text" class="ch9cp_tooltip"
       id="ch9cp_date"
       name="ch9cp_date" />
```

10. Again, in the `ch9cp_date_meta_box` function, add the following highlighted block of code to the existing block of JavaScript code:

```
<script type='text/javascript'>
    jQuery( document ).ready( function() {
        jQuery( '#ch9cp_date' ).datepicker( { minDate: '+0',
                dateFormat: 'yy-mm-dd', showOn: 'both',
                constrainInput: true } );
        jQuery( '.ch9cp_tooltip' ).each( function() {
                jQuery( this ).tipTip();
            }
        );
    });
</script>
```

11. Save and close the plugin file.
12. Select any item in the **Posts** management section and edit it.
13. Move the mouse over the date field to see the new tooltip appear:

How it works...

The TipTip library turns regular HTML `title` tags into nice looking tooltips that appear when users position their mouse cursor over an item or select it.

This recipe starts by downloading the TipTip script from the plugin author's website. Once downloaded, we only extract two of the three files that the archive contains. The third file is not needed, as it is a non-compact version of the script.

Once we have the desired files in place, we load them in the admin page header by adding calls to the `wp_enqueue_script` and `wp_enqueue_style` functions in the callback that was already associated with the `admin_enqueue_script` action hook. Similar to `wp_enqueue_style`, the `wp_enqueue_script` function has five parameters, which indicate the name of the script, the location of the script file, a list of any dependencies for the script, a version number, and an option to indicate if the script should be loaded in the site header or footer.

Once the library is loaded, activating the tooltips is quite simple. First, we select a class name for our items and add it to all the items that are destined to have help text associated with them. Then, we add the help text in a `title` tag on each item. Note that the item in question could be anything from a div to a form input component or a table row. Finally, we make a call to a jQuery function to find all the items that have the right class and execute the TipTip function on them. After execution, all the selected items will have their title text appear as tooltips.

See also

- The *Displaying a calendar day selector using the Datepicker plugin* recipe

Using AJAX to dynamically update partial page contents

When users create complex websites with lots of dynamic content, such as Twitter widgets or other components that fetch external data, refreshing the entire page every time a user interacts with the website can quickly become a gruelling experience for visitors.

In such situations, using **Asynchronous JavaScript and XML (AJAX)** can greatly accelerate user navigation by only displaying subsets of data on visitor-facing pages and dynamically retrieving updates to isolated sections. More specifically, AJAX allows the browser to send requests to a web server, including data parameters, and to insert the data that it receives back in the web page, replacing or augmenting the original content.

This recipe shows how to add AJAX support to the bug tracking system created in Chapter 8, *Creating Custom MySQL Database Tables*.

Getting ready

You should have already followed the *Importing data from a user file into custom tables* recipe in Chapter 8, *Creating Custom MySQL Database Tables*, to have a starting point for this recipe. Alternatively, you can get the resulting code (Chapter 8/ch8-bug-tracker/ch8-bug-tracker-v8.php) from the code bundle and rename the file as ch8-bug-tracker.php.

How to do it...

1. Navigate to the WordPress plugin directory of your development installation.
2. Navigate to the ch8-bug-tracker directory and edit ch8-bug-tracker.php.
3. Locate the ch8bt_shortcode_list function and find the section where the SQL query is being prepared.
4. Add an extra line to the query (the highlighted line of code in the following code block) to show only open bugs (bugs with a bug_status field set to 0):

```
$bug_query = 'select * from ' . $wpdb->get_blog_prefix();
$bug_query .= 'ch8_bug_data ';
$bug_query .= 'where bug_status = 0 ';
```

5. Make the change highlighted in the following code to the code building the search query:

```
if ( $search_mode ) {
    $search_term = '%' . $search_string . '%';
    $bug_query .= "and ( bug_title like '%s' ";
    $bug_query .= "or bug_description like '%s' ) ";
}
```

6. Find the code responsible for drawing the search form, and add the following highlighted block of code after it to display a link to be clicked to show closed bugs:

```
$output .= '</form></div>';

$output .= '<div class="show_closed_bugs">';
$output .= 'Show closed bugs';
$output .= '</div>';

$output .= '<div class="bug-tracker-list"><table>';
```

7. Insert this code segment after the bug display table to add the JavaScript responsible for providing the AJAX-based data replacement functionality:

```
$output .= "<script type='text/javascript'>";
$nonce = wp_create_nonce( 'ch8bt_ajax' );
$output .= "function replacecontent( bug_status )" .
           "{ jQuery.ajax( {" .
           "    type: 'POST', url: ajax_url," .
           "    data: { action: 'ch8bt_buglist_ajax'," .
           "            _ajax_nonce: '" . $nonce . "'," .
           "            bug_status: bug_status }," .
           "    success: function( data ) {" .
           "            jQuery('.bug-tracker-list').html( data );"
.
           "            }" .
           "    });" .
           "};";

$output .= "jQuery( document ).ready( function() {";
$output .= "jQuery('.show_closed_bugs').click( function()
                                  { replacecontent( 1 ); } ";
$output .= ")})" ;";
$output .= "</script>";
```

8. Add the following line of code at the end of the plugin file to register a function to add content to the page header:

```
add_action( 'wp_head', 'ch8bt_declare_ajaxurl' );
```

9. Append the following block of code to provide an implementation for the ch8bt_declare_ajaxurl function:

```
function ch8bt_declare_ajaxurl() { ?>
    <script type="text/javascript">
        var ajax_url =
            '<?php echo admin_url( 'admin-ajax.php' ); ?>';
    </script>
<?php }
```

10. Insert the following lines of code to register functions that will be called when AJAX requests are received from public or logged in users with an action variable set to ch8bt_buglist_ajax:

```
add_action( 'wp_ajax_ch8bt_buglist_ajax', 'ch8bt_buglist_ajax' );
add_action( 'wp_ajax_nopriv_ch8bt_buglist_ajax',
            'ch8bt_buglist_ajax' );
```

11. Add the following block of code to provide an implementation for the ch8bt_buglist_ajax function:

```
function ch8bt_buglist_ajax() {
    check_ajax_referer( 'ch8bt_ajax' );

    if ( isset( $_POST['bug_status'] ) &&
         is_numeric( $_POST['bug_status'] ) ) {
        global $wpdb;

        // Prepare query to retrieve bugs from database
        $bug_query = 'select * from ' . $wpdb->get_blog_prefix();
        $bug_query .= 'ch8_bug_data where bug_status = ';
        $bug_query .= intval( $_POST['bug_status'] );
        $bug_query .= ' ORDER by bug_id DESC';

        $bug_items = $wpdb->get_results(
            $wpdb->prepare( $bug_query ), ARRAY_A );

        // Prepare output to be returned to AJAX requestor
        $output = '<div class="bug-tracker-list"><table>';

        // Check if any bugs were found
        if ( $bug_items ) {
            $output .= '<tr><th style="width: 80px">ID</th>';
            $output .= '<th style="width: 300px">';
            $output .= 'Title / Desc</th><th>Version</th></tr>';

            // Create row in table for each bug
```

```
            foreach ( $bug_items as $bug_item ) {
                $output .= '<tr style="background: #FFF">';
                $output .= '<td>' . $bug_item['bug_id'] . '</td>';
                $output .= '<td>' . $bug_item['bug_title'];
                $output .= '</td><td>' . $bug_item['bug_version'];
                $output .= '</td></tr>';
                $output .= '<tr><td></td><td colspan="2">';
                $output .= $bug_item['bug_description'];
                $output .= '</td></tr>';
            }
        } else {
            // Message displayed if no bugs are found
            $output .= '<tr style="background: #FFF">';
            $output .= '<td colspan="3">No Bugs to Display</td>';
        }
        $output .= '</table></div><br />';
        echo $output;
    }
    die();
}
```

12. Add the following line of code to register a function to be called when scripts are being queued up:

```
add_action( 'wp_enqueue_scripts', 'ch8bt_load_jquery' );
```

13. Insert the following code block to provide an implementation for the ch8bt_load_query function:

```
function ch8bt_load_jquery() {
    wp_enqueue_script( 'jquery' );
    wp_enqueue_style( 'bug_tracker_css',
                      plugins_url( 'stylesheet.css', __FILE__ ),
                      array(), '1.0' );
}
```

14. Save and close the plugin file.

15. Create a new text file named `stylesheet.css` in the plugin directory and insert the following content in the file:

```css
.show_closed_bugs {
    cursor: pointer;
    color: #00c;
}
```

16. Visit the bug listing page that was previously created to see that only opened bugs are displayed.

17. Click on the link to display closed bugs to see how the list gets quickly replaced with closed issues:

How it works...

AJAX page interactions are powered by JavaScript code and allow users to create pages with content that gets dynamically updated. To add this functionality to our bug tracking system, we start this recipe by modifying the existing shortcode bug query to only retrieve entries that have an open status (value of 0).

Once this is done, we move on to add two new elements to the initial shortcode output, a link to display closed bugs and a block of JavaScript code. The link itself is quite simple, containing a class name and a text label that visitors will be able to click. The JavaScript code is a bit more complex. Essentially, the script makes a request for the replacecontent function to be called when the show_closed_bugs link is clicked by visitors. In turn, the replacecontent function contains a single call to the jQuery ajax function. This function takes a number of arguments, starting with the type of operation, which is set to POST. This indicates that all the variables sent in the request URL will be stored in a standard $_POST variable array.

The second parameter is the URL to which the request should be sent. The variable used here is defined in the header code that is generated by the `ch8bt_declare_ajaxurl` function and points to the WordPress `admin-ajax.php` script URL. While the name of this script starts with the word `admin`, it can also be used to process AJAX requests from visitor-facing pages.

After these first two arguments is a `data` array that contains a number of data elements, such as the name of the action, a nonce field to secure the request, and the status of the bugs that should be retrieved. Finally, the `success` parameter indicates that the data received back from the AJAX request should be used to replace the HTML content of the `bug-tracker-list` div section of the existing page.

To process this request, our plugin goes on to register the function `ch8bt_buglist_ajax` to be called when one of two variable name actions are matched: `wp_ajax_<actionname>` or `wp_ajax_nopriv_<actionname>`. In both cases, `<actionname>` is the string that was sent as part of the data parameters in the AJAX request. Upon receiving the request, the callback generates an updated bug table, echoes the resulting HTML code, and makes a call to the standard PHP `die()` function. While this last step might seem strange, it is needed to avoid having a trailing `1` at the end of the new HTML, indicating that AJAX processing was successfully performed by WordPress.

While the `ch8bt_buglist_ajax` function shares a lot of code with the existing `ch8bt_shortcode_list` function, it is easier to create a separate code block that only contains the necessary elements for this example. That being said, combining the two functions would make future updates to the table layout easier to maintain.

See also

- The *Importing data from a user file into custom tables* recipe in `Chapter 8`, *Creating Custom MySQL Database Tables*

10
Adding New Widgets to the WordPress Library

In this chapter, you will learn how to create your own widget through the following topics:

- Creating a new widget in WordPress
- Displaying configuration options
- Validating configuration options
- Implementing the widget display function
- Adding a custom dashboard widget
- Adding a custom widget to the network dashboard

Introduction

Widgets have been present in WordPress from the early days of the platform. They allow users to easily populate sidebars or other areas of their website theme with blocks of content that are provided by WordPress itself (post or page data), or by any plugins that have been installed (for example, bug tracking system information). Looking at a WordPress installation, the default set of widgets include the Archives widget, which lists monthly post archives, and the Recent Comments widget, which provides an easy way to display visitor comments stored on your WordPress website.

Following its open design, WordPress provides functions that allow plugin developers to create new widgets that users will be able to add to their page design. This chapter shows how to use the widget class to create a custom widget. It also covers the second type of widget, the dashboard widget, which can be used to display plugin-specific information on the front page of the administrative area.

Creating a new widget in WordPress

The first step in creating a custom widget is to define its name and indicate which class contains all of its implementation functions. Once the new element has been registered with the system, it will immediately appear in the widget list, where users will be able to drag and drop it to their sidebars.

This recipe defines a new widget that displays recent book reviews from the custom post type category created in Chapter 4, *The Power of Custom Post Types*.

Getting ready

You should have already followed the *Updating page title to include custom post data using plugin filters* recipe from Chapter 4, *The Power of Custom Post Types*, to have a starting point for this recipe. Alternatively, you can get the resulting code (Chapter 4/ch4-book-reviews/ch4-book-reviews-v11.php) from the code bundle and activate the Chapter 4 - Book Reviews plugin.

How to do it...

1. Navigate to the WordPress plugin directory of your development installation.
2. Create a new directory called ch10-book-review-widget.
3. Navigate to the directory and create a text file called ch10-book-review-widget.php.
4. Open the new file in a code editor and add an appropriate header at the top of the plugin file, naming the plugin Chapter 10 - Book Review Widget.
5. Add the following line of code to register a function to be called when widgets are initialized:

```
add_action( 'widgets_init', 'ch10brw_create_widgets' );
```

6. Add the following code segment to provide an implementation for the `ch10brw_create_widgets` function:

```
function ch10brw_create_widgets() {
    register_widget( 'Book_Reviews' );
}
```

7. Insert the following block of code to declare the `Book_Reviews` class along with its constructor method:

```
class Book_Reviews extends WP_Widget {
    // Construction function
    function __construct () {
        parent::__construct( 'book_reviews', 'Book Reviews',
            array( 'description' =>
                    'Displays list of recent book reviews' ) );
    }
}
```

8. Save and close the plugin file.
9. Navigate to the **Plugins** management page and **Activate** the Chapter 10 – Book Review Widget plugin.
10. Visit the **Widgets** section of the **Appearance** administration page to see the newly created **Book Reviews** widget appear as part of the list of **Available Widgets**.
11. Drag and drop the new widget to one of the available sidebars listed on the right-hand side to create a widget instance, and see that the widget currently has no available options to configure it:

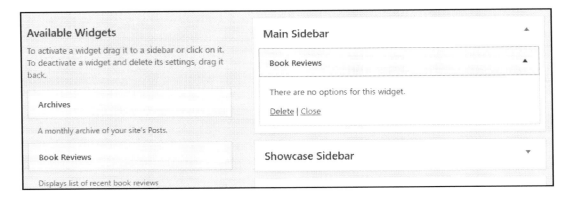

How it works...

The `widgets_init` action hook is used to register a function to be executed when widgets are being created by WordPress. When the callback occurs, we create a new widget by calling the simple `register_widget` function. As can be seen in the recipe, this function requires a single argument that indicates the name of the class that contains the widget definition.

The rest of the recipe declares the widget implementation class, which extends the WordPress `WP_Widget` class. While the class has many potential member methods, this recipe only defines the class constructor, which initializes the object instance by specifying a unique identifier, a title, and a description embedded within an array of optional parameters. As with any other functions declared in plugins, it is important to give unique names to the widget class and widget identifier in order to avoid conflict with other plugins.

When the plugin is activated, users can see the new widget immediately and are able to add one or more instances of the new element as part of a sidebar's content. However, the new widget will not render anything other than an error message on website pages until its `widget` method is implemented in a later recipe in this chapter.

There's more...

As you may have noticed, this recipe creates a separate plugin file and directory from the main book review plugin created in `Chapter 4`, *The Power of Custom Post Types*.

Plugins extending other plugins

While we could have placed the widget creation code in the same file as the book review plugin, placing it in a separate file is just as valid. Some plugins distributed on the official `wordpress.org` repository actually use that technique to break up their functionality into more manageable code segments. The only thing to be careful of with this technique is to be sure that all the elements that a secondary plugin is dependent upon are loaded before referring to them in callback functions.

In this case, since widgets are created late in the WordPress initialization process, the custom post type that will be required by the widget will be available.

See also

- The *Updating page title to include custom post data using plugin filters* recipe in `Chapter 4`, *The Power of Custom Post Types*

Displaying configuration options

Similar to the plugin configuration pages, widgets can have one or more options to allow users to specify how some aspects of the component will behave. These options can be configured individually for each instance of a widget that is added to a website layout. To handle all of the logistics around multiple possible widget instances, WordPress actually takes care of most of the data handling and storage tasks.

This recipe shows how to add a new method to the book review widget class to display configuration options.

Getting ready

You should have already followed the *Creating a new widget in WordPress* recipe to have a starting point for this recipe. Alternatively, you can get the resulting code (`Chapter 10/ch10-book-review-widget/ch10-book-review-widget-v1.php`) from the code bundle and rename the file as `ch10-book-review-widget.php`.

How to do it...

1. Navigate to the WordPress plugin directory of your development installation.
2. Navigate to the `ch10-book-review-widget` directory and edit `ch10-book-review-widget.php`.
3. Find the `Book_Reviews` class and add the following block of code within the class to define the `form` method:

```
function form( $instance ) {
    // Retrieve previous values from instance
    // or set default values if not present
    $render_widget = ( !empty( $instance['render_widget'] ) ?
                        $instance['render_widget'] : 'true' );

    $nb_book_reviews = ( !empty( $instance['nb_book_reviews'] ) ?
```

```php
                                          $instance['nb_book_reviews'] : 5 );

    $widget_title = ( !empty( $instance['widget_title'] ) ?
                      esc_attr( $instance['widget_title'] ) :
                      'Book Reviews' );
    ?>

    <!-- Display fields to specify title and item count -->
    <p>
        <label for="<?php echo
                    $this->get_field_id( 'render_widget' ); ?>">
        <?php echo 'Display Widget'; ?>
        <select id="<?php echo
                    $this->get_field_id( 'render_widget' ); ?>"
                name="<?php echo
                $this->get_field_name( 'render_widget' ); ?>">
            <option value="true"
                <?php selected( $render_widget, 'true' ); ?>>
            Yes</option>
            <option value="false"
                <?php selected( $render_widget, 'false' ); ?>>
            No</option>
        </select>
        </label>
    </p>
    <p>
        <label for="<?php echo
                    $this->get_field_id( 'widget_title' ); ?>">
        <?php echo 'Widget Title:'; ?>
        <input type="text"
                id="<?php echo
                    $this->get_field_id( 'widget_title' );?>"
                name="<?php
                echo $this->get_field_name( 'widget_title' ); ?>"
                value="<?php echo $widget_title; ?>" />
        </label>
    </p>
    <p>
        <label for="<?php echo
                    $this->get_field_id( 'nb_book_reviews' ); ?>">
        <?php echo 'Number of reviews to display:'; ?>
        <input type="text"
                id="<?php echo
                    $this->get_field_id( 'nb_book_reviews' ); ?>"
                name="<?php echo
                $this->get_field_name( 'nb_book_reviews' ); ?>"
                value="<?php echo $nb_book_reviews; ?>" />
        </label>
```

```
            </p>
        <?php  }
```

4. Save and close the plugin file.
5. Refresh the **Appearance** | **Widgets** administration page and expand the **Book Reviews** widget instance to see the newly created options.
6. Change the widget options and click on **Save** to update its configuration:

How it works...

When users create a new widget instance, WordPress automatically manages configuration options for that element using an array variable. It also calls the widget class' `form` method, if present, to render the widget instance's options in a configuration panel.

The first few lines of code in the `form` method verify that the `instance` array contains proper values that specify whether the widget should be displayed, the number of book reviews to be shown, and the title that should be displayed at the beginning of the widget. If any of these options are missing, we use the PHP ternary conditional operator (`? :`) to assign default values to the `render_widget`, `nb_book_reviews`, and `widget_title` functions. This operator expects three expressions, ordered as follows: `(expr1)?(expr2):(expr3)`. It will then return `expr2` if `expr1` is true and `expr3` if it's false.

With these variables in place, the rest of the `form` method's code uses a mix of HTML and PHP code to render the configuration fields that are shown in the widget editor. The `get_field_id` and `get_field_name` methods, seen throughout this code, are used to generate unique identifiers that will help WordPress to store data separately for all widget instances.

As can be seen in this recipe, the widget class is able to automatically process and save widget configuration parameters. However, it should be noted that allowing WordPress to handle this task by itself means that no validation will be performed on the data entered. This could cause problems if a user enters text instead of the number of reviews to be displayed. The next recipe shows how to handle data validation.

See also

- The *Creating a new widget in WordPress* recipe

Validating configuration options

The widget configuration panel that was put in place in the previous recipe was functional, allowing users to change options and save updated values in the website database. That being said, all WordPress does by default when the user saves a widget is store values directly to the site database. Since accepting user data blindly can lead to functionality problems and security risks if wrong or malicious values are entered, it is preferable to add data validation rules through the creation of an `update` method that will be able to verify configuration data before it is saved. This recipe shows how to implement a widget's `update` method.

Getting ready

You should have already followed the *Displaying configuration options* recipe to have a starting point for this recipe. Alternatively, you can get the resulting code (`Chapter 10/ch10-book-review-widget/ch10-book-review-widget-v2.php`) from the code bundle and rename the file as `ch10-book-review-widget.php`.

How to do it...

1. Navigate to the WordPress plugin directory of your development installation.
2. Navigate to the ch10-book-review-widget directory and edit ch10-book-review-widget.php.
3. Find the Book_Reviews class and add the following block of code within the class to define the update method:

```
function update( $new_instance, $instance ) {
    // Only allow numeric values
    if ( is_numeric ( $new_instance['nb_book_reviews'] ) ) {
        $instance['nb_book_reviews'] =
            intval( $new_instance['nb_book_reviews'] );
    } else {
        $instance['nb_book_reviews'] =
            $instance['nb_book_reviews'];
    }
    $instance['widget_title'] =
        sanitize_text_field( $new_instance['widget_title'] );

    $instance['render_widget'] =
        sanitize_text_field( $new_instance['render_widget'] );

    return $instance;
}
```

4. Save and close the plugin file.
5. Visit the **Widgets** section of the **Appearance** administration page and expand the **Book Reviews** widget instance.
6. Enter a textual value in the **Number of reviews to display** field and save the widget. You will see that the field's value reverts to the last valid number saved for this field.

How it works...

The update method receives two arrays of data and must return a single array to be saved in the website database. The two incoming arrays contain the new option values entered by the user and the values that were previously stored for the widget, respectively.

To start from known values, the method's implementation starts by making a copy of the old values to a new variable called `$instance`. It follows this initialization by calling the `sanitize_text_field` function to remove potentially harmful HTML or PHP tags from text fields, saving the return value in the `$instance` array. It also calls the PHP `is_numeric` and `intval` functions on entry, indicating the number of reviews to be displayed to make sure that it's a numeric value. If anything other than a number is entered, the previous field value will be saved and displayed back to the user. Unfortunately, it is not possible to display an error message when this type of validation of widget options is performed.

See also

- The *Displaying configuration options* recipe

Implementing the widget display function

For all of the widget creation work that we have done so far, our new creation does not display any content on the website yet. When displaying an area that contains widgets, WordPress tries to call a method named `widget` for each user-selected widget to output the desired content to the browser.

This recipe shows how to implement a `widget` method to display a list of recent book reviews when the widget is instantiated in a sidebar.

Getting ready

You should have already followed the *Validating configuration options* recipe to have a starting point for this recipe. Alternatively, you can get the resulting code (`Chapter 10/ch10-book-review-widget/ch10-book-review-widget-v3.php`) from the code bundle and rename the file as `ch10-book-review-widget.php`.

How to do it...

1. Navigate to the WordPress plugin directory of your development installation.
2. Navigate to the `ch10-book-review-widget` directory and edit `ch10-book-review-widget.php`.
3. Find the `Book_Reviews` class and add the following block of code within the class to define the `widget` method:

```
function widget( $args, $instance ) {
    if ( 'true' == $instance['render_widget'] ) {
        // Extract members of args array as individual variables
        extract( $args );

        // Retrieve widget configuration options
        $nb_book_reviews =
            ( !empty( $instance['nb_book_reviews'] ) ?
                $instance['nb_book_reviews'] : 5 );

        $widget_title = ( !empty( $instance['widget_title'] ) ?
                esc_attr( $instance['widget_title'] ) :
                'Book Reviews' );

        // Preparation of query string to retrieve book reviews
        $query_array = array( 'post_type' => 'book_reviews',
                            'post_status' => 'publish',
                            'posts_per_page' =>
                                $nb_book_reviews );

        // Execution of post query
        $book_review_query = new WP_Query();
        $book_review_query->query( $query_array );

        // Display widget title
        echo $before_widget . $before_title;
        echo apply_filters( 'widget_title', $widget_title );
        echo $after_title;

        // Check if any posts were returned by query
        if ( $book_review_query->have_posts() ) {
            // Display posts in unordered list layout
            echo '<ul>';

            // Cycle through all items retrieved
            while ( $book_review_query->have_posts() ) {
                $book_review_query->the_post();
                echo '<li><a href="' . get_permalink() . '">';
```

```
                           echo get_the_title( get_the_ID() ) . '</a></li>';
                }
                echo '</ul>';
        }
        wp_reset_query();
        echo $after_widget;
    }
}
```

4. Save and close the plugin file.
5. Visit the website's front page to see the newly added widget contents displayed in the sidebar:

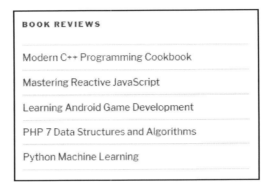

How it works...

Similar to action hooks that we have seen in the earlier chapters, the `widget` method is meant to directly output HTML code to the browser that will be displayed when an instance of the new widget has been created in a sidebar.

The `widget` method starts by checking whether or not the widget should be displayed. If it should, it continues by calling the standard PHP `extract` function on the first parameter received, an array named `$args`. Calling this function parses the array and creates variables for each element found, making it easier for the following code to access the elements that should be placed before and after the widget title and widget content.

After this initial statement, the recipe continues by retrieving the number of items to display and the widget title from the `$instance` array, which has been received as the second method parameter using the same technique that was shown when implementing the `form` method.

The rest of the code is very similar to the book review shortcode created in *Chapter 4, The Power of Custom Post Types* (displaying custom post type data in shortcodes), where we assemble a query string that indicates the type and maximum quantity of data that we want to retrieve from the database. The resulting query is executed by creating a new instance of the WordPress `WP_Query` object. If results are found, the following recipe code cycles through all the entries and outputs code to render an unordered list of all the items found. Last, but not least, the recipe formats the widget content by outputting the values of the `$before_widget`, `$after_widget`, `$before_title`, and `$after_title` widget class variables, and the user-specified widget title in the right places.

See also

- The *Creating a new widget in WordPress* recipe

Adding a custom dashboard widget

While widgets are primarily used by website administrators to easily add content to their front-facing websites, WordPress contains another type of widget that plugin developers can use to enhance user experience. Dashboard plugins are sections that appear on the front page of a website's administration area. These sections can offer any kind of functionality, from simple information displays indicating how much data is stored in a plugin to forms that allow website administrators to quickly perform configuration tasks.

This recipe shows how to add a new dashboard widget that indicates how many book reviews are stored in the system, along with links to quickly access them.

Getting ready

You should have already followed the *Updating page title to include custom post data using plugin filters* recipe from Chapter 4, *The Power of Custom Post Types*, to have a starting point for this recipe. Alternatively, you can get the resulting code (Chapter 4/ch4-book-reviews/ch4-book-reviews-v11.php) from the code bundle and activate the Chapter 4 - Book Reviews plugin.

How to do it...

1. Navigate to the WordPress plugin directory of your development installation.
2. Create a new directory called `ch10-book-review-dashboard-widget`.
3. Navigate to the directory and create a text file called `ch10-book-review-dashboard-widget.php`.
4. Open the new file in a code editor and add an appropriate header at the top of the plugin file, naming the plugin `Chapter 10 - Book Review Dashboard Widget`.
5. Add the following line of code to register a function to be called when the dashboard contents are being prepared:

```
add_action( 'wp_dashboard_setup',
            'ch10brdw_add_dashboard_widget' );
```

6. Add the following code segment to provide an implementation for the `ch10brdw_add_dashboard_widget` function:

```
function ch10brdw_add_dashboard_widget() {
    wp_add_dashboard_widget( 'book_reviews_dashboard_widget',
                             'Book Reviews',
                             'ch10brdw_dashboard_widget' );
}
```

7. Insert the following block of code to implement the `ch10brdw_dashboard_widget` function declared in the previous step:

```
function ch10brdw_dashboard_widget() {
    $book_review_count = wp_count_posts( 'book_reviews' );
    if ( !empty( (array) $book_review_count ) ) {
    ?>
    <a href="<?php echo add_query_arg( array(
                                'post_status' => 'publish',
                                'post_type' => 'book_reviews' ),
                                admin_url( 'edit.php' ) ); ?>">
    <strong>
        <?php echo $book_review_count->publish; ?>
    </strong> Published
    </a>
    <br />
    <a href="<?php echo add_query_arg( array(
                                'post_status' => 'draft',
                                'post_type' => 'book_reviews' ),
                                admin_url( 'edit.php' ) ); ?>">
```

```
<strong>
    <?php echo $book_review_count->draft; ?>
</strong> Draft
</a>
<?php }
}
```

8. Save and close the plugin file.
9. Navigate to the **Plugins** management page and **Activate** the Chapter 10 – Book Review Dashboard Widget plugin.
10. Navigate to the website's **Dashboard** to see the new **Book Reviews** widget at the bottom of the page, as shown in the following screenshot:

How it works...

Any plugin can register its own dashboard widget when WordPress is putting together content for this administrative landing page. After registering a function to be called during the dashboard setup phase, our recipe makes a call to the wp_add_dashboard_widget function to add our own element to the website when the callback is executed. The wp_add_dashboard_widget function requires three parameters that need to provide a unique identifier for the new item, a title to be displayed at the top of the widget, and a function that will be responsible for generating the widget's contents. The wp_add_dashboard_widget function also has an optional fourth parameter that can be used when the widget needs to process form data as part of the dashboard widget contents.

As can be seen in the previous screenshot, dashboard widgets are displayed using WordPress meta boxes, where any HTML code echoed by the content display function directly appears in the box.

While the display function is mostly composed of HTML code, we also make a call to the wp_count_posts utility function, which easily returns the number of posts for a given post type.

The new widget can be hidden and moved to a new location on the Dashboard, like any other built-in widget. Just like the front-facing widget plugin created earlier in this chapter, it should be noted that all the code in this plugin is in a separate file to the original book review plugin, to organize its code separately from the original plugin file created in `Chapter 4`, *The Power of Custom Post Types*.

See also

- The *Updating page title to include custom post data using plugin filters* recipe in `Chapter 4`, *The Power of Custom Post Types*

Adding a custom widget to the network dashboard

As discussed in the recipe titled *Creating network-level admin pages* back in `Chapter 3`, *User Settings and Administration Pages*, WordPress offers a very powerful mode called Network mode, which allows for multiple websites to be served from a single installation of the platform. When creating a plugin, developers need to think if it would make sense for their plugin to offer a dashboard widget that would only be seen in the network administrator's dashboard instead of being seen in individual website dashboards, or if their plugin's scope is really more relevant at each website's level. The following recipe shows how to modify the dashboard widget defined in the previous recipe so that it appears in the network administration panel on network installations, while still appearing in the administration dashboard in single site installations.

Getting ready

You should have already followed the *Adding a custom dashboard widget* recipe to have a starting point for this recipe. Alternatively, you can get the resulting code (`Chapter 10/ch10-book-review-dashboard-widget/ch10-book-review-dashboard-widget-v1.php`) from the code bundle and rename the file `ch10-book-review-dashboard-widget.php`. You should also have access to a network site configured as a Network to test all of this plugin's functionality.

How to do it...

1. Navigate to the WordPress plugin directory of your development installation.
2. Create a new directory called `ch10-book-review-dashboard-widget` and edit `ch10-book-review-dashboard-widget.php`.
3. Locate the `add_action` call that was first added at the top of the plugin and add the following highlighted lines of code around the existing function call:

```
if ( is_multisite() ) {
    add_action( 'wp_network_dashboard_setup',
                'ch10brdw_add_dashboard_widget' );
} else {
    add_action( 'wp_dashboard_setup',
                'ch10brdw_add_dashboard_widget' );
}
```

4. Locate the `ch10brdw_dashboard_widget` function and add the following code to the function around the existing implementation of the function. The new lines of code are shown in bold:

```
function ch10brdw_dashboard_widget() {
    if ( is_multisite() ) {
        $sites_list = get_sites();
    } else {
        $sites_list = array( 'blog_id' => 1 );
    }

    foreach( $sites_list as $site ) {
        if ( is_multisite() ) {
            switch_to_blog( $site->blog_id );
        }
        $site_name = get_bloginfo( 'name' );
        echo '<div>' . $site_name . '</div>';
        $book_review_count = wp_count_posts( 'book_reviews' );
        ?>
        // REST OF PREVIOUS CODE GOES HERE
        <?php }
    }
    if ( is_multisite() ) {
        restore_current_blog();
    }
}
```

5. Save and close the plugin file.

6. Navigate to the website **Dashboard** (on a single site installation) or to the Network-level **Dashboard** (in a network installation) to see the same widget as before or to see the network-level dashboard, respectively:

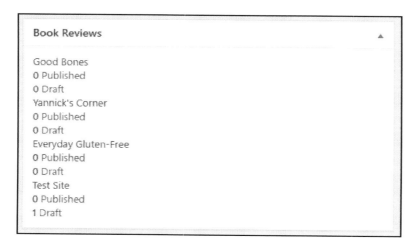

How it works...

The initial change made in this recipe is to check whether the plugin is running on a single site or network installation of WordPress and associate a callback function with the appropriate action hook depending on the result. As you can see, we use the same callback function in both cases, since the widget registering function should call `wp_add_dashboard_widget` to register a widget with the system in either case.

The widget rendering function is also shared between both modes. When running in a network installation, the rendering code first gets a list of all sites using the `get_sites` function, then cycles through the list of sites and uses the `switch_to_blog` function to access data from each site's database tables. Once all the blogs have been processed, we use the `restore_current_blog` function to go back to the original site that is configured as the top-level site in the network.

 It is important to restore the current blog to avoid leaving some internal variables pointing to the wrong site.

When running on a single site installation of WordPress, we create a dummy list of sites that contains a single entry to allow us to use the same `foreach` loop control structure. We then avoid calling the functions that are related to network site operations when WordPress is not configured in the multisite mode. Otherwise, the actual code that queries how many book reviews are present and displays them is identical between both versions of the widget.

See also

- The *Adding a custom dashboard widget* recipe

11
Enabling Plugin Internationalization

In this chapter, you will learn about plugin localization through the following topics:

- Changing the WordPress language configuration
- Adapting default user settings for translation
- Making admin page code ready for translation
- Modifying shortcode output for translation
- Translating text strings using Poedit
- Loading a language file in the plugin initialization

Introduction

WordPress is a worldwide phenomenon, with users embracing the platform all around the globe. To create a more specific experience for users in different locales, WordPress offers the ability to translate all of its user- and visitor-facing content, resulting in numerous localizations becoming available for download online. Like most other functionalities in the platform, internationalization is also available to plugin developers through a set of easy-to-use functions--the main difference being that plugin translations are typically included with the extension, instead of being downloaded separately as is the case with WordPress.

To prepare their plugin to be localized, developers must use special internationalization functions when dealing with text elements. Once this structure is in place, any users can create localizations by themselves for languages that they know and submit them back to the plugin author for inclusion in a future update to the extension. WordPress.org also offers an online interface for users to be able to contribute translations without requiring to use offline tools.

This chapter explains how to prepare a plugin to be translated and shows how to use the Poedit tool to create a new language file for a simple plugin.

Changing the WordPress language configuration

The first step to translate a plugin is to configure WordPress to a different language setting other than English. This will automatically trigger mechanisms in the platform to look for alternate language content for any internationalized string.

In this recipe, we will set the site to **French**.

Getting ready

You should have access to a WordPress development environment.

How to do it...

1. Open your site **Dashboard** and navigate to the **General** section of the **Settings** menu.
2. Set the **Site Language** to **Français du Canada** and click on **Save Changes**.

How it works...

The **Site Language** configuration option of WordPress allows you to select the language that will be seen by visitors when they go to your website. As can be seen in the drop-down list of languages, WordPress has a single language installed by default, shown at the top of the list. The remainder of the list indicates languages that can be added to your website. When you set a new language, translation files are automatically downloaded for the selected language and the new selection becomes the default for visitors. If you look inside the `wp-content/languages` directory of your WordPress installation, you will see that a number of files with `.po` and `.mo` extensions were downloaded for the selected language. Portable object (`.po`) files are ASCII text files that contain a list of all the original English text from the WordPress source code, while machine object (`.mo`) files are binary versions of the translation table that have been compiled to be efficiently loaded by PHP as a website is rendered.

 If you are not presented with a list of languages to install automatically in the **General** section of the **Dashboard**, visit `https://codex.wordpress.org/Installing_WordPress_in_Your_Language` to learn how to manually download and install translation files for WordPress.

Adapting default user settings for translation

Before we can create translation files for our own plugins, their code needs to be specifically written to allow text items to be translated. This work starts in the plugin's activation routine, where default plugin option values are set, to find alternate values when a language other than English is specified in the website's configuration file.

This recipe shows how to assign a translated string to a plugin's default options array on initialization.

Getting ready

You should have already followed the *Changing the WordPress language configuration* recipe to have a specified translation language for the website.

How to do it...

1. Navigate to the WordPress plugin directory of your development installation.
2. Create a new directory called `ch11-hello-world`.
3. Navigate to the directory and create a text file called `ch11-hello-world.php`.
4. Open the new file in a code editor and add an appropriate header at the top of the plugin file, naming the plugin `Chapter 11 - Hello World`.
5. Add the following line of code to register a function to be called when the plugin is activated:

```
register_activation_hook( __FILE__,
                          'ch11hw_set_default_options_array' );
```

6. Insert the following block of code to provide an implementation for the `ch11hw_set_default_options_array` function:

```
function ch11hw_set_default_options_array() {
    if ( false === get_option( 'ch11hw_options' ) ) {
        $new_options = array();
        $new_options['default_text'] = __( 'Hello World',
                                         'ch11hw_hello_world' );
        add_option( 'ch11hw_options', $new_options );
    }
}
```

7. Save and close the plugin file.
8. Navigate to the **Extensions** (Plugins in French) management page and click on the **Activer** (Activate in French) link for the `Chapter 11 - Hello World` plugin.
9. Using phpMyAdmin, find the `options` table entry where the `option_name` field has a value of `ch11hw_options` to see the newly created option:

How it works...

The __ function (that's two underscores) is a WordPress utility function that tries to find a translation for the text that it receives in its first argument within the text domain specified in the second argument. A text domain is essentially a subsection of the global translation table that is managed by WordPress. In this example, the text to be translated is the string `Hello World`, for which the system tries to find a translation in the `ch11hw_hello_world` domain. Since this domain is not available at this time, the function returns the original string that it received as its first parameter. The plugin code assigns the value it receives to the default configuration array.

It should be noted that the __ function is actually an alias for the `translate` function. While both functions have the same functionality, using __ makes the code shorter when it contains a lot of text elements to be translated.

 While it may be tempting for developers to use a variable or constant in the first parameter of the __ function if they need to display the same text multiple times, this should not be done, as it will cause problems with the translation lookup mechanism.

See also

- The *Changing the WordPress language configuration* recipe

Making admin page code ready for translation

While the previous recipe showed how to look up the translation of a text item and return its value for further processing in the plugin code, there are many instances where it is more practical to display the translated content immediately.

This recipe shows how to translate the contents of a simple administration page for immediate display.

Getting ready

You should have already followed the *Adapting default user settings for translation* recipe to have a starting point for this recipe. Alternatively, you can get the resulting code (Chapter 11/ch11-hello-world/ch11-hello-world-v1.php) for that recipe from the code bundle. You should rename the file to ch11-hello-world.php before starting.

How to do it...

1. Navigate to the ch11-hello-world folder of the WordPress plugin directory of your development installation.
2. Open the ch11-hello-world.php file in a text editor.
3. Add the following line of code at the end of the file to register a function to be called when WordPress is building the administration page's menu:

```
add_action( 'admin_menu', 'ch11hw_settings_menu' );
```

4. Add the following code section to provide an implementation for the ch11hw_settings_menu function:

```
function ch11hw_settings_menu() {
    add_options_page(
        __( 'Hello World Configuration', 'ch11hw_hello_world' ),
        __( 'Hello World', 'ch11hw_hello_world' ),
        'manage_options',
        'ch11hw-hello-world', 'ch11hw_config_page' );
}
```

5. Insert the following block of code to create the ch11hw_config_page function declared in the call to add_options_page:

```
function ch11hw_config_page() {
    $options = get_option( 'ch11hw_options' );
    ?>

    <div id="ch11hw-general" class="wrap">
    <!-- Echo translation for "Hello World" to the browser -->
    <h2><?php _e( 'Hello World', 'ch11hw_hello_world' ); ?></h2>
    <form method="post" action="admin-post.php">
    <input type="hidden" name="action"
           value="save_ch11hw_options" />
    <?php wp_nonce_field( 'ch11hw' ); ?>
```

```
<!-- Echo translation for "Hello World" to the browser -->
<?php _e( 'Default Text', 'ch11hw_hello_world' ); ?>:
<input type="text" name="default_text"
        value="<?php echo
                esc_html( $options['default_text'] ); ?>"/>
<br />
<input type="submit" value="<?php _e( 'Submit',
    'ch11hw_hello_world' ); ?>" class="button-primary"/>
</form>
</div>
<?php }
```

6. Add the following line of code to register a function to be executed when the administration panel is being prepared to be displayed:

```
add_action( 'admin_init', 'ch11hw_admin_init' );
```

7. Append the following code segment to provide an implementation for the ch11hw_admin_init function:

```
function ch11hw_admin_init() {
    add_action( 'admin_post_save_ch11hw_options',
                'process_ch11hw_options' );
}
```

8. Provide code for the process_ch11hw_options function, declared in the previous step, by inserting the following code:

```
function process_ch11hw_options() {
    if ( !current_user_can( 'manage_options' ) ) {
        wp_die( 'Not allowed' );
    }

    check_admin_referer( 'ch11hw' );

    $options = get_option( 'ch11hw_options' );
    $options['default_text'] = $_POST['default_text'];

    update_option( 'ch11hw_options', $options );
    wp_redirect( add_query_arg( 'page', 'ch11hw-hello-world',
                    admin_url( 'options-general.php' ) ) );
    exit;
}
```

9. Save and close the plugin file.

10. Navigate to the administration page of your development WordPress installation.

11. Click on the **Réglages** (Settings in French) section on the left-hand navigation menu to expand it. You will see a new menu item called **Hello World** in the tree. Selecting the new entry displays the plugin's simple configuration form, as shown in the following screenshot:

How it works...

This recipe makes use of the ___ function, covered in the previous recipe, along with the _e function. This second function's purpose is similar to ___, except that it immediately echoes the outcome of the translation lookup to the browser. It should be used for all text elements that would previously have just been simple text in HTML code. Of course, making a call to this function requires the presence of standard opening and closing PHP tags (<? and ?>) to be executed among the surrounding HTML.

The rest of this plugin's code takes care of storing user updates in the website database, as covered previously in Chapter 3, *User Settings and Administration Pages*.

See also

- The *Adapting default user settings for translation* recipe

Modifying shortcode output for translation

As we have seen in numerous recipes, shortcodes are powerful tools that provide an easy way for users to add content to their website posts and pages. Since this content is presented to users, it can benefit from a translation just as much as the website's administration pages.

This recipe shows how to translate shortcode output before it is displayed. It also explains how to deal with variable data elements that can be positioned differently between languages.

Getting ready

You should have already followed the *Making admin page code ready for translation* recipe to have a starting point for this recipe. Alternatively, you can get the resulting code (Chapter 11/ch11-hello-world/ch11-hello-world-v2.php) for that recipe from the code bundle. You should rename the file to ch11-hello-world.php before starting.

How to do it...

1. Navigate to the ch11-hello-world folder of the WordPress plugin directory of your development installation.
2. Open the ch11-hello-world.php file in a text editor.
3. Add the following line of code at the end of the file to declare a new shortcode that will be available to content authors:

```
add_shortcode( 'hello-world', 'ch11hw_hello_world_shortcode' );
```

4. Add the following code section to provide an implementation for the ch11hw_hello_world_shortcode function:

```
function ch11hw_hello_world_shortcode() {
    $options = get_option( 'ch11hw_options' );
    $output = sprintf( __( 'The current text string is: %s.',
                       'ch11hw_hello_world' ),
                       $options['default_text'] );
    return $output;
}
```

5. Save and close the plugin file.
6. Create a new page (using the **Ajouter** item of the **Pages** menu) and insert the new shortcode [hello-world] in the content, then publish the page (**Publier**).

7. View the page (**Voir la page**) to see the output of the shortcode:

HELLO WORLD   The current text string is: Hello World.
Edit

How it works...

This recipe shows something that's a bit more complex than the previous two, as we want the shortcode output to be a combination of static text with a dynamic element, and we want that element to appear in different places based on the grammatical structure of the target language. The way to achieve this functionality is to combine the __ internationalization function with the `sprintf` standard PHP function.

The purpose of the `sprintf` function is to insert a variable in a string. It performs this task by looking for a placeholder in the target string sent in the first argument, and replaces it with the variable that it receives as its second argument. Some examples of placeholders are `%s` for a string and `%d` for an integer. With this functionality in mind, we use a placeholder as part of the string to be translated so that users who create localization files can choose where the value will be placed as part of the sentence structure. Once the translation has been obtained by the __ function, we can immediately send the alternate language string to `sprintf` to create the final text.

See also

- The *Adapting default user settings for translation* recipe

Translating text strings using Poedit

After inserting all the necessary code to look up translations for text elements, we need to create the actual translation files. While there are multiple tools available to perform this task, we will focus our efforts around the most popular one, the free multiplatform Poedit.

This recipe shows how to extract all the strings to be translated from the plugin's code using Poedit, translate them, and save the resulting language file under the plugin directory.

Getting ready

You should have already followed the *Modifying shortcode output for translation* recipe to have a starting point for this recipe. Alternatively, you can get the resulting code (Chapter 11/ch11-hello-world/ch11-hello-world-v3.php) for that recipe from the code bundle. You should rename the file to ch11-hello-world.php before starting.

How to do it...

1. Navigate to the ch11-hello-world folder of the WordPress plugin directory of your development installation.
2. Create a new subdirectory named languages.
3. Navigate to the Poedit download page and download the appropriate version of the tool for your computer (https://www.poedit.net/download).
4. Install and start the Poedit application.
5. Select the **New...** menu item under the application's **File** menu.

 While Poedit offers an automated way to create translations for WordPress themes or plugins, we will focus on the free version of Poedit and highlight all steps required to create a translation in this mode.

6. Select **French (Canada)** as **Language of the translation**.
7. Click on the **Save** button from the toolbar, navigate to the languages folder created earlier in this recipe, and set the filename to ch11hw_hello_world-fr_CA.po.
8. Click on the **Extract from sources** button in the main interface window to open the **Catalog Properties** window, which will default to the **Sources paths** tab.

TIP

If the Poedit window is too small, it will not display the main interface section. Simply make the window larger to see the **Extract from sources** button.

9. Create a new entry in the **Paths** list by pressing the **New item** button.
10. Set the value of the new path entry to . . (two period characters).
11. Switch to the **Sources keywords** tab and add two new items to the list of **Additional keywords** and set their values to __ and _e.
12. Switch to the **Translation** properties tab and set the **Project name and version** field to Hello World.
13. Click on the **OK** button to close the **Catalog properties** dialog, then click on **Save** from the toolbar to be able to start editing entries in the file.
14. Select the items one by one in order to display them in the lower section of the window.
15. Enter a translation for each text element in the lower dialog box. The following screenshot shows the translations of each item to French:

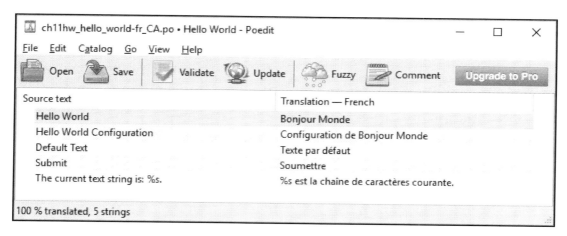

16. Save the translation file once completed.

How it works...

The Poedit tool searches through PHP files, looking for functions that have specific names, as specified in the **Keywords** configuration section. It looks through all the files located in the same directory as the catalog itself and in any additional folders specified under the **Paths** section of the catalog settings. By specifying `..` as an additional path, we tell Poedit to look one directory up from the `languages` folder, where the plugin files are located.

Based on the configuration that we specified, Poedit is able to find all the instances of the `__` and `_e` functions in the plugin code and retrieve the text strings that are set as the first argument to these functions. Once all the strings have been found, Poedit provides a simple interface to provide translations for each string and saves the resulting translation file. Upon saving, Poedit actually creates two files, the portable object file and the machine object file.

The name of the language files is made from two parts: the name of the text domain, `ch11hw_hello_world`, which was used in all of our calls to the `__` and `_e` functions in the previous recipes, and the target language code, `fr_CA`, to match the language configuration that we set earlier in this chapter. To support all the variants of the French language that WordPress supports, you can copy the translation files, changing the language code each time in the Poedit catalog configuration, as well as in the file names (`ch11hw_hello_world-fr_CA.po` and `ch11hw_hello_world-fr_BE.po`).

There's more...

If you are only comfortable with English, create a template file that users will be able to import to start their translation.

Translation template file

When you are only familiar with English, you can create a translation template that only contains the text to be translated by saving the catalog as a `.pot` file instead of a `.po`/`.mo` combination. In addition to the special extension, the filename should not contain a language tag (for example, `ch11hw_hello_world.pot`).

See also

- The *Adapting default user settings for translation* recipe

Loading a language file in the plugin initialization

The final step to plugin translation is to put the code in place to load a translation file. This is done by registering an action hook callback and calling a single function when it gets executed.

This recipe shows how to load the translation file created in the previous recipe.

Getting ready

You should have already followed the *Making admin page code ready for translation* and *Translating text strings using Poedit* recipes to have the proper files required for this recipe. Alternatively, you can get the resulting code (Chapter 11/ch11-hello-world/ch11-hello-world-v3.php and Chapter 11/ch11-hello-world/languages folder) for these recipes from the code bundle. You should rename the file ch11-hello-world-v3.php to ch11-hello-world.php and copy the languages folder next to the renamed file before starting the recipe.

How to do it...

1. Navigate to the ch11-hello-world folder of the WordPress plugin directory of your development installation.
2. Open the ch11-hello-world.php file in a text editor.
3. Add the following line of code at the end of the file to register a function to be called when the plugin is initialized:

```
add_action( 'init', 'ch11hw_plugin_init' );
```

4. Add the following code section to provide an implementation for the `ch11hw_plugin_init` function:

```
function ch11hw_plugin_init() {
    load_plugin_textdomain( 'ch11hw_hello_world', false,
                            dirname( plugin_basename( __FILE__ ) )
                            . '/languages' );
}
```

5. Locate the `ch11hw_set_default_options_array` function and add the same call to `load_plugin_textdomain` at the top of the function before the `if` statement:

```
load_plugin_textdomain( 'ch11hw_hello_world', false,
                        dirname( plugin_basename( __FILE__ ) )
                        . '/languages' );
```

6. Save and close the plugin file.
7. Navigate to the **Réglages** menu to see if the plugin's menu item has changed.
8. Select the **Bonjour Monde** item to see the translated configuration page:

How it works...

The `load_plugin_textdomain` function has three arguments. When called, it looks in the folder specified in the last parameter for a `.mo` file with a name starting with the text domain specified in the first parameter, followed by the current language set in the WordPress configuration file. If found, the translation file is loaded in memory and is used to search for translations every time the `__` or `_e` functions are encountered during execution. The middle argument, set to a `false` value, is obsolete but is still needed for backward compatibility.

Once all the hooks are in place in the plugin code, and a first translation file (or template) is made available with the plugin, users can easily modify text elements to other languages, which they can use immediately. They can also provide these new translations back to the plugin author for inclusion in future updates. We added a second call to `load_plugin_textdomain` in the activation hook, since the `init` action hook is not executed when activation hooks execute.

There's more…

As a plugin evolves over time, new text items may need to be translated. There may also be a need to use more advanced translation functions and translate JavaScript code.

Updating a translation file

When new calls to the __ or _e functions are made in a plugin, the translation file needs to be updated to take new text elements into account. To do this, start the Poedit tool and open the existing catalog. Then, select **Update** from the toolbar. This will extract all the text items and identify new entries. Once this is done, new items can be translated and saved back to the catalog file.

Advanced translation functions

While we used the most common internationalization functions in this chapter, there are a few more advanced functions that may be useful in your efforts:

- `_n( $singular, $plural, $number, $domain )`: This function will look up one of the first two strings received, depending on whether the number is one or more.
- `_x( $text, $context, $domain )`: Adds a parameter to the localization lookup to add a context parameter. This is useful when dealing with words that have the same spelling but different meanings.
- `_ex( $text, $context, $domain )`: Same as _x but echoes the result of the lookup.
- `_nx( $singular, $plural, $number, $context, $domain)`: Same as _n with the additional context parameter from _x.

There are also a number of functions that will perform a localization lookup immediately, followed by the escape of the resulting string. These functions include `esc_attr__()`, `esc_attr_e()`, `esc_html__()`, `esc_html_x()`, and many more. For a full list of internationalization functions, visit `https://codex.wordpress.org/L10n`.

Localizing JavaScript files

JavaScript files are a bit more tricky to translate, as they are often read from an external file that cannot contain any PHP code. The solution to this is the `wp_localize_script` function. When called, this function declares new variables in scripts that have already been queued up to be loaded, and populates these variables with localized strings. Upon execution, the code will be able to access and display the proper text on screen. The following code snippet is an example showing how to use the function:

```
wp_enqueue_script( 'script_handle' );
$translation_vars = array( 'string_val' =>
                    __( 'Text to be translated' ) );
wp_localize_script( 'script_handle', 'javascript_object',
              $translation_vars );
```

In the previous code example, a new object called `javascript_object` will be created inside the `script_handle` script, with a data member called `string_val` that contains a translation of the target text in the current WordPress language, if available.

See also

- The *Translating text strings using Poedit* recipe

12
Distributing Your Plugin on wordpress.org

In this chapter, we will discuss how to distribute your creations, covering the following topics:

- Creating a readme file for your plugin
- Applying for your plugin to be hosted on wordpress.org
- Uploading your plugin using Subversion
- Providing plugin banner and thumbnail images

Introduction

Once you have a version of your new plugin that is ready to be distributed to the masses, you need to decide whether you will join the official WordPress repository or self-publish it.

In most cases, the preferred option is to add your new extension to the official WordPress plugin repository, where you have many benefits, including free hosting, built-in notification of new updates, and a powerful search engine that users can access on https://wordpress.org or from the **Plugins** section of their website's administration pages. Other benefits of hosting on the official repository include download statistics and the creation of a free forum to facilitate user support. To qualify for this hosting, your work must be free and open source, as well as comply with the GNU General Public License, Version 2 (also known as GPL v2), a common open source software license that WordPress itself uses.

This includes any code you wrote, along with any third-party PHP or Javascript libraries that you have included in your work. To learn more about the GPL v2 license, visit `https://www.gnu.org/licenses/gpl-2.0.html`. It is also possible to publish a plugin with paid premium features on the official repository, but you cannot move free features behind a paywall over time.

In comparison, self-hosting gives you full control over pricing, distribution license, and general presentation of your work, but it makes it harder for people to find your plugin and relies on implementing a custom update notification mechanism yourself, using third-party libraries to add equivalent functionality or having users manually download updates when available. There are also a number of popular plugin digital marketplaces that can help alleviate some of these drawbacks, but your work will still have less visibility than it would on the official repository.

Before making your plugin publicly available, you should also be sure that you are ready to deal with user feedback and questions. Once your creation is available for download, WordPress website administrators will quickly download it, install it, and may find that your work covers most, but not all, of their needs. When this happens, you will start getting requests to add functionality. This interaction with users is usually a great experience that can bring new ideas to the table that will enhance your work, but you should also be ready to accept criticism and invest time in fixing issues and implementing new features. You also need to think of the time that will be involved in testing your extension against new versions of WordPress, which typically come out two to three times a year.

This chapter explains how to prepare your work to be uploaded to the official plugin repository, including the application for an account, the actual code submission using Subversion, and how to customize your plugin page to give it a unique look.

Creating a README file for your plugin

If you look at any plugins on the official WordPress repository, you will see that their page contains a lot of information, including a description of the extension, a list of frequently asked questions, and installation notes. As you may have noticed from the work that we have done so far, this data does not reside in the main plugin's code file. Instead, the official WordPress repository looks for this information in a specially formatted `readme.txt` file that needs to be included with the plugin.

This recipe shows how to create a `readme.txt` file for the Book Reviews plugin that we created in *Chapter 4*, *The Power of Custom Post Types*.

Getting ready

You should have already followed the *Updating page title to include custom post data using plugin filters* recipe from *Chapter 4*, *The Power of Custom Post Types*, to have a starting point for this recipe. Alternatively, you can get the resulting code (`Chapter 4/ch4-book-reviews/ch4-book-reviews-v11.php`) for that recipe from the code bundle.

How to do it...

1. Navigate to the `ch4-book-reviews` folder of your WordPress plugins directory.
2. Create a new text file named `readme.txt` and open it in a code editor.
3. Insert the following text in the file:

```
=== Book Reviews ===
Contributors: ylefebvre
Donate link: http://ylefebvre.ca/wordpress-plugins/book-reviews
Tags: book, reviews
Requires at least: 4.0
Tested up to: 4.8
Stable tag: trunk
License: GPLv2 or later
License URI: https://www.gnu.org/licenses/gpl-2.0.html

Create your own book review web site!

== Description ==

This plugin lets you add a book review system to your WordPress
site. Using custom post types, administrators will be able to
create and edit book reviews to be published on your site.

== Installation ==

1. Download the plugin
1. Upload the book-reviews folder to your site's wp-content/plugins
directory
1. Activate the plugin in the WordPress Admin Panel
1. Start creating new book reviews!
1. Use the [book-review-list] shortcode to list reviews on a page.
```

```
== Changelog ==

= 1.0 =
* First version of the plugin.

== Frequently Asked Questions ==

There are currently no FAQs at this time.

== Screenshots ==

1. The review edition page
```

4. Save and close the text file.
5. Navigate to the **Book Reviews** edition page and take a screenshot using a third-party screen capture tool or your operating system's built-in function.
6. Save the resulting image as `screenshot-1.jpg` in the plugin directory.

How it works...

The `readme.txt` file uses a wiki-like syntax, with the number of equal signs (=) indicating the level of each section header. The first and most important section is the header, which contains important information, such as the plugin's name, the author's `https://wordpress.org` username, donation link, search tags, supported versions, along with a one-line description of its functionality. This last item will always be visible as users navigate through your plugin's pages.

The initial header is followed by multiple sections, which correspond to the various sections that appear within a plugin's display pages. More specifically, these sections contain a complete description of the extension's capability, a step-by-step guide to installing and using your work, a change log containing a list of all the versions with a summary of changes for each of them, frequently asked questions, and screenshots. It is also possible for plugin authors to create their own arbitrary section using the same syntax.

As with the standard wiki syntax, the repeating 1. in front of each installation step will be converted to incrementing values when the system displays these bullets using an ordered list on the live website. Finally, if screenshots are listed in the readme.txt file, the https://wordpress.org website will search for files whose names start with the keyword screenshot-, followed by a number corresponding to the values listed in the screenshot section, and display them with the associated text as a legend. When taking screenshots of your plugin in action, make sure that they are clear and meaningful, as visitors will often decide whether they will download your creations based on these images.

You can find more details about the readme.txt file format in the https://wordpress.org plugin handbook (https://developer.wordpress.org/plugins/wordpress-org/how-you r-readme-txt-works/).

There's more...

To keep plugin code files more organized and have complete control over releases, you should consider using Subversion tags.

Releasing specific plugin versions using tags

Tags are a Subversion concept that allows developers to identify a group of files at a specific point in time and label them with a name. This name can be used to specify the version of your plugin that https://wordpress.org visitors will be able to download. While this recipe specifies a value of trunk as the Stable Tag, indicating that the latest version of the files uploaded to the plugin's trunk folder will be released, it's possible to indicate any other tag name in this field. In addition to keeping your work more organized, working with tags allows you to commit partially implemented new plugin features to your repository without having them automatically available for all to access.

Applying for your plugin to be hosted on WordPress.org

After creating proper documentation for your creation, the next step toward its publication on the official plugin repository is to apply for hosting. This is simply done by submitting a request form in the **Developer Center** section on `http://wordpress.org`.

This recipe shows how to apply for plugin hosting and offers tips to follow for quick acceptance.

How to do it...

1. Create a zip archive containing your entire plugin directory, including the `readme.txt` file created in the previous recipe.
2. Log into the `https://wordpress.org` website using the form at the top of the plugin submission page with your existing credentials or create a new account if you don't currently have one.
3. Point your web browser to the plugin hosting request form page, which is available at `https://wordpress.org/plugins/developers/add/`.
4. Select your ZIP file and upload it to the site.

How it works...

Plugin submission is a fairly simple process, giving developers access to a Subversion repository that they can use to upload their work and share it with the community.

Before submitting your plugin, you should search through existing plugins to be sure that you have not selected a name that already exists in the repository, as that will result in your request being turned down. You can do this by using the website's search engine, as well as trying to access an address that was named based on your plugin name. For example, following our **Book Reviews** plugin example, you could check to see whether the address `https://wordpress.org/plugins/book-reviews` exists.

It should be noted that your plugin needs to be functional when you apply to be listed on the repository. Once your plugin has been approved, you will get access to a hosted Subversion version control repository to easily keep backups of all the versions of your work during development and easily publish your work. If you work on a plugin with one or more people, this infrastructure will make it very easy to exchange code between all contributors.

See also

- The *Creating a README file for your plugin* recipe

Uploading your plugin using Subversion

If you thought that using Subversion in the recipes of `Chapter 1`, *Preparing a Local Development Environment*, was overkill when you're working on a plugin locally, you will see that this knowledge comes in very handy once your hosting request has been approved by the WordPress team, as the system's backend relies on that version control system.

This recipe shows how to submit your creation to the `https://wordpress.org` website once a repository has been created for you.

Getting ready

You should have already followed the *Applying for your plugin to be hosted on WordPress.org* recipe to have an approved repository on the official website. You should have also installed a Subversion client, as shown in the *Creating a local Subversion repository* recipe in `Chapter 1`, *Preparing a Local Development Environment*. Finally, you should have plugin files ready for upload.

How to do it...

1. Right-click on a file explorer and select the **TortoiseSVN | Repo-browser** menu.
2. Enter the address of your new repository, as indicated in your hosting approval email. For example, for a plugin named **Book Reviews**, the address would be `http://plugins.svn.wordpress.org/book-reviews`:

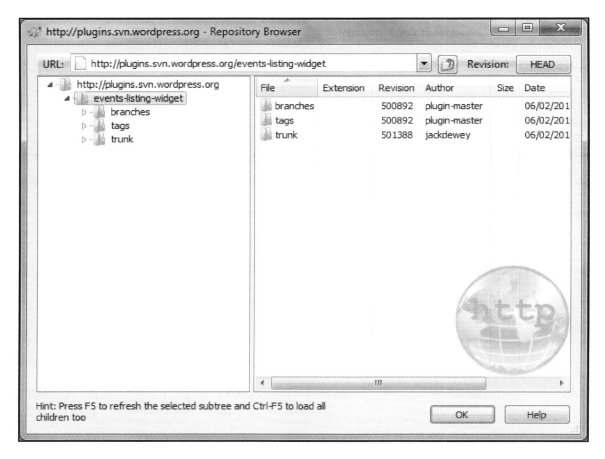

3. Right-click on the plugin's name on the left-hand side tree view and select the **Checkout** option.
4. Select a local folder on your computer as the **Checkout directory**.

5. Click on **OK** to create a local copy of the server structure with the accompanying version control data.

6. Copy your plugin's files to the `trunk` folder of the resulting directory structure if it is empty, or update existing files with newer versions if you continued working on them after submission.

7. If you added any new files, right-click on them, and select the **TortoiseSVN | Add...** menu.

8. Right-click on the `trunk` folder and select the **SVN Commit...** menu option.

9. Enter a message indicating that you are uploading new files to the plugin repository and what changes have been made.

10. Click on **OK** to upload your files to the official repository.

11. When prompted for authentication, use your `https://wordpress.org`**Username** and **Password**. Click on the **Save authentication** checkbox to avoid providing these credentials each time.

12. After committing files, you will receive an email confirming that they have been uploaded to the repository, along with information on any changes that were made to each file. You will then be able to visit your plugin's page and download it. For our example, the **Book Reviews** plugin, the address of the page would be `https://wordpress.org/plugins/book-reviews`:

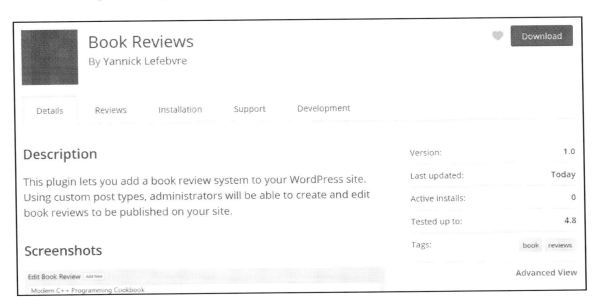

How it works…

The official WordPress plugin repository uses Subversion to manage all code files, provide version control services to developers, and find information to populate the extension's page. When your new repository is created, it contains three main directories: `trunk`, `tags`, and `branches`.

The `trunk` directory is usually the main location where you place the latest version of your plugin files. Following the steps in the recipe, we copy our files to this location and commit them to the server. Once uploaded, the WordPress.org servers take care of creating a zipped copy of your work.

The `tags` directory is designed to hold pointers to various versions of your creation over time, as discussed in the *Creating a README file for your plugin* recipe. This functionality used in conjunction with the **Stable tag** field of your plugin's `readme.txt` file allows you to redirect users to a known working version of your work while you commit and test potentially unstable work to the `trunk`. New tags are created using the **Branch/Tag** item of the **TortoiseSVN** menu and associating a name to a specific revision. The `branches` directory has a similar function to `tags`, but is more focused toward the creation of alternate versions of plugins or in-development revisions that include specific functionality.

There's more…

If you want to execute your plugin's code in a local WordPress development installation as you are writing it, the following section shows you how to manage your code.

Checking out plugins to your development installation

When checking out the complete plugin directory, you end up with a structure that cannot be executed directly in a local development installation of WordPress for testing and development purposes. Instead of checking out the entire directory structure, you can limit your selection to the `trunk` directory. This will only copy the contents of that specific folder to your system and you can set the target folder to be located directly under the plugins directory.

See also

- The *Creating a README file for your plugin* recipe
- The *Checking out files from a Subversion repository* recipe in `Chapter 1`, *Preparing a Local Development Environment*
- The *Committing changes to a Subversion repository* recipe in `Chapter 1`, *Preparing a Local Development Environment*

Providing plugin banner and thumbnail images

While the plugin listing that we put in place by creating a `readme.txt` file and uploading it to the official plugin repository is perfectly functional, it does not really stand out among the sea of extensions that are available on the website. Thankfully, `https://wordpress.org` introduced a mechanism allowing plugin developers to add a banner image to their listing. This image can be anything from a simple picture to a complex graphic to advertise your creation.

This recipe explains how to prepare images for your plugin and how to upload them to your repository.

Getting ready

You should have already followed the *Applying for your plugin to be hosted on wordpress.org* and *Uploading your plugin using Subversion* recipes to have an approved repository on the official repository and plugin files uploaded to the server.

How to do it...

1. Create a new image that is exactly 772 x 250 pixels.
2. Save the image as a PNG file with the name `banner-772x250.png`.
3. Right-click on a file explorer and select the **TortoiseSVN** | **Repo-Browser** menu.

4. Enter the address of your plugin repository. For example, for a plugin named **Book Reviews**, the address would be `http://plugins.svn.wordpress.org/book-reviews`.

5. Create a new top-level directory named `assets`, at the same level as `trunk`, `tags`, and `branches`.

6. Select the `assets` directory, then drag and drop the new image file in the folder to upload it to the server.

7. Specify a Log Message in the dialog that appears to explain why the file is being uploaded.

8. Create smaller images that are exactly 256 x 256 pixels and 128 x 128 pixels in size and name the files `icon-256x256.png` and `icon-128x128.png`, respectively. The larger icon should be a higher resolution version of the exact content of the smaller one, since it will be used to replace the smaller one on high DPI displays.

9. Repeat steps 6 and 7 to upload the two icons to the `assets` directory.

10. Visit your plugin's page on `https://wordpress.org` to see the images in place:

11. Search for your plugin through the `https://wordpress.org/plugins`page or the **Add New** section of the **Plugins** management interface of WordPress to see how the icon and short plugin description are used:

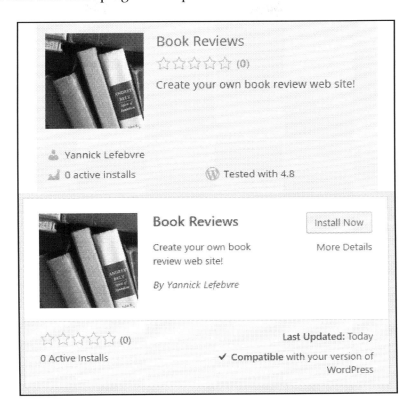

How it works…

When files are uploaded to the plugin repositories, the `https://wordpress.org` website checks for the presence of specific image files with specific names for the plugin banner and icon. If these files are present, it changes the layout of the plugin page to incorporate the images. It is important to respect the image format and specified dimensions when creating a plugin banner and icons to make sure that they are displayed properly on the website.

See also

- The *Uploading your plugin using Subversion* recipe

Index

A

action hooks
  online listings 43
  user settings, accessing 116
admin code
  splitting, for site optimization from plugin file 124,
    125, 126
admin page contents
  rendering, with HTML 95, 96, 97
  rendering, with Settings API 108, 109, 111, 113,
    114
  wp_nonce_field function 98
admin page
  code, creating for translation 327, 328, 330
  custom table data, displaying 256, 258, 259
  formatting, with meta boxes 118, 120, 121, 122,
    123, 124
  multiple sets of user settings, managing 132,
    133, 136, 138
  tooltips, adding to form fields with TipTip plugin
    293, 294, 296
administration page menu item
  creating, in settings menu 84, 85, 87
Akismet API
  URL 228
Application Programming Interface (API) 74
application security risks
  reference 97
arrays
  user settings, storing 78, 79, 80, 81
Asynchronous JavaScript and XML (AJAX)
  about 297
  used, for updating partial page contents 296,
    297, 298, 300, 301, 302

B

built-in ThickBox plugin
  used, for displaying pop-up dialog 283, 284, 285

C

calendar day selector
  displaying, with Datepicker plugin 290, 291, 292,
    293
CAPTCHA
  implementing, on user forms with local library
    225, 227, 228
  implementing, on user forms with online service
    221, 222, 223, 225
  URL, for downloading 226
client-side content submission form
  creating 210, 213
coding errors
  troubleshooting 56, 57, 59, 60
Comma-Separated Values (CSV) 275
confirmation message
  displaying 102, 103, 104
Cornerstone
  URL 21
CSSTidy
  URL 132
custom categories
  filters, adding to custom post list page 177, 178,
    179, 180
  Quick Edit fields, adding 180, 187
custom dashboard widget
  adding 315, 318
custom database table data
  displaying, in shortcode 269, 271
Custom Field section
  hiding, in post editor 199, 200, 201
custom fields

adding, to categories 166, 167, 169
adding, to user editor 229, 230, 232
custom help pages
  adding 104, 105, 106, 107
custom meta boxes
  information, capturing 192, 193, 194, 195
  information, displaying 192, 193, 194, 195
  meta box, adding to all post types 196
custom post data
  displaying, with filter functions 196, 198
  page title, updating with plugin filters 187, 189
custom post list page
  additional columns, displaying 173, 177
  filters, adding for custom categories 177, 178, 179, 180
custom post type editor
  category editor, hiding 170, 171
  section, adding 150, 151, 153, 154
custom post type
  creating 144, 146, 147, 148, 149
  custom categories, adding 163, 164, 165, 166
  data, displaying in shortcodes 158, 160, 162
  items, displaying with custom layout 154, 155, 157, 158
  permalinks slug, modifying 149
  reference 149
  user-submitted content, saving 213, 214, 216, 217
custom table data
  displaying, on admin page 256, 258, 259
  retrieving, with search function 272, 273, 274
custom table structure
  updating, on plugin upgrade 253, 255
custom tables
  data, importing from user file 275, 278
  deleting, on plugin removal 251, 252, 253
  records, deleting 265, 266, 268
  records, inserting 259, 262, 264
  records, updating 259, 262, 264
custom user data
  used, in containing shortcode 240
custom widget
  adding, to network dashboard 318, 319, 320, 321

D

database tables
  code creation, simplifying with phpMyAdmin 248, 249
  creating 244, 245, 246, 247
  creating, in network installation 249, 251
Datepicker plugin
  URL 291
  used, for displaying calendar day selector 290, 291, 292, 293
deactivation function 77
Debug Bar plugin
  URL 60
debugging features
  SAVEQUERIES 61
  WP_DEBUG_DISPLAY 61
  WP_DEBUG_LOG 61
dedicated code editor
  installing 31, 32, 34
default user settings
  creating, on plugin initialization 74, 76, 77

E

EasyPHP
  URL 13
email icon
  URL, for downloading 51
email notifications
  sending, upon new submissions 218, 219, 220
enclosing shortcode
  creating 66, 67
external files
  loading, with WordPress path utility functions 44, 45, 46
external images
  loading, with WordPress path utility functions 44, 45, 46

F

filter functions
  used, for displaying custom post data 196, 198
filter hooks
  user settings, accessing 116
filters

adding, to custom categories to custom post list
    page 177, 178, 179, 180

G

Git
    URL 22
Google Images
    URL 147
Google reCAPTCHA
    URL 222
GPL v2 license
    URL 342

H

hooks
    about 36
    searching, in WordPress source code 43
    URL 43
HTML
    used, for rendering admin page contents 95, 96,
    97

I

IconArchive
    URL 89, 146, 157
internationalization functions
    URL 339
items
    hiding, from unauthorized users 93, 94

J

JavaScript files
    localizing 339
jQuery
    loading, onto WordPress web pages 280, 281,
    282
    noconflict mode 282

L

language file
    loading, in plugin initialization 336, 337, 338
link statistics tracking code
    inserting, in page body with plugin filters 53, 54,
    56

local library
    used, for implementing CAPTCHA on user forms
    225, 227, 228
local Subversion repository
    creating 19, 20, 21
    initial files, importing 22, 24
    manual repository, creating 22
    other version control systems 22
local WordPress installation
    configuring 14, 15, 16, 18, 19
    downloading 14, 15, 16, 18, 19

M

MAMP
    URL 13
menu items
    adding, to external pages 91, 92
Mercurial
    URL 22
meta boxes
    adding, to all post types 196
    used, for formatting admin pages 118, 120, 121,
    122, 123, 124
multi-level administration menu
    creating 88, 90, 91
multisite network
    reference 139

N

network dashboard
    custom widget, adding to 318, 319, 320, 321
network-level admin pages
    creating 139, 140, 141, 142
Notepad++
    URL 32

O

object-oriented PHP
    used, for writing plugins 70, 71
online service
    used, for implementing CAPTCHA on user forms
    221, 222, 223, 225

P

PagaVCS
  URL 21
page headers
  output content, adding with plugin actions 40, 41, 42
partial page contents
  updating, with AJAX 296, 297, 298, 300, 301, 302
Permalinks 88
phpMyAdmin
  used, for simplifying code creation 248, 249
plugin actions
  action hooks, online listings 43
  hooks, searching in WordPress source code 43
  used, for adding output content to page headers 40, 41, 42
plugin banner
  providing 351, 352, 353
plugin configuration data
  processing 98, 99, 101, 102
  storing 98, 99, 101, 102
plugin data
  removing, on deletion 81, 82, 83, 84
plugin file
  creating 36, 38, 39
plugin filters
  apply_filters function, using 49, 50
  filter hooks, listing 49, 50
  get_permalink() function 53
  get_the_title() function 53
  link statistics tracking code, inserting in page body 53, 54, 56
  text, adding after each item's content 50, 52
  used, for modifying site generator meta tag 47, 48, 49
  used, for updating page title to include custom post data 187, 189
plugin header
  creating 36, 38, 39
plugin initialization
  advanced translation functions 338
  deactivation function 77
  default user settings, creating 74, 76, 77
  JavaScript files, localizing 339

  language file, loading 336, 337, 338
  translation file, updating 338
plugin output
  formatting, with style sheet 68
plugins
  checking out, to development installation 350
  extending, other plugins 306
  hosting, on WordPress.org 346, 347
  README file, creating 342, 344, 345
  specific plugin versions, releasing with tags 345
  uploading, with Subversion 347, 348, 350
  writing, with object-oriented PHP 70, 71
Poedit
  URL 333
  used, for translating text strings 332, 333, 334, 335
pop-up dialog
  dialog close button, removing 286
  display, controlling with shortcodes 287, 288, 290
  displaying, on selected pages 286, 287
  displaying, with built-in ThickBox plugin 283, 284, 285
post editor
  Custom Field section, hiding 199, 200, 201
  users, allowing to upload files directly 201, 202, 203, 206, 207
post types
  meta box, adding 196
Programmer's Notepad
  URL 32

Q

Quick Edit fields
  adding, for custom categories 180, 187

R

README file
  creating, for plugin 342, 344, 345
  reference 345
register_taxonomy function
  URL 166
remote web development environment
  creating 13

S

SAVEQUERIES
URL 61
Screem
URL 32
search function
implementing, to retrieve custom table data 272, 273, 274
Settings API
drop-down list settings field, rendering 114
text area settings field, rendering 115
used, for rendering admin page contents 108, 109, 111, 113, 114
Settings menu
administration page menu item, creating 84, 85, 87
menu order, determining 88
shortcode
about 61
creating 61, 62, 63
creating, with parameters 63, 65
custom database table data, displaying 269, 271
custom post type data, displaying 158, 160, 162
custom user data, using 240
do_shortcode function 163
enclosing shortcode, creating 66, 67
output, modifying for translation 330, 331, 332
used, for controlling pop-up dialog display 287, 288, 290
site generator meta tag
modifying, with plugin filters 47, 48, 49
site performance optimization
via splitting admin code from plugin file 124, 125, 126
SmartSVN
URL 21
Structured Query Language (SQL) 244
style sheet
data storing, in user settings 127, 131, 132
loading, to format plugin output 68
Sublime Text
URL 32
Subversion client for Mac
URL 21
Subversion file, statuses

Added 27
Conflicted 27
Deleted 27
Ignored 27
Modified 27
Non-versioned 27
Normal 26
Subversion repository
changes, committing 27, 28, 29, 30
differences, viewing in modified files 30
file history, viewing 31
files, checking out 24, 25, 26
files, updating to latest repository version 31
uncommitted file changes, reverting 31
Subversion
URL 22
used, for uploading plugins 347, 348, 350

T

tags
used, for releasing specific plugin versions 345
taxonomy 163
text editor
installing 31, 32, 34
text strings
translating, with Poedit 332, 333, 334, 335
translation template file, creating 335
TextMate
URL 32
TextWrangler
URL 32
thumbnail images
providing 351, 352, 353
TipTip plugin
URL 294
used, for adding tooltips to admin page form fields 293, 294, 296
TortoiseSVN
installing 20
URL 19
translation files
URL 325
translation
admin page code, creating 327, 328, 330
default user settings, adapting 325, 326, 327

shortcode output, modifying 330, 331, 332
troubleshooting
  built-in WordPress debugging features 60
  coding errors 56, 57, 59, 60

U

User Access Control (UAC) 9
user capability 87
user custom data
  processing 233
  storing 233
user data
  displaying, in user list page 235, 236, 238, 239
user editor
  custom fields, adding 229, 230, 232
user file
  data, importing into custom tables 275, 278
user forms
  CAPTCHA, implementing with local library 225, 227, 228
  CAPTCHA, implementing with online service 221, 222, 223, 225
user settings
  accessing, from action hook 116
  accessing, from filter hook 116
  multiple sets, managing from admin page 132, 133, 136, 138
  storing, with arrays 78, 79, 80, 81
  style sheet data, storing 127, 131, 132
user-submitted content
  moderating 217
  saving, in custom post types 213, 214, 216, 217
users
  allowing, to upload files directly from post editor 201, 202, 203, 206, 207

V

variable content
  printing 56, 57, 59, 60
Varying Vagrant Vagrants (VVV)
  about 13
  URL 13
Visual Studio Code
  URL 32

W

WampServer
  URL 13
web server
  installing 8, 9, 10, 11, 12
  remote web development environment, creating 13
widget
  configuration options, displaying 307, 310
  configuration options, validating 310, 312
  creating, in WordPress 304, 306
  display function, implementing 312, 314, 315
  plugins, extending other plugins 306
WordPress Codex
  about 43
  URL 43, 49
WordPress path utility functions
  admin_url() 46
  content_url() 46
  get_template_directory_uri() 46
  get_theme_root() 46
  home_url() 47
  includes_url() 47
  plugins_url function 46
  site_url() 47
  used, for loading external files and images 44, 45, 46
  wp_upload_dir() 47
WordPress source code
  hooks, searching 43
WordPress web pages
  jQuery, loading 280, 281, 282
WordPress.org
  plugins, hosting 346, 347
WordPress
  language configuration, modifying 324, 325
  URL 15
wp_enqueue_script function
  about 282
  URL 282
wp_insert_post function
  URL 217

X

XAMPP
  about 8

URL 8
XnViewMP tool
  URL 157

Printed in Great Britain
by Amazon